POCKET WORLD IN FIGURES
2008 EDITION

The
Economist

Pocket
World in
Figures

2008 Edition

THE ECONOMIST IN ASSOCIATION WITH
PROFILE BOOKS LTD

Published by Profile Books Ltd,
3A Exmouth House, Pine Street, London EC1R OJH

This edition published by Profile Books in association with
The Economist, 2007

Material researched and compiled by
Andrea Burgess, Ulrika Davies, Mark Doyle, Andrew Gilbert,
Conrad Heine, Carol Howard, Stella Jones, Rishad Jonuschat,
David McKelvey, Keith Potter, Christopher Wilson, Simon Wright

The greatest care has been taken in compiling this book. However,
no responsibility can be accepted by the publishers or compilers
for the accuracy of the information presented.

Typeset in Officina by MacGuru Ltd
info@macguru.org.uk

Printed in Italy by
Graphicom

A CIP catalogue record for this book is available
from the British Library

ISBN 978 1 86197 844 8

Contents

CONTENTS

CONTENTS

107 Part II   Country Profiles

Notes

This 2008 edition of *The Economist Pocket World in Figures*
includes new rankings on such things as such things as
contraception use, populations over 80, increases in
commodity prices and house prices, brain drains, maritime
traders, children's well-being, murders, executions and
several environmental measures. The world rankings consider
183 countries; all those with a population of at least 1m or a
GDP of at least $1bn; they are listed on pages 248–52. The
country profiles cover 67 major countries. Also included are
profiles of the euro area and the world. The extent and quality
of the statistics available varies from country to country. Every
care has been taken to specify the broad definitions on which
the data are based and to indicate cases where data quality or
technical difficulties are such that interpretation of the
figures is likely to be seriously affected. Nevertheless, figures
from individual countries may differ from standard
international statistical definitions. The term "country" can
also refer to territories or economic entities.

Some country definitions

Macedonia is officially known as the Former Yugoslav Republic
of Macedonia. Serbia includes Montenegro. Data for Cyprus
normally refer to Greek Cyprus only. Data for China do not
include Hong Kong or Macau. For countries such as Morocco
they exclude disputed areas. Congo-Kinshasa refers to the
Democratic Republic of Congo, formerly known as Zaire.
Congo-Brazzaville refers to the other Congo. Data for the EU
refer to the 25 members as at May 2004: Austria, Belgium,
Denmark, Finland, France, Germany, Greece, Ireland, Italy,
Luxembourg, Netherlands, Portugal, Spain, Sweden and the
United Kingdom plus Cyprus, Czech Republic, Estonia,
Hungary, Latvia, Lithuania, Malta, Poland, Slovakia and
Slovenia. The euro area includes all of the first 15 in that list
except Denmark, Sweden and the United Kingdom.

Statistical basis

The all-important factor in a book of this kind is to be able to
make reliable comparisons between countries. Although this
is never quite possible for the reasons stated above, the best
route, which this book takes, is to compare data for the same
year or period and to use actual, not estimated, figures
wherever possible. Where a country's data is excessively out of
date, it is excluded, which is the reason there is no country
profile of Iraq in this edition. The research for this edition of

The Economist Pocket World in Figures was carried out in 2007 using the latest available sources that present data on an internationally comparable basis. Data, therefore, unless otherwise indicated, refer to the year ending December 31 2005.

In the country profiles, life expectancy, crude birth, death and fertility rates are based on 2005–10 averages; human development indices and energy data are for 2004; marriage and divorce data refer to the latest year for which figures are available. Employment, health and education data are for the latest year between 2000 and 2005.

Other definitions
Data shown in country profiles may not always be consistent with those shown in the world rankings because the definitions or years covered can differ. Data may also differ between two different rankings.

Most countries' national accounts are now compiled on a GDP basis so, for simplicity, the term GDP has been used interchangeably with GNP or GNI.

Statistics for principal exports and principal imports are normally based on customs statistics. These are generally compiled on different definitions to the visible exports and imports figures shown in the balance of payments section.

Definitions of the statistics shown are given on the relevant page or in the glossary on page 246. Figures may not add exactly to totals, or percentages to 100, because of rounding or, in the case of GDP, statistical adjustment. Sums of money have generally been converted to US dollars at the official exchange rate ruling at the time to which the figures refer.

Energy consumption data are not always reliable, particularly for the major oil producing countries; consumption per head data may therefore be higher than in reality. Energy exports can exceed production and imports can exceed consumption if transit operations distort trade data or oil is imported for refining and re-exported.

Abbreviations

bn	billion (one thousand million)	ha	hectare
EU	European Union	m	million
kg	kilogram	PPP	Purchasing power parity
km	kilometre	TOE	tonnes of oil equivalent
GDP	Gross domestic product	trn	trillion (one thousand billion)
GNI	Gross national income	...	not available
GNP	Gross national product		

World rankings

Countries: natural facts

Countries: *the largest*[a]
'000 sq km

1	Russia	17,075		31	Tanzania	945
2	Canada	9,971		32	Nigeria	924
3	China	9,561		33	Venezuela	912
4	United States	9,373		34	Namibia	824
5	Brazil	8,512		35	Pakistan	804
6	Australia	7,682		36	Mozambique	799
7	India	3,287		37	Turkey	779
8	Argentina	2,767		38	Chile	757
9	Kazakhstan	2,717		39	Zambia	753
10	Sudan	2,506		40	Myanmar	677
11	Algeria	2,382		41	Afghanistan	652
12	Congo	2,345		42	Somalia	638
13	Saudi Arabia	2,200		43	Central African Rep	622
14	Greenland	2,176		44	Ukraine	604
15	Mexico	1,973		45	Madagascar	587
16	Indonesia	1,904		46	Kenya	583
17	Libya	1,760		47	Botswana	581
18	Iran	1,648		48	France	544
19	Mongolia	1,565		49	Yemen	528
20	Peru	1,285		50	Thailand	513
21	Chad	1,284		51	Spain	505
22	Niger	1,267		52	Turkmenistan	488
23	Angola	1,247		53	Cameroon	475
24	Mali	1,240		54	Papua New Guinea	463
25	South Africa	1,226		55	Sweden	450
26	Colombia	1,142		56	Morocco	447
27	Ethiopia	1,134			Uzbekistan	447
28	Bolivia	1,099		58	Iraq	438
29	Mauritania	1,031		59	Paraguay	407
30	Egypt	1,000		60	Zimbabwe	391

Mountains: *the highest*[b]

	Name	Location	Height (m)
1	Everest	Nepal-China	8,848
2	K2 (Godwin Austen)	Pakistan	8,611
3	Kangchenjunga	Nepal-Sikkim	8,586
4	Lhotse	Nepal-China	8,516
5	Makalu	Nepal-China	8,463
6	Cho Oyu	Nepal-China	8,201
7	Dhaulagiri	Nepal	8,167
8	Manaslu	Nepal	8,163
9	Nanga Parbat	Pakistan	8,125
10	Annapurna I	Nepal	8,091
11	Gasherbrum I	Pakistan-China	8,068
12	Broad Peak	Pakistan-China	8,047
13	Xixabangma (Gosainthan)	China	8,046
14	Gasherbrum II	Pakistan-China	8,035

a Includes freshwater.
b Includes separate peaks which are part of the same massif.

Rivers: *the longest*

Name	Location	Length (km)
1 Nile	Africa	6,695
2 Amazon	South America	6,516
3 Yangtze	Asia	6,380
4 Mississippi-Missouri system	North America	6,019
5 Ob'-Irtysh	Asia	5,570
6 Yenisey-Angara	Asia	5,550
7 Hwang He (Yellow)	Asia	5,464
8 Congo	Africa	4,667
9 Parana	South America	4,500
10 Mekong	Asia	4,425

Deserts: *the largest*

Name	Location	Area ('000 sq km)
1 Sahara	Northern Africa	8,600
2 Arabia	SW Asia	2,300
3 Gobi	Mongolia/China	1,166
4 Patagonian	Argentina	673
5 Great Victoria	W and S Australia	647
6 Great Basin	SW United States	492
7 Chihuahuan	N Mexico	450
8 Great Sandy	W Australia	400

Lakes: *the largest*

Name	Location	Area ('000 sq km)
1 Caspian Sea	Central Asia	371
2 Superior	Canada/US	82
3 Victoria	E Africa	69
4 Huron	Canada/US	60
5 Michigan	US	58
6 Tanganyika	E Africa	33
7 Baikal	Russia	32
8 Great Bear	Canada	31

Islands: *the largest*

Name	Location	Area ('000 sq km)
1 Greenland	North Atlantic Ocean	2,176
2 New Guinea	South-west Pacific Ocean	809
3 Borneo	Western Pacific Ocean	746
4 Madagascar	Indian Ocean	587
5 Baffin	North Atlantic Ocean	507
6 Sumatra	North-east Indian Ocean	474
7 Honshu	Sea of Japan-Pacific Ocean	227
8 Great Britain	Off coast of north-west Europe	218

Notes: Estimates of the lengths of rivers vary widely depending on eg, the path to take through a delta. The definition of a desert is normally a mean annual precipitation value equal to 250ml or less. Australia (7.69 sq km) is defined as a continent rather than an island.

Population: size and growth

Largest populations
Millions, 2005

1	China	1,315.8	34	Kenya	34.3
2	India	1,103.4	35	Algeria	32.9
3	United States	298.2	36	Canada	32.3
4	Indonesia	222.8	37	Morocco	31.5
5	Brazil	186.4	38	Afghanistan	29.9
6	Pakistan	157.9	39	Iraq	28.8
7	Russia	143.2		Uganda	28.8
8	Bangladesh	141.8	41	Peru	28.0
9	Nigeria	131.5	42	Nepal	27.1
10	Japan	128.1	43	Venezuela	26.7
11	Mexico	107.0	44	Uzbekistan	26.6
12	Vietnam	84.2	45	Malaysia	25.3
13	Philippines	83.1	46	Saudi Arabia	24.6
14	Germany	82.7	47	Taiwan	22.9
15	Ethiopia	77.4	48	North Korea	22.5
16	Egypt	74.0	49	Ghana	22.1
17	Turkey	73.2	50	Romania	21.7
18	Iran	69.5	51	Yemen	21.0
19	Thailand	64.2	52	Sri Lanka	20.7
20	France	60.5	53	Australia	20.2
21	United Kingdom	59.7	54	Mozambique	19.8
22	Italy	58.1	55	Syria	19.0
23	Congo-Kinshasa	57.5	56	Madagascar	18.6
24	Myanmar	50.5	57	Côte d'Ivoire	18.2
25	South Korea	47.8	58	Cameroon	16.3
26	South Africa	47.4		Chile	16.3
27	Ukraine	46.5		Netherlands	16.3
28	Colombia	45.6	61	Angola	15.9
29	Spain	43.1	62	Kazakhstan	14.8
30	Argentina	38.7	63	Cambodia	14.1
31	Poland	38.5	64	Niger	14.0
32	Tanzania	38.3	65	Mali	13.5
33	Sudan	36.2			

Largest populations
Millions, 2025

1	India	1,447.5	15	Vietnam	106.4
2	China	1,445.8	16	Egypt	98.5
3	United States	354.9	17	Turkey	89.6
4	Indonesia	271.2	18	Iran	88.0
5	Brazil	228.8	19	Germany	80.3
6	Pakistan	225.0	20	Thailand	68.8
7	Nigeria	210.1	21	France	65.8
8	Bangladesh	206.0	22	United Kingdom	65.2
9	Russia	128.2	23	Italy	58.1
10	Ethiopia	125.0	24	Kenya	57.2
11	Mexico	124.7	25	Colombia	55.6
12	Japan	121.6	26	Myanmar	55.4
13	Philippines	115.9	27	Sudan	54.3
14	Congo-Kinshasa	107.5	28	Ukraine	54.0

Fastest growing populations
Average annual % change, 2005–10

1	Liberia	4.50	25	Mauritania	2.53
2	Burundi	3.90	26	Syria	2.52
3	Afghanistan	3.85	27	Ethiopia	2.51
4	Niger	3.49	28	Guatemala	2.47
5	Eritrea	3.24		Tanzania	2.47
	Uganda	3.24	30	Senegal	2.46
7	Congo-Kinshasa	3.22	31	Kuwait	2.44
8	West Bank and Gaza	3.18	32	Equatorial Guinea	2.38
9	Jordan	3.04	33	Nigeria	2.27
10	Benin	3.02	34	Saudi Arabia	2.24
	Mali	3.02	35	Sudan	2.22
12	Guinea-Bissau	2.98	36	Guinea	2.16
13	Yemen	2.97	37	Congo-Brazzaville	2.11
14	Somalia	2.92		Qatar	2.11
15	Burkina Faso	2.89	39	Belize	2.08
16	Chad	2.88	40	Brunei	2.05
17	United Arab Emirates	2.85	41	Sierra Leone	2.04
18	Angola	2.78	42	Cameroon	2.00
19	Rwanda	2.76		Papua New Guinea	2.00
20	Madagascar	2.66	44	Ghana	1.99
21	Kenya	2.65	45	Libya	1.97
	Togo	2.65		Nepal	1.97
23	Gambia, The	2.63		Oman	1.97
24	Malawi	2.57			

Slowest growing populations
Average annual % change, 2005–10

1	Moldova	-0.90	24	Bosnia	0.13
2	Georgia	-0.79		Italy	0.13
3	Ukraine	-0.76		Serbia	0.13
4	Bulgaria	-0.72	27	Channel Islands	0.19
5	Belarus	-0.55	28	Denmark	0.21
6	Lithuania	-0.53		Greece	0.21
7	Latvia	-0.52		Netherlands	0.21
8	Russia	-0.51	31	Belgium	0.24
9	Romania	-0.45	32	Bermuda	0.25
10	Estonia	-0.35	33	Martinique	0.28
11	Hungary	-0.29	34	Finland	0.29
12	Armenia	-0.21		Uruguay	0.29
13	Poland	-0.15	36	Barbados	0.32
14	Croatia	-0.09	37	South Korea	0.33
15	Germany	-0.07	38	North Korea	0.34
16	Czech Republic	-0.03	39	Andorra	0.36
	Virgin Islands (US)	-0.03		Austria	0.36
18	Japan	-0.02	41	Portugal	0.37
19	Cuba	-0.01		Trinidad & Tobago	0.37
	Aruba	0.01	43	Switzerland	0.38
	Slovenia	0.01	44	United Kingdom	0.42
22	Slovakia	0.03	45	Malta	0.43
23	Macedonia	0.08	46	Sweden	0.45

Population: matters of breeding

Fertility rates, 2005–10

Highest av. no. of children per woman		Lowest av. no. of children per woman	
1 Niger	7.19	1 Macau	0.91
2 Afghanistan	7.07	2 Hong Kong	0.97
Guinea-Bissau	7.07	3 Belarus	1.20
4 Burundi	6.80	4 South Korea	1.21
5 Liberia	6.77	5 Ukraine	1.22
6 Congo-Kinshasa	6.70	6 Bosnia	1.23
7 Mali	6.52	Poland	1.23
8 Sierra Leone	6.47	8 Czech Republic	1.24
9 Uganda	6.46	9 Slovakia	1.25
10 Angola	6.43	10 Lithuania	1.26
11 Chad	6.20	Singapore	1.26
12 Somalia	6.04	12 Japan	1.27
13 Burkina Faso	6.00	13 Hungary	1.28
14 Rwanda	5.92	Slovenia	1.28
15 Malawi	5.59	15 Latvia	1.29
16 Yemen	5.50	16 Romania	1.30
17 Guinea	5.44	17 Greece	1.33
18 Benin	5.42	18 Russia	1.34
19 Equatorial Guinea	5.36	19 Croatia	1.35
20 Nigeria	5.32	20 Germany	1.36

Women[a] who use modern methods of contraception[b]

Highest, %		Lowest, %	
1 China	83.3	1 Chad	2.1
2 United Kingdom	81.0	2 Afghanistan	3.6
3 Hong Kong	79.7	3 Guinea-Bissau	3.6
4 Switzerland	77.5	4 Sierra Leone	3.9
5 Netherlands	75.6	5 Guinea	4.2
6 Finland	75.4	6 Niger	4.3
7 Belgium	74.3	Rwanda	4.3
8 Canada	73.3	8 Congo-Kinshasa	4.4
9 Australia	72.2	9 Angola	4.5
10 Cuba	72.1	10 Eritrea	5.1
11 Denmark	72.0	Mauritania	5.1
New Zealand	72.0	12 Liberia	5.5
13 Germany	71.8	13 Mali	5.7
14 Costa Rica	70.7	14 Ethiopia	6.3
15 United States	70.5	15 Central African Republic	6.9
16 Brazil	70.3	Sudan	6.9
17 Thailand	69.8	17 Benin	7.2
18 France	69.3	18 Côte d'Ivoire	7.3
19 Norway	69.2	19 Albania	7.9
20 Hungary	68.4	20 Nigeria	8.2
21 Puerto Rico	67.6	Senegal	8.2
22 Spain	67.4	22 Burkina Faso	8.6
23 South Korea	66.9	23 Gambia, The	8.9
24 Nicaragua	66.1	24 Togo	9.3
25 Dominican Republic	65.8	25 Yemen	9.8

a Aged 15–49, married or in a relationship.
b Excludes traditional methods of contraception, such as the rhythm method.

Crude birth rates
Average no. of live births per 1,000 population, 2005–10

Highest			Lowest		
1	Congo-Kinshasa	49.6	1	Macau	7.5
	Guinea-Bissau	49.6	2	Hong Kong	7.6
	Liberia	49.6	3	Germany	8.2
4	Niger	49.0		Singapore	8.2
5	Afghanistan	48.2	5	Japan	8.3
6	Mali	48.1	6	Bosnia	8.8
7	Angola	47.3	7	Bulgaria	8.9
8	Burundi	47.1	8	Andorra	9.0
9	Uganda	46.6		Croatia	9.0
10	Sierra Leone	46.2		Slovenia	9.0
11	Chad	45.5	11	Lithuania	9.1
12	Rwanda	44.5	12	Austria	9.2
13	Burkina Faso	44.0		Czech Republic	9.2
14	Somalia	42.9		Italy	9.2
15	Malawi	40.7		Switzerland	9.2
16	Benin	40.2		Ukraine	9.2
17	Nigeria	39.9	17	Greece	9.3
18	Guinea	39.8		Hungary	9.3
19	Mozambique	39.5		Latvia	9.3
20	Eritrea	39.3		South Korea	9.3
	Zambia	39.3	21	Belarus	9.4
22	Kenya	39.2	22	Channel Islands	9.5
23	Tanzania	39.0		Poland	9.5

Births per 1,000 women aged 15–19
2005–10

Highest			Lowest		
1	Niger	258	1	North Korea	2
2	Congo-Kinshasa	226	2	Japan	4
3	Liberia	223		South Korea	4
4	Uganda	207	4	China	5
5	Mali	199		Hong Kong	5
6	Guinea-Bissau	193		Netherlands	5
7	Chad	192		Switzerland	5
8	Guinea	189	8	Singapore	6
9	Sierra Leone	176		Slovenia	6
10	Burkina Faso	158	10	Denmark	7
11	Malawi	157		Italy	7
12	Congo-Brazzaville	145		Sweden	7
13	Angola	141		Tunisia	7
14	Nigeria	140	14	Algeria	8
15	Benin	128		Belgium	8
	Zambia	128		France	8
17	Central African Rep	124		Libya	8
18	Afghanistan	123	18	Greece	9
19	Madagascar	122	19	Finland	10
20	Bangladesh	120		Germany	10
	Côte d'Ivoire	120		Norway	10
22	Nicaragua	119		Spain	10

Population: age

Median age[a]

Highest, 2005

1	Japan	42.9
2	Germany	42.1
3	Italy	42.0
4	Finland	40.9
5	Bulgaria	40.8
6	Croatia	40.6
7	Belgium	40.3
8	Slovenia	40.2
	Sweden	40.2
10	Austria	40.1
	Greece	40.1
	Switzerland	40.1
13	Andorra	40.0
	Channel Islands	40.0
15	Denmark	39.5
16	Latvia	39.3
17	Netherlands	39.1
	Portugal	39.1
19	Bermuda	39.0
20	Czech Republic	38.9
	Estonia	38.9
	France	38.9
	Hong Kong	38.9
	Ukraine	38.9
	United Kingdom	38.9
26	Spain	38.8
27	Hungary	38.7
28	Canada	38.6
29	Luxembourg	38.3
30	Norway	38.0
31	Lithuania	37.9
32	Malta	37.6
33	Singapore	37.5
34	Belarus	37.4
35	Russia	37.3
36	Bosnia	37.1
37	Cayman Islands	37.0

Lowest, 2005

1	Uganda	15.3
2	Mali	16.0
	Niger	16.0
4	Guinea-Bissau	16.2
5	Congo-Kinshasa	16.3
6	Afghanistan	16.4
	Liberia	16.4
	Malawi	16.4
9	Angola	16.6
10	Yemen	16.7
11	Burkina Faso	16.8
	Chad	16.8
13	West Bank and Gaza	16.9
	Zambia	16.9
15	Burundi	17.0
16	Rwanda	17.4
17	Ethiopia	17.5
	Tanzania	17.5
19	Nigeria	17.6
20	Benin	17.7
	Mozambique	17.7
22	Madagascar	17.9
	Somalia	17.9
24	Eritrea	18.1
	Guinea	18.1
	Kenya	18.1
	Togo	18.1
28	Guatemala	18.2
29	Central African Rep	18.3
30	Côte d'Ivoire	18.5
	Senegal	18.5
	Sierra Leone	18.5
33	Cameroon	18.7
	Equatorial Guinea	18.7
35	Congo-Brazzaville	18.8
	Lesotho	18.8

Highest, 2050

1	Macau	55.5
2	Japan	54.9
	South Korea	54.9
4	Singapore	53.7
5	Martinique	53.0
6	Poland	52.4
7	Bulgaria	52.3
8	Slovenia	52.2
9	Cuba	52.1
	Hong Kong	52.1

Lowest, 2050

1	Burundi	20.8
2	Niger	21.1
3	Liberia	21.2
4	Guinea-Bissau	21.5
5	Congo-Kinshasa	22.5
6	Afghanistan	23.0
7	Angola	23.2
8	Uganda	23.3
9	Sierra Leone	24.0
10	Chad	24.3

a Age at which there are an equal number of people above and below.

Population aged 0–14
Highest, %

1	Uganda	49.4		19	Benin	44.2
2	Niger	48.0			Mozambique	44.2
3	Mali	47.7		21	Somalia	44.1
4	Guinea-Bissau	47.4		22	Madagascar	43.8
5	Congo-Kinshasa	47.2		23	Rwanda	43.5
6	Malawi	47.1		24	Guinea	43.4
7	Afghanistan	47.0		25	Togo	43.3
8	Liberia	46.9		26	Guatemala	43.1
9	Angola	46.4		27	Eritrea	43.0
10	Burkina Faso	46.2		28	Sierra Leone	42.8
	Chad	46.2		29	Central African Rep	42.7
12	West Bank and Gaza	45.9		30	Kenya	42.6
	Yemen	45.9		31	Equatorial Guinea	42.4
14	Zambia	45.7		32	Senegal	42.2
15	Burundi	45.1		33	Congo-Brazzaville	41.9
16	Ethiopia	44.5		34	Cameroon	41.8
17	Tanzania	44.4		35	Côte d'Ivoire	41.7
18	Nigeria	44.3		36	Iraq	41.5

Population aged 60 and over
Highest, %

1	Japan	26.4			Hungary	20.8
2	Italy	25.3		20	Ukraine	20.6
3	Germany	25.1		21	Slovenia	20.5
4	Sweden	23.4		22	Lithuania	20.3
5	Greece	23.3		23	Czech Republic	19.9
6	Bulgaria	22.9		24	Channel Islands	19.7
7	Latvia	22.4			Norway	19.7
8	Belgium	22.1		26	Netherlands	19.3
	Croatia	22.1			Romania	19.3
	Portugal	22.1		28	Bosnia	19.1
11	Austria	21.9		29	Faroe Islands	18.9
12	Spain	21.7			Serbia	18.9
13	Estonia	21.6		31	Luxembourg	18.7
14	Finland	21.4		32	Andorra	18.5
15	Denmark	21.2		33	Malta	18.4
	United Kingdom	21.2		34	Belarus	18.1
17	Switzerland	21.1		35	Georgia	17.9
18	France	20.8				

Population aged 80 and over
Highest, %

1	Sweden	5.3			Belgium	4.3
2	Italy	5.1			Spain	4.3
3	Japan	4.8			Switzerland	4.3
4	France	4.6		12	Denmark	4.1
	Norway	4.6		13	Faroe Islands	4.0
6	United Kingdom	4.5			Finland	4.0
7	Germany	4.4		15	Andorra	3.7
8	Austria	4.3			Portugal	3.7

City living

Biggest cities[a]
Population m, 2005

1	Tokyo, Japan	35.2	16	Cairo, Egypt	11.1
2	Mexico City, Mexico	19.4	17	Lagos, Nigeria	10.9
3	New York, US	18.7	18	Beijing, China	10.7
4	São Paulo, Brazil	18.3		Manila, Philippines	10.7
5	Mumbai, India	18.2	20	Moscow, Russia	10.6
6	Delhi, India	15.0	21	Paris, France	9.8
7	Shanghai, China	14.5	22	Istanbul, Turkey	9.7
8	Kolkata, India	14.3	23	Seoul, South Korea	9.6
9	Jakarta, Indonesia	13.2	24	Chicago, US	8.8
10	Buenos Aires, Argentina	12.6	25	London, UK	8.5
11	Dhaka, Bangladesh	12.4	26	Guangzhou, China	8.4
12	Los Angeles, US	12.3	27	Bogotá, Colombia	7.7
13	Karachi, Pakistan	11.6	28	Tehran, Iran	7.3
14	Rio de Janeiro, Brazil	11.5	29	Lima, Peru	7.2
15	Osaka, Japan	11.3		Shenzhen, China	7.2

Fastest growing cities[b]
Average annual growth, 2005–10, %

1	Kigali, Rwanda	7.73	15	Florianópolis, Brazil	4.03
2	Tuxtla Gutiérrez, Mexico	6.06	16	Kampala, Uganda	4.02
3	Ouagadougou, Burkina Faso	4.66	17	Phnom Penh, Cambodia	3.98
4	Kathmandu, Nepal	4.65	18	Ascunción, Paraguay	3.95
5	Valencia, Venezuela	4.64		Dar es Salaam, Tanzania	3.95
6	Mbuji-Mayi, Congo-Kin.	4.63	20	Tijuana, Mexico	3.90
7	Niamey, Niger	4.62	21	Monrovia, Liberia	3.75
8	Lubumbashi, Congo-Kin.	4.61	22	Maputo, Mozambique	3.67
9	Kolwezi, Congo-Kin.	4.60	23	Nairobi, Kenya	3.64
10	Kabul, Afghanistan	4.52	24	Kumasi, Ghana	3.62
11	Kinshasa, Congo-Kin.	4.37	25	Ciudad Juárez, Mexico	3.57
12	Bamako, Mali	4.34	26	Chittagong, Bangladesh	3.55
13	N'Djaména, Chad	4.24		Luanda, Angola	3.55
14	Lomé, Togo	4.08	28	Mombasa, Kenya	3.53
			29	Brazzaville, Congo-Braz.	3.40

Slowest growing cities[b]
Average annual growth, 2005–10, %

1	Yueyang, China	-0.63	12	Havana, Cuba	-0.27
2	Dnipropetrovsk, Ukraine	-0.58	13	Lodz, Poland	-0.26
3	Sofia, Bulgaria	-0.56	14	Puebla, Mexico	-0.25
4	Donetsk, Ukraine	-0.51	15	Belgrade, Serbia	-0.22
5	Kharkiv, Ukraine	-0.50	16	Chelyabinsk, Russia	-0.20
6	Zaporizhzhya, Ukraine	-0.45	17	Seoul, South Korea	-0.19
7	Tbilisi, Georgia	-0.44	18	Turin, Italy	-0.18
8	Odessa, Ukraine	-0.39		Yekaterinburg, Russia	-0.18
9	Nizhniy Novgorod, Russia	-0.34	20	Voronezh, Russia	-0.16
10	Perm, Russia	-0.31	21	Pusan, South Korea	-0.14
	Samara, Russia	-0.31		Ufa, Russia	-0.14

a Urban agglomerations. Data may change from year-to-year based on reassessments of agglomeration boundaries.
b Urban agglomerations of more than 750,000.

Population living in urban areas

Highest, % *Lowest, %*

	Highest	%		Lowest	%
1	Bermuda	100.0	1	Burundi	10.0
	Cayman Islands	100.0	2	Bhutan	11.1
	Hong Kong	100.0	3	Trinidad & Tobago	12.2
	Macau	100.0	4	Uganda	12.6
	Singapore	100.0	5	Papua New Guinea	13.4
6	Guadeloupe	99.8	6	Sri Lanka	15.1
7	Kuwait	98.3	7	Nepal	15.8
8	Martinique	97.9	8	Ethiopia	16.0
9	Puerto Rico	97.6	9	Niger	16.8
10	Belgium	97.2	10	Malawi	17.2
11	Bahrain	96.5	11	Burkina Faso	18.3
12	Qatar	95.4	12	Lesotho	18.7
13	Malta	95.3	13	Rwanda	19.3
14	Virgin Islands (US)	94.2	14	Eritrea	19.4
15	Guam	94.0	15	Cambodia	19.7
16	Venezuela	93.4	16	Laos	20.6
17	Iceland	92.8	17	Kenya	20.7
18	Réunion	92.4	18	Afghanistan	22.9
19	Uruguay	92.0	19	Swaziland	24.1
20	Israel	91.6	20	Tanzania	24.2
21	Andorra	90.6	21	Tajikistan	24.7
22	Bahamas	90.4	22	Bangladesh	25.1
23	Argentina	90.1	23	Chad	25.3
24	United Kingdom	89.7	24	Vietnam	26.4
25	Australia	88.2	25	Madagascar	26.8
26	Chile	87.6	26	Yemen	27.3
27	Lebanon	86.6	27	India	28.7
28	New Zealand	86.2	28	Guinea-Bissau	29.6
29	Denmark	85.6	29	Channel Islands	30.5
30	Libya	84.8		Mali	30.5

Proportion of a country's population residing in a single city[a]

%

		%			%
1	Singapore	100.0	15	Brazzaville, Congo-Braz.	29.3
	Hong Kong	100.0	16	Athens, Greece	29.0
3	San Juan, Puerto Rico	65.9	17	Monrovia, Liberia	28.5
4	Kuwait City, Kuwait	49.7		Auckland, New Zealand	28.5
5	Tel Aviv, Israel	44.8	19	San José, Costa Rica	28.1
6	Panama City, Panama	37.4	20	Vienna, Austria	27.6
7	Yerevan, Armenia	36.6	21	Tokyo, Japan	27.5
8	Montevideo, Uruguay	36.5	22	Lisbon, Portugal	26.3
9	Tripoli, Libya	35.8	23	Lima, Peru	25.7
10	Santiago, Chile	34.9	24	Port-au-Prince, Haiti	25.0
11	Ulan Bator, Mongolia	32.6		Dublin, Ireland	25.0
12	Buenos Aires, Argentina	32.4	26	Tbilisi, Georgia	23.4
13	Asunción, Paraguay	30.2	27	Santo Domingo, Dom. Rep.	22.7
14	Dubai, UAE	29.6		Amman, Jordan	22.7

a Urban agglomerations over 750,000.

Quality of life index[a]
New York=100, Nov. 2006
Highest

	Highest	
1	Zurich, Switzerland	108.1
2	Geneva, Switzerland	108.0
3	Vancouver, Canada	107.7
	Vienna, Austria	107.7
5	Auckland, New Zealand	107.3
	Dusseldorf, Germany	107.3
7	Frankfurt, Germany	107.1
8	Munich, Germany	106.9
9	Bern, Switzerland	106.5
	Sydney, Australia	106.5
11	Copenhagen, Denmark	106.2
12	Wellington, New Zealand	105.8
13	Amsterdam, Netherlands	105.7
14	Brussels, Belgium	105.6
15	Toronto, Canada	105.4
16	Berlin, Germany	105.2
17	Melbourne, Australia	105.0
18	Luxembourg, Lux.	104.8
	Ottawa, Canada	104.8
20	Stockholm, Sweden	104.7
21	Perth, Australia	104.5
22	Montreal, Canada	104.3
23	Nuremberg, Germany	104.2
24	Calgary, Canada	103.6
	Hamburg, Germany	103.6
26	Oslo, Norway	103.5
27	Dublin, Ireland	103.3
	Honolulu, US	103.3
29	San Francisco, US	103.2
30	Adelaide, Australia	103.1
	Helsinki, Finland	103.1
32	Brisbane, Australia	102.8
33	Paris, France	102.7
34	Singapore	102.5
35	Tokyo, Japan	102.3
36	Boston, US	101.9
	Lyon, France	101.9
38	Yokohama, Japan	101.7
39	London, UK	101.2
40	Kobe, Japan	101.0
41	Barcelona, Spain	100.6
42	Madrid, Spain	100.5
	Osaka, Japan	100.5
44	Chicago, US	100.4
	Washington, DC, US	100.4
46	Portland, Oregon, US	100.3
47	Lisbon, Portugal	100.1

	Lowest	
1	Baghdad, Iraq	14.5
2	Brazzaville, Congo-Braz.	29.5
3	Bangui, Central Afr. Rep.	30.6
4	Khartoum, Sudan	31.0
5	Pointe Noire, Congo-Braz.	33.0
6	Ndjamena, Chad	34.0
7	Port Harcourt, Nigeria	38.2
	Sanaa, Yemen	38.2
9	Kinshasa, Congo-Kin.	38.3
10	Nouakchott, Mauritania	39.0
11	Conakry, Guinea	40.4
12	Dhaka, Bangladesh	40.5
	Ouagadougou, Burk. Faso	40.5
14	Niamey, Niger	40.8
15	Antananarivo, Madag.	41.1
16	Port au Prince, Haiti	41.4
17	Lagos, Nigeria	41.8
18	Tashkent, Uzbekistan	43.0
19	Addis Ababa, Ethiopia	43.1
20	Luanda, Angola	43.4
21	Abidjan, Côte d'Ivoire	43.7
22	Bamako, Mali	43.9
23	Lomé, Togo	45.1
24	Kazan, Russia	46.7
25	Dar es Salaam, Tanzania	47.4
26	Havana, Cuba	47.8
27	Novosibirsk, Russia	47.9
28	Maputo, Mozambique	48.7
29	Douala, Cameroon	49.2
30	Yangon, Myanmar	49.3
31	Almaty, Kazakhstan	49.4
32	Minsk, Belarus	49.5
33	Yaoundé, Cameroon	51.3
34	Tirana, Albania	51.7
35	San Pedro Sula, Honduras	51.8
36	Beirut, Lebanon	52.5
37	Algiers, Algeria	52.6
38	Damascus, Syria	52.8
	Tehran, Iran	52.8
40	Karachi, Pakistan	52.9
41	Tripoli, Libya	54.2
42	Cotonou, Benin	54.3
43	Moscow, Russia	54.4
44	Managua, Nicaragua	54.9
45	Vientiane, Laos	55.0
46	Harare, Zimbabwe	55.2
47	Kiev, Ukraine	56.2

a Based on 39 factors ranging from recreation to political stability.

Refugees and asylum seekers[a]

Largest refugee nationalities
'000

1	Afghanistan	1,908.1	11	Angola	215.8
2	Sudan	693.2	12	Serbia[b]	189.9
3	Burundi	438.7	13	Turkey	170.1
4	Congo-Kinshasa	430.6	14	Myanmar	164.9
5	Somalia	394.8	15	Eritrea	143.6
6	Vietnam	358.2	16	China	124.0
7	West Bank and Gaza	349.7	17	Croatia	119.1
8	Iraq	262.1	18	Bosnia	109.9
9	Azerbaijan	233.7	19	Sri Lanka	108.1
10	Liberia	231.1	20	Bhutan	106.5

Countries with largest refugee populations
'000

1	Pakistan	1,084.7	11	Saudi Arabia	240.7
2	Iran	716.4	12	Armenia	219.6
3	Germany	700.0	13	Congo-Kinshasa	204.3
4	Tanzania	548.8	14	Zambia	155.7
5	United States	379.3	15	Serbia[b]	148.3
6	China	301.0	16	Sudan	147.3
7	United Kingdom	293.5	17	Canada	147.2
8	Chad	275.4	18	India	139.3
9	Uganda	257.3	19	France	137.3
10	Kenya	251.3	20	Nepal	126.4

Origin of asylum applications to indust. countries
'000

1	Serbia[b]	22.1	11	Congo-Kinshasa	7.5
2	Russia	21.6		India	7.5
3	China	18.4	13	Georgia	7.1
4	Iraq	12.5		Somalia	7.1
5	Turkey	12.0	15	Sri Lanka	5.6
6	Haiti	10.8	16	Colombia	5.4
7	Iran	9.2	17	Mexico	5.1
8	Nigeria	8.0	18	Armenia	5.0
9	Pakistan	7.8	19	Moldova	4.7
10	Afghanistan	7.7	20	Bangladesh	4.5

Asylum applications in industrialised countries
'000

1	France	49.7	10	Netherlands	12.4
2	United States	48.8	11	Italy	9.6
3	United Kingdom	30.8	12	Greece	9.1
4	Germany	28.9	13	Cyprus	7.8
5	Sweden	23.2	14	Poland	6.9
6	Austria	22.5	15	Norway	5.4
7	Canada	19.7	16	Spain	5.3
8	Belgium	16.0	17	Ireland	4.3
9	Switzerland	14.3	18	Czech Republic	4.2

a As reported by UNHCR.   b Includes Montenegro.

The world economy

Biggest economies
GDP, $bn

1	United States	12,417	25	Norway	296
2	Japan	4,534	26	Indonesia	287
3	Germany	2,795	27	Denmark	259
4	China	2,234	28	South Africa	240
5	United Kingdom	2,199	29	Greece	225
6	France[a]	2,127	30	Ireland	202
7	Italy	1,763	31	Finland	193
8	Spain	1,125	32	Iran	190
9	Canada	1,114	33	Argentina	183
10	India	806		Portugal	183
11	Brazil	796	35	Hong Kong	178
12	South Korea	788	36	Thailand	177
13	Mexico	768	37	Venezuela	140
14	Russia	764	38	Malaysia	130
15	Australia	733		United Arab Emirates	130
16	Netherlands	624	40	Czech Republic	124
17	Belgium	371	41	Israel	123
18	Switzerland	367	42	Colombia	122
19	Turkey	363	43	Singapore	117
20	Sweden	358	44	Chile	115
21	Taiwan	346	45	Pakistan	111
22	Saudi Arabia	310	46	Hungary	109
23	Austria	306		New Zealand	109
24	Poland	303	48	Algeria	102

Biggest economies by purchasing power
GDP PPP, $bn

1	United States	12,417	21	Iran	544
2	China	8,815	22	Netherlands	533
3	Japan	3,995	23	Poland	528
4	India	3,779	24	South Africa	521
5	Germany	2,430	25	Philippines	427
6	United Kingdom	2,002	26	Pakistan	369
7	France	1,850	27	Saudi Arabia	363
8	Italy	1,672	28	Belgium	337
9	Brazil	1,566	29	Colombia	333
10	Russia	1,552	30	Ukraine	322
11	Spain	1,179	31	Egypt	321
12	Mexico	1,108	32	Sweden	294
13	Canada	1,078	33	Bangladesh	291
14	South Korea	1,064	34	Austria	277
15	Indonesia	848	35	Malaysia	276
16	Taiwan	664	36	Switzerland	265
17	Australia	646	37	Greece	260
18	Turkey	606	38	Vietnam	255
19	Thailand	557	39	Hong Kong	242
20	Argentina	553	40	Algeria	232

Note: For a list of 183 countries with their GDPs, see pages 248–252.
a Includes overseas departments.

Regional GDP

$bn		*% annual growth 2000–05*	
World	44,688	World	4.0
Advanced economies	34,143	Advanced economies	2.1
G7	27,068	G7	1.9
Euro area	10,007	Euro area	1.4
Asia[a]	4,004	Asia[a]	7.9
Latin America	2,539	Latin America	2.7
Eastern Europe[b]	2,189	Eastern Europe[b]	5.5
Middle East	1,004	Middle East	4.9
Africa	809	Africa	4.8

Regional purchasing power

GDP, % of total		*$ per head*	
World	100.0	World	9,480
Advanced economies	52.3	Advanced economies	32,830
G7	41.2	G7	34,270
Euro area	14.8	Euro area	27,350
Asia[a]	27.1	Asia[a]	4,840
Latin America	7.4	Latin America	8,620
Eastern Europe[b]	7.1	Eastern Europe[b]	9,530
Middle East	2.8	Middle East	7,360
Africa	3.3	Africa	2,540

Regional population

% of total (6.5bn)		*No. of countries[c]*	
Advanced economies	15.3	Advanced economies	29
G7	11.4	G7	7
Euro area	4.9	Euro area	12
Asia[a]	52.3	Asia[a]	23
Latin America	8.5	Latin America	33
Eastern Europe[b]	7.3	Eastern Europe[b]	28
Middle East	3.7	Middle East	13
Africa	12.8	Africa	48

Regional international trade

Exports of goods and services, % of tot.		*Current account balances, $bn*	
Advanced economies	69.1	Advanced economies	-473.4
G7	40.4	G7	-586.9
Euro area	29.7	Euro area	8.1
Asia[a]	12.0	Asia[a]	165.2
Latin America	4.5	Latin America	34.6
Eastern Europe[b]	7.4	Eastern Europe[b]	24.5
Middle East	4.5	Middle East	189.0
Africa	2.5	Africa	14.6

a Excludes Hong Kong, Japan, Singapore, South Korea and Taiwan.
b Includes Russia and other CIS, Turkey and Malta.
c IMF definition.

Living standards

Highest GDP per head
$

1	Luxembourg	77,760	36	Cyprus	21,400
2	Bermuda[ab]	69,230	37	Greece	20,290
3	Norway	64,240	38	Martinique[b]	19,880
4	Iceland	53,230	39	Bahamas	19,440
5	Switzerland	50,280	40	Guadeloupe[b]	19,340
6	Ireland	49,220	41	Bahrain	18,760
7	Qatar	49,200	42	Israel	18,420
8	Denmark	47,910	43	Puerto Rico[a]	18,090
9	Cayman Islands[ab]	43,090	44	Réunion[b]	17,580
10	United States	41,640	45	Portugal	17,460
11	Sweden	39,740	46	Slovenia	17,180
12	Andorra[a]	39,010	47	French Polynesia[ac]	16,960
13	Netherlands	38,290	48	South Korea	16,480
14	Austria	37,330	49	New Caledonia[ac]	15,280
15	Finland	37,150	50	Taiwan	15,110
16	United Kingdom	36,830	51	Guam[a]	14,790
17	Australia	36,260	52	Virgin Islands (US)[ab]	14,470
18	Faroe Islands[a]	36,170	53	Malta	13,960
19	Belgium	35,660	54	Netherlands Antilles[ab]	12,730
20	Japan	35,390	55	Saudi Arabia	12,590
21	France	35,150	56	Czech Republic	12,190
22	Canada	34,480	57	Oman	11,860
23	Germany	33,800	58	Barbados	11,080
24	Greenland[a]	30,360	59	Trinidad & Tobago	11,050
25	Italy	30,340	60	Hungary	10,820
26	Kuwait	29,920	61	Estonia	10,080
27	Aruba[b]	29,630	62	Slovakia	8,590
28	United Arab Emirates	28,820	63	Croatia	8,370
29	Channel Islands[a]	28,470	64	Poland	7,880
30	New Zealand	27,320	65	Lithuania	7,540
31	Singapore	27,150	66	Mexico	7,180
32	Spain	26,090	67	Chile	7,070
33	Macau[a]	25,690	68	Latvia	6,880
34	Brunei[a]	25,620	69	Libya	6,570
35	Hong Kong	25,390	70	Equatorial Guinea	6,110

Lowest GDP per head
$

1	Congo-Brazzaville	90		Niger	240
2	Burundi	110		Rwanda	240
3	Ethiopia	140	13	Zimbabwe	260
4	Myanmar[a]	150	14	Madagascar	270
5	Malawi	160		Nepal	270
6	Liberia	170	16	Uganda	300
7	Guinea-Bissau	190	17	Gambia, The	310
8	Eritrea	220	18	Tanzania	320
	Sierra Leone	220	19	Central African Rep	340
10	Afghanistan	240		Mozambique	340

a Estimate. b 2004 c 2003

Highest purchasing power
GDP per head in PPP (USA = 100)

1	Bermuda[ab]	166.9	36	Greece	55.8
2	Luxembourg	143.8	37	Slovenia	53.2
3	Channel Islands[a]	123.7	38	Cyprus[a]	52.6
4	Cayman Islands[ab]	104.6	39	South Korea	52.6
5	United States	100.0	40	Aruba[ab]	52.0
6	Norway	98.9	41	Bahrain	51.3
7	Andorra[a]	92.6	42	Czech Republic	49.0
8	Ireland	91.9	43	Portugal	48.7
9	Macau	87.3	44	Greenland[ac]	47.7
10	Iceland	87.2	45	Martinique	47.3
11	Switzerland	85.1	46	Malta	45.8
12	Hong Kong	83.2	47	Puerto Rico[a]	44.4
13	Denmark	81.1	48	Hungary	42.7
14	Austria	80.4	49	Guadeloupe	42.6
15	Canada	79.7	50	French Polynesia[ad]	41.8
16	United Kingdom	79.3	51	Bahamas[e]	40.6
17	Netherlands	78.0	52	Barbados[a]	40.6
18	Sweden	77.6	53	Réunion	38.6
19	Finland	76.8	54	Seychelles	38.4
20	Belgium	76.7	55	Netherlands Antilles[ab]	38.2
21	Australia	75.9	56	Slovakia	37.9
22	Japan	74.6	57	Saudi Arabia	37.5
23	Faroe Islands[ac]	74.0	58	Estonia	36.9
24	France	72.5	59	Oman	36.2
25	Singapore	70.8	60	Guam[a]	35.8
26	Germany	70.3		New Caledonia[ad]	35.8
27	Taiwan	70.0	62	Trinidad & Tobago	34.9
28	Italy	68.1	63	Lithuania	34.6
29	Qatar[a]	65.4		Virgin Islands (US)[ab]	34.6
30	Spain	64.9	65	Argentina	34.1
31	Kuwait	62.8	66	Poland	33.1
32	Israel	61.7	67	Latvia	32.6
33	Brunei[a]	61.1	68	Croatia	31.1
34	United Arab Emirates	60.9	69	Mauritius	30.4
35	New Zealand	59.7	70	Botswana	29.6

Lowest purchasing power
GDP per head in PPP (USA = 100)

1	Somalia[a]	1.4	10	Madagascar	2.2
2	Malawi	1.6		Yemen	2.2
3	Burundi	1.7	12	Liberia[a]	2.4
	Congo-Kinshasa	1.7		Zambia	2.4
5	Tanzania	1.8	14	Ethiopia	2.5
6	Afghanistan[ab]	1.9		Mali	2.5
	Niger	1.9	16	Eritrea	2.6
	Sierra Leone	1.9	17	Benin	2.7
9	Guinea-Bissau	2.0		Nigeria	2.7

Note: for definition of purchasing power parity see page 247.
a Estimate.   b 2004   c 2001   d 2003   e 2002

The quality of life

Human development index[a]
Highest, 2004

1	Norway	96.5	31	Barbados	87.9
2	Iceland	96.0	32	Malta	87.5
3	Australia	95.7	33	Brunei	87.1
4	Ireland	95.6		Kuwait	87.1
5	Sweden	95.1	35	Hungary	86.9
6	Canada	95.0	36	Argentina	86.3
7	Japan	94.9	37	Poland	86.2
8	United States	94.8	38	Bahrain	85.9
9	Finland	94.7		Chile	85.9
	Netherlands	94.7	40	Estonia	85.8
	Switzerland	94.7	41	Lithuania	85.7
12	Belgium	94.5	42	Slovakia	85.6
	Luxembourg	94.5	43	Uruguay	85.1
14	Austria	94.4	44	Croatia	84.6
15	Denmark	94.3	45	Latvia	84.5
16	France	94.2	46	Qatar	84.4
17	Italy	94.0	47	Costa Rica	84.1
	United Kingdom	94.0	48	United Arab Emirates	83.9
19	Spain	93.8	49	Cuba	82.6
20	New Zealand	93.6	50	Bahamas	82.5
21	Germany	93.2	51	Mexico	82.1
22	Israel	92.7	52	Bulgaria	81.6
	Hong Kong	92.7	53	Oman	81.0
24	Greece	92.1	54	Panama	80.9
25	Singapore	91.6		Trinidad & Tobago	80.9
26	South Korea	91.2	56	Malaysia	80.5
27	Slovenia	91.0		Romania	80.5
28	Portugal	90.4	58	Bosnia	80.0
29	Cyprus	90.3		Mauritius	80.0
30	Czech Republic	88.5	60	Libya	79.8

Human development index[a]
Lowest, 2004

1	Niger	31.1	10	Mozambique	39.0
2	Sierra Leone	33.5	11	Congo-Kinshasa	39.1
3	Mali	33.8	12	Malawi	40.0
4	Burkina Faso	34.2	13	Zambia	40.7
5	Guinea-Bissau	34.9	14	Côte d'Ivoire	42.1
6	Central African Rep	35.3	15	Benin	42.8
7	Chad	36.8	16	Tanzania	43.0
8	Ethiopia	37.1	17	Angola	43.9
9	Burundi	38.4	18	Guinea	44.5

a GDP or GDP per head is often taken as a measure of how developed a country is, but its usefulness is limited as it refers only to economic welfare. In 1990 the UN Development Programme published its first estimate of a Human Development Index, which combined statistics on two other indicators – adult literacy and life expectancy – with income levels to give a better, though still far from perfect, indicator of human development. In 1991 average years of schooling was combined with adult literacy to give a knowledge variable. The HDI is shown here scaled from 0 to 100; countries scoring over 80 are considered to have high human development, those scoring from 50 to 79 medium and those under 50 low.

Economic freedom index[b]

1	Hong Kong	89.3	21	Sweden	72.6
2	Singapore	85.7	22	Lithuania	72.0
3	Australia	82.7	23	Bahamas	71.4
4	United States	82.0		Trinidad & Tobago	71.4
5	New Zealand	81.6	25	Austria	71.3
	United Kingdom	81.6	26	Taiwan	71.1
7	Ireland	81.3	27	Spain	70.9
8	Luxembourg	79.3	28	Barbados	70.5
9	Switzerland	79.1	29	El Salvador	70.3
10	Canada	78.7	30	Norway	70.1
11	Chile	78.3	31	Czech Republic	69.7
12	Estonia	78.1	32	Armenia	69.4
13	Denmark	77.6	33	Uruguay	69.3
14	Iceland	77.1	34	Mauritius	69.0
	Netherlands	77.1	35	Georgia	68.7
16	Finland	76.5	36	South Korea	68.6
17	Belgium	74.5	37	Bahrain	68.4
18	Japan	73.6		Botswana	68.4
19	Germany	73.5		Israel	68.4
20	Cyprus	73.1		Slovakia	68.4

Gender-related development index[c]

1	Norway	96.2	21	Germany	92.8
2	Iceland	95.8	22	Israel	92.5
3	Australia	95.6	23	Greece	91.7
4	Ireland	95.1	24	Slovenia	90.8
5	Luxembourg	94.9	25	South Korea	90.5
	Sweden	94.9	26	Portugal	90.2
7	Canada	94.7	27	Cyprus	90.0
8	United States	94.6	28	Czech Republic	88.1
9	Netherlands	94.5	29	Malta	86.9
10	Switzerland	94.4	30	Hungary	86.7
11	Belgium	94.3	31	Kuwait	86.4
	Finland	94.3	32	Argentina	85.9
13	Japan	94.2		Poland	85.9
14	Denmark	94.0	34	Estonia	85.6
	France	94.0		Lithuania	85.6
16	United Kingdom	93.8	36	Slovakia	85.3
17	Austria	93.7	37	Chile	85.0
18	Italy	93.4	38	Bahrain	84.9
19	Spain	93.3	39	Uruguay	84.7
20	New Zealand	93.2	40	Croatia	84.4

b Ranks countries on the basis of indicators of how government intervention can restrict the economic relations between individuals, published by the Heritage Foundation. The methodology changed in 2007 and now includes data on labour and business freedom as well as trade policy, taxation, monetary policy, the banking system, foreign-investment rules, property rights, the amount of economic output consumed by the government, regulation policy, the size of the black market and the extent of wage and price controls. Countries are scored from 80–100 (free) to 0–49.9 (repressed).
c Combines similar data to the HDI (and also published by the UNDP) to give an indicator of the disparities in human development between men and women in individual countries. The lower the index, the greater the disparity.

Economic growth

Highest economic growth, 1995–2005
Average annual % increase in real GDP

1	Equatorial Guinea[a]	21.6		28	Botswana	5.7
2	Bosnia	15.7			Mali	5.7
3	Liberia	13.9		30	Belize	5.5
4	Azerbaijan	10.2			Tanzania	5.5
5	China	9.0			Yemen	5.5
6	Armenia	8.6		33	Albania	5.4
7	Mozambique	8.4		34	Bangladesh	5.3
8	Myanmar	8.3		35	Bahrain	5.1
9	Chad	7.9			Dominican Republic	5.1
10	Angola	7.8			Luxembourg	5.1
11	Ireland	7.4			Singapore	5.1
	Rwanda	7.4		39	Tunisia	5.0
13	Vietnam	7.2		40	Mauritania	4.9
14	Cambodia	6.9		41	Ethiopia	4.8
	Belarus	6.9		42	Benin	4.7
	Latvia	6.9			Burkina Faso	4.7
17	Bhutan	6.7			Egypt	4.7
18	Estonia	6.6			Ghana	4.7
	Georgia	6.6			Mauritius	4.7
20	United Arab Emirates	6.4			Senegal	4.7
21	India	6.3			Tajikistan	4.7
	Kazakhstan	6.3		49	Iran	4.6
	Sudan	6.3			Jordan	4.6
	Trinidad & Tobago	6.3			Kyrgyzstan	4.6
25	Laos	6.2			Malaysia	4.6
26	Uganda	6.0			Uzbekistan	4.6
27	Lithuania	5.9				

Lowest economic growth, 1995–2005
Average annual % change in real GDP

1	Zimbabwe	-2.6		20	Austria	2.1
2	Guinea-Bissau	-0.2			Belgium	2.1
3	Congo-Kinshasa	0.0			Denmark	2.1
4	Burundi	0.4			Portugal	2.1
5	Dominica	0.6			Romania	2.1
6	Jamaica	0.7		25	Brazil	2.2
7	Central African Republic	0.8			Colombia	2.2
8	Haiti	1.0			France	2.2
9	Papua New Guinea	1.1			Macedonia	2.2
10	Italy	1.3			Malta	2.2
	Japan	1.3			Moldova	2.2
	Paraguay	1.3			Netherlands	2.2
13	Germany	1.4		32	Argentina	2.3
	Côte d'Ivoire	1.4			Fiji	2.3
15	Switzerland	1.5		34	Eritrea	2.4
	Uruguay	1.5		35	Czech Republic	2.5
	Venezuela	1.5			Kenya	2.5
18	Gabon	1.7		37	El Salvador	2.6
19	Bulgaria	2.0				

a 1995–2004

Highest economic growth, 1985–95
Average annual % increase in real GDP

1	China	10.0	11	Macau	7.4
2	Thailand	9.5	12	Bhutan	6.7
3	Singapore	8.7	13	Swaziland	6.5
	South Korea	8.7		Vietnam	6.5
5	Malaysia	8.2	15	Hong Kong	6.4
	Taiwan	8.2		New Caledonia	6.4
7	Belize	7.8	17	Mauritius	6.2
	Botswana	7.8	18	Uganda	6.0
9	Chile	7.7	19	Malta	5.8
10	Indonesia	7.5			

Lowest economic growth, 1985–95
Lowest annual % change in real GDP

1	Liberia	-20.9	12	Romania	-2.0
2	Georgia	-14.1	13	Albania	-1.0
3	Tajikistan	-8.5	14	Hungary	-0.9
4	Moldova	-7.5	15	Nicaragua	-0.8
5	Latvia	-4.6		Slovakia	-0.8
6	Congo-Kinshasa	-3.7	17	Angola	-0.7
	Rwanda	-3.7	18	Bulgaria	-0.6
8	Estonia	-3.2	19	Trinidad & Tobago	-0.4
9	Haiti	-2.4	20	Zambia	0.1
10	Sierra Leone	-2.3	21	Congo-Brazzaville	0.2
11	Cameroon	-2.1		Suriname	0.2

Highest services growth, 1995–2005[a]
Average annual % increase in real terms

1	Bosnia	16.1	9	Azerbaijan	7.3
2	China	9.7	10	Rwanda	7.2
3	Equatorial Guinea	8.6	11	Albania	7.1
4	Georgia	8.4		Mozambique	7.1
5	India	8.3	13	Laos	6.5
6	Bhutan	8.0	14	Kazakhstan	6.4
	Burkina Faso	8.0	15	Latvia	6.3
8	Mauritania	7.7	16	Belize	6.2

Lowest services growth, 1995–2005[a]
Average annual % increase in real terms

1	Central African Rep	-6.2	9	Seychelles	0.8
2	Congo-Kinshasa	-1.4	10	Japan	0.9
3	Papua New Guinea	-0.5	11	Gabon	1.0
4	Guinea-Bissau	0.0	12	Argentina	1.3
5	Brazil	0.2		Jamaica	1.3
6	Paraguay	0.5		Peru	1.3
7	Malaysia	0.6	15	Chile	1.4
8	Bulgaria	0.7		Poland	1.4

a Or nearest available years.
Note: Rankings of highest and lowest industrial growth 2000–2005 can be found on page 46 and highest and lowest agricultural growth 1995–2005 on page 49.

Trading places

Biggest exporters
% of total world exports (goods, services and income)

1	Euro area	16.36	23	Malaysia	1.13
2	United States	11.89	24	India	1.10
3	Germany	8.83	25	Australia	1.05
4	United Kingdom	6.33	26	Norway	1.03
5	China	5.95	27	Denmark	1.01
6	Japan	5.56	28	Hong Kong	1.00
7	France	4.69	29	Brazil	0.93
8	Netherlands	3.57	30	Thailand	0.90
9	Italy	3.56	31	Luxembourg	0.87
10	Canada	3.18	32	Poland	0.78
11	Belgium	2.56		United Arab Emirates	0.78
12	South Korea	2.34	34	Turkey	0.72
13	Spain	2.22	35	Indonesia	0.69
14	Switzerland	2.07	36	Finland	0.66
15	Russia	1.94	37	Czech Republic	0.64
16	Taiwan	1.64	38	Hungary	0.52
17	Mexico	1.60	39	South Africa	0.48
18	Ireland	1.46	40	Israel	0.42
19	Sweden	1.45	41	Iran	0.41
20	Singapore	1.35		Kuwait	0.41
21	Austria	1.33		Portugal	0.41
22	Saudi Arabia	1.26		Venezuela	0.41

Most trade dependent
Trade as % of GDP[a]

1	Aruba	164.5
2	Equatorial Guinea	139.3
3	Liberia	126.7
4	Malaysia	96.2
5	Singapore	94.0
6	United Arab Emirates	89.5
7	Suriname	89.4
8	Slovakia	71.6
9	Belgium	71.3
10	Iraq	70.7
11	Bahrain	68.2
12	Estonia	66.4
13	Puerto Rico	65.9
14	Lesotho	65.7
15	Swaziland	65.6
16	Cambodia	63.4
17	Czech Republic	63.2
18	Turkmenistan	62.9
19	Vietnam	62.7
20	Zimbabwe	61.7
21	Thailand	60.9

Least trade dependent
Trade as % of GDP[a]

1	North Korea	5.1
2	Bermuda	7.6
3	Somalia	9.6
4	Central African Rep	10.2
5	United States	10.3
6	Rwanda	11.3
7	Japan	11.6
8	Brazil	12.1
9	Cuba	12.2
10	Hong Kong	13.6
11	Benin	13.8
12	Euro area	15.1
	Niger[b]	15.1
14	Uganda	15.2
15	India	15.8
16	Australia	16.2
17	Greece	16.3
18	Cameroon	16.8
	Pakistan	16.8
20	Colombia	17.1
21	Burkina Faso	17.4

Notes: The figures are drawn from balance of payment statistics so have differing definitions from trade statistics taken from customs or similar sources. For Hong Kong and Singapore, domestic exports and retained imports only are used.

Biggest traders of goods
% of world exports of goods

1	Euro area	15.16	24	United Arab Emirates	1.15
2	Germany	9.72	25	Thailand	1.09
3	United States	8.98	26	Australia	1.07
4	China	7.63	27	Ireland	1.04
5	Japan	5.68		Norway	1.04
6	France	4.39	29	India	0.99
7	United Kingdom	3.84	30	Poland	0.96
8	Canada	3.74	31	Indonesia	0.86
9	Italy	3.73	32	Denmark	0.83
10	Netherlands	3.48	33	Czech Republic	0.78
11	South Korea	2.89	34	Turkey	0.77
12	Belgium	2.63	35	Finland	0.65
13	Russia	2.44	36	Hungary	0.62
14	Mexico	2.14	37	Iran	0.60
15	Taiwan	1.98	38	Puerto Rico	0.57
16	Spain	1.95	39	South Africa	0.55
17	Saudi Arabia	1.75		Venezuela	0.55
18	Switzerland	1.51	41	Nigeria	0.48
19	Malaysia	1.42	42	Kuwait	0.47
20	Sweden	1.35	43	Chile	0.41
21	Singapore	1.25	44	Argentina	0.40
22	Brazil	1.18		Israel	0.40
23	Austria	1.17		Philippines	0.40

Biggest traders of services and income
% of world exports of services and income

1	Euro area	18.88	24	Australia	1.00
2	United States	18.02	25	Taiwan	0.92
3	United Kingdom	11.59	26	Russia	0.89
4	Germany	6.93	27	Greece	0.81
5	France	5.32	28	Finland	0.66
	Japan	5.32	29	Turkey	0.63
7	Netherlands	3.75	30	Malaysia	0.53
8	Switzerland	3.26	31	Thailand	0.51
9	Italy	3.20	32	Israel	0.48
10	Spain	2.80		Portugal	0.48
11	Hong Kong	2.69	34	Mexico	0.46
12	Belgium	2.41	35	Brazil	0.41
13	China	2.40	36	Poland	0.40
	Luxembourg	2.40	37	Egypt	0.34
15	Ireland	2.35	38	Czech Republic	0.33
16	Canada	1.98		South Africa	0.33
17	Austria	1.65	40	Hungary	0.32
	Sweden	1.65		Indonesia	0.32
19	Singapore	1.57	42	Kuwait	0.30
20	Denmark	1.40	43	Lebanon	0.28
21	India	1.32	44	Croatia	0.27
22	South Korea	1.18	45	Saudi Arabia	0.23
23	Norway	1.02	46	Argentina	0.22

a Average of imports plus exports of goods as % of GDP.   b 2004

Balance of payments: current account

Largest surpluses
$m

1	Japan	165,780		26	Belgium	9,328
2	China	160,818		27	Denmark	8,616
3	Germany	116,030		28	Argentina	5,395
4	Saudi Arabia	87,131		29	Brunei	5,339
5	Russia	83,348		30	Angola	5,138
6	Switzerland	60,973		31	Oman	4,717
7	Netherlands	48,936		32	Luxembourg	4,267
8	Norway	46,560		33	Austria	4,252
9	Singapore	33,212		34	Israel	3,756
10	Kuwait	32,634		35	Trinidad & Tobago	3,594
11	United Arab Emirates	27,238		36	Macau	3,367
12	Canada	26,555		37	Ukraine	2,531
13	Venezuela	25,533		38	Philippines	2,338
14	Nigeria	24,202		39	Egypt	2,103
15	Sweden	23,643		40	Uzbekistan	1,949
16	Algeria	21,183		41	Bahrain	1,575
17	Hong Kong	20,284		42	Botswana	1,469
18	Malaysia	19,980		43	Yemen	1,215
19	South Korea	16,559		44	Peru	1,030
20	Taiwan	16,116		45	Morocco	1,018
21	Libya	14,945		46	Indonesia	929
22	Brazil	14,199		47	Gabon[a]	925
23	Iran	14,000		48	Congo-Brazzaville	903
24	Qatar	10,713		49	Turkmenistan	875
25	Finland	9,517		50	Chile	703

Largest deficits
$m

1	United States	-791,510		21	Thailand	-3,670
2	Spain	-83,136		22	Pakistan	-3,608
3	United Kingdom	-53,350		23	Sudan	-3,013
4	Australia	-40,977		24	Bulgaria	-3,004
5	France	-33,290		25	Iceland	-2,627
6	Euro area	-28,060		26	Croatia	-2,585
7	Italy	-27,724		27	Serbia	-2,500
8	Turkey	-23,155		28	Czech Republic	-2,495
9	Greece	-17,879		29	Jordan	-2,311
10	Portugal	-17,007		30	Bosnia	-2,156
11	India	-11,415		31	Latvia	-2,002
12	Iraq[a]	-9,728		32	Colombia	-1,886
13	New Zealand	-9,622		33	Lebanon	-1,881
14	South Africa	-9,142		34	Lithuania	-1,831
15	Romania	-8,621		35	Ethiopia	-1,568
16	Hungary	-8,106		36	Estonia	-1,445
17	Ireland	-5,331		37	Guatemala	-1,387
18	Poland	-5,105		38	Equatorial Guinea[b]	-1,164
19	Mexico	-5,054		39	Jamaica	-1,079
20	Slovakia	-4,090		40	Syria	-1,065

Largest surpluses as % of GDP
%

1	Brunei	56.0	26	Russia	10.9
2	Kuwait	43.7	27	Papua New Guinea	8.9
3	Libya	38.6	28	Yemen	8.4
4	Macau	29.1	29	Netherlands	8.2
5	Singapore	28.4	30	China	7.2
6	Saudi Arabia	28.1	31	Iran	7.1
7	United Arab Emirates	26.1		Namibia	7.1
8	Qatar	25.2	33	Sweden	6.7
9	Nigeria	24.5	34	Bolivia	5.3
10	Trinidad & Tobago	24.3	35	Finland	4.9
11	Algeria	20.7	36	Taiwan	4.7
12	Venezuela	18.4	37	Germany	4.2
13	Angola	18.3	38	Japan	3.7
14	Congo-Brazzaville	17.7	39	Denmark	3.4
15	Switzerland	16.7	40	Ukraine	3.1
16	Norway	16.4	41	Israel	3.0
17	Botswana	15.7	42	Argentina	2.9
18	Malaysia	15.4	43	Belgium	2.6
19	Oman	15.3	44	Canada	2.4
20	Uzbekistan	14.3		Egypt	2.4
21	Turkmenistan	12.9		Philippines	2.4
22	Luxembourg	12.6	47	South Korea	2.1
23	Bahrain	12.1	48	Morocco	2.0
24	Gabon[a]	11.5	49	Brazil	1.8
25	Hong Kong	11.4	50	Swaziland	1.7

Largest deficits as % of GDP
%

1	Mauritania	-46.5	21	Mozambique	-11.5
2	Equatorial Guinea[b]	-36.0	22	Bulgaria	-11.3
3	Burundi	-32.8	23	Jamaica	-11.1
4	Iraq[a]	-28.9	24	Estonia	-11.0
5	Bosnia	-23.0	25	Gambia, The	-10.9
6	Laos	-20.2		Sudan	-10.9
7	Jordan	-18.0	27	Malta	-10.7
8	Iceland	-17.5		Suriname	-10.7
9	Zimbabwe	-16.9	29	Togo	-10.6
10	Nicaragua	-16.3	30	Portugal	-9.8
11	Malawi	-16.2	31	Kyrgyzstan	-9.3
12	Belize	-14.4	32	Serbia	-9.2
13	Sierra Leone	-14.1	33	Moldova	-9.1
14	Ethiopia	-14.0	34	New Zealand	-8.8
15	Bahamas	-13.0		Slovakia	-8.8
	Barbados	-13.0	36	Romania	-8.7
17	Burkina Faso	-12.8	37	Mali	-8.6
18	Latvia	-12.7	38	Lebanon	-8.5
19	Aruba	-12.1	39	Greece	-8.4
20	Georgia	-11.8	40	Senegal	-8.3

a 2004   b 2003

Workers' remittances
$m, 2006

1	Mexico	25,038	24	Portugal	3,017
2	India	23,548	25	Austria	2,941
3	China	22,492	26	United States	2,924
4	Philippines	14,923	27	Dominican Republic	2,915
5	France	12,742	28	Australia	2,858
6	Spain	7,927	29	Jordan	2,681
7	Belgium	7,158	30	Algeria	2,527
8	United Kingdom	6,722	31	Honduras	2,400
9	Germany	6,542	32	Italy	2,398
10	Lebanon	5,723	33	Nigeria	2,273
11	Morocco	5,196	34	Netherlands	2,227
12	Bangladesh	4,810	35	Bulgaria	2,037
13	Serbia	4,703	36	Jamaica	1,959
14	Pakistan	4,600	37	Switzerland	1,910
15	Romania	4,466	38	Indonesia	1,865
16	Russia	3,642	39	Bosnia	1,849
17	Poland	3,547	40	Peru	1,846
18	Brazil	3,540	41	Ecuador	1,749
19	Colombia	3,510	42	Sri Lanka	1,590
20	Guatemala	3,439	43	Albania	1,435
21	Egypt	3,341	44	Tunisia	1,393
22	Vietnam	3,200	45	Yemen	1,283
23	El Salvador	3,124			

Official reserves[a]
$m, end-2005

1	Japan	846,895	24	Libya	41,880
2	China	831,410	25	Indonesia	34,579
3	Taiwan	253,295	26	Denmark	34,028
4	South Korea	210,552	27	Canada	33,018
5	United States	188,255	28	Venezuela	29,803
6	Russia	182,272	29	Czech Republic	29,556
7	India	137,825	30	Saudi Arabia	28,888
8	Hong Kong	124,274	31	Nigeria	28,632
9	Singapore	115,794	32	Argentina	28,082
10	Germany	101,678	33	Israel	28,059
11	France	74,359	34	Sweden	24,867
12	Mexico	74,109	35	Egypt	21,856
13	Malaysia	70,450	36	Romania	21,601
14	Italy	65,955	37	UAE	21,010
15	Algeria	59,166	38	South Africa	20,626
16	Switzerland	57,576	39	Netherlands	20,446
17	Brazil	53,800	40	Ukraine	19,389
18	Turkey	52,494	41	Hungary	18,590
19	Thailand	52,076	42	Philippines	18,475
20	Norway	46,986	43	Spain	17,229
21	United Kingdom	43,595	44	Chile	16,933
22	Australia	43,259	45	Lebanon	16,618
23	Poland	42,561	46	Morocco	16,550

a Foreign exchange, SDRs, IMF position and gold at market prices.

Exchange rates

The Economist's Big Mac index

		Big Mac prices		Implied	Actual $	Under (−)/
		in local currency	in $	PPP[a] of the $	exchange rate	over (+) valuation against $, %

Countries with the most under-valued currencies, January 2007

		in local currency	in $	PPP[a] of the $	Actual $ exchange rate	Under (−)/over (+) valuation against $, %
1	China	11.00	1.41	3.42	7.77	−56
2	Hong Kong	12.00	1.54	3.73	7.81	−52
3	Malaysia	5.50	1.57	1.71	3.50	−51
	Venezuela	6,800.00	1.58	2,111.80	4,306.85	−51
5	Egypt	9.09	1.60	2.82	5.70	−50
6	Ukraine	9.00	1.71	2.80	5.27	−47
7	Indonesia	15,900.00	1.75	4,937.89	9,100.00	−46
	Philippines	85.00	1.74	26.40	48.90	−46
	Sri Lanka	190.00	1.75	59.01	108.59	−46
10	Thailand	62.00	1.78	19.25	34.74	−45
11	Russia	49.00	1.85	15.22	26.51	−43
12	Paraguay	10,000.00	1.90	3,105.59	5,250.00	−41
13	Slovakia	57.98	2.13	18.01	27.19	−34
	South Africa	15.50	2.14	4.81	7.25	−34
15	Uruguay	55.00	2.17	17.08	25.33	−33
16	Costa Rica	1,130.00	2.18	350.93	519.08	−32
17	Poland	6.90	2.29	2.14	3.01	−29
	Taiwan	75.00	2.28	23.29	32.93	−29
19	Japan	280.00	2.31	86.96	120.96	−28
	Pakistan	140.00	2.31	43.48	60.73	−28

Countries with the most over-valued or least under-valued currencies, Jan. 2007

		in local currency	in $	PPP[a] of the $	Actual $ exchange rate	Under (−)/over (+) valuation against $, %
1	Iceland	509.00	7.44	158.07	68.45	+131
2	Norway	41.50	6.63	12.89	6.26	+106
3	Switzerland	6.30	5.05	1.96	1.25	+57
4	Denmark	27.75	4.84	8.62	5.74	+50
5	Sweden	32.00	4.59	9.94	6.97	+43
6	United Kingdom	1.99	3.90	1.62[b]	1.96[b]	+21
7	Euro area[c]	2.94	3.82	1.10[d]	1.30[d]	+19
8	Turkey	4.55	3.22	1.41	1.41	0
9	New Zealand	4.60	3.16	1.43	1.45	−2
10	Canada	3.63	3.08	1.13	1.18	−4
	South Korea	2,900.00	3.08	900.62	941.50	−4
12	Chile	1,670.00	3.07	518.63	544.45	−5
	Colombia	6,900.00	3.06	2,142.86	2,253.53	−5
14	Brazil	6.40	3.01	1.99	2.13	−6
15	Hungary	590.00	3.00	183.23	196.84	−7
16	Peru	9.50	2.97	2.95	3.20	−8
17	UAE	10.00	2.72	3.11	3.67	−15
18	Australia	3.45	2.67	1.07	1.29	−17
	Mexico	29.00	2.66	9.01	10.89	−17

a Purchasing-power parity: local price divided by price in United States ($3.22, average of four cities).
b Dollars per pound.
c Weighted average of prices in euro area.
d Dollars per euro.

Inflation

Consumer price inflation

Highest, 2006, %			Lowest, 2006, %		
1	Zimbabwe	1016.7	1	Gabon[a]	0.0
2	Guinea[a]	31.4	2	Niger	0.1
3	Angola[a]	23.0	3	Japan	0.2
4	Yemen	21.6	4	Singapore[a]	0.5
5	Uzbekistan[a]	21.0	5	Taiwan	0.6
6	Zambia[a]	18.3	6	Poland	1.0
7	Jamaica[a]	15.3		Seychelles[a]	1.0
8	Haiti	14.2		Switzerland	1.0
9	Kenya	14.1	9	Belarus	1.1
10	Venezuela	13.6		Brunei	1.1
11	Burundia	13.4	11	Finland	1.3
12	Afghanistan[a]	13.2	12	China	1.5
	Congo-Kinshasa	13.2		Gambia, The	1.5
	Mozambique	13.2		Sweden	1.5
15	Indonesia	13.1	15	Austria	1.7
16	Serbia	12.7		Netherlands	1.7
17	Eritrea[a]	12.5		Senegal[a]	1.7
18	Ethiopia	12.3	18	Germany	1.8
19	Irana	12.1	19	Denmark	1.9
20	Moldova[a]	11.9		France	1.9
21	Qatar	11.8		Mali	1.9
22	Costa Rica	11.5			

Inflation, 2001–06

Highest average annual consumer price inflation, %			Lowest average annual consumer price inflation, %		
1	Zimbabwe	349.8	1	Libya[b]	-3.1
2	Angolaa	64.5	2	Hong Kong	-0.6
3	Belarusa	24.3	3	Japan	-0.3
4	Myanmar[b]	22.6	4	Brunei[b]	0.0
5	Uzbekistan[b]	21.5	5	Oman[c]	0.2
6	Venezuela	20.8	6	Singapore[b]	0.6
7	Zambia[b]	20.0	7	Gabon[b]	0.7
8	Haiti	19.7	8	Lithuania[b]	0.8
9	Eritrea[b]	19.2		Saudi Arabia	0.8
10	Dominican Republic	17.9		Switzerland	0.8
11	Turkey	17.8		Taiwan	0.8
12	Ghana	15.9	12	Kuwait[c]	1.0
13	Guinea[b]	15.8	13	Finland	1.1
14	Congo - Kinshasa	15.1	14	Panama[b]	1.2
15	Iran[b]	14.7	15	Senegal[b]	1.3
16	Serbia	14.2	16	China	1.5
17	Afghanistan[b]	13.9		Macedonia	1.5
19	Nigeria	13.7		Sweden	1.5
	Yemen	13.7	19	Germany	1.6
21	Suriname	13.6		Norway	1.6
22	Romania	12.9	21	Mali	1.7
23	Argentina	12.6		United Kingdom	1.7
24	Russia	12.5			

a 2005   b 2001–05   c 2001–04

Commodity prices

2006, % change on a year earlier		2000–06, % change	
1 Zinc	136.9	1 Copper	271.4
2 Copper	83.0	2 Zinc	189.7
3 Nickel	64.3	3 Lead	182.5
4 Sugar	49.4	4 Nickel	180.4
5 Gold	35.8	5 Rubber	119.1
6 Rubber	35.7	6 Oil[a]	117.7
7 Aluminium	35.4	7 Gold	116.3
8 Lead	31.2	8 Sugar	80.5
9 Tea	27.8	9 Cocoa	78.8
10 Wheat	26.2	10 Aluminium	65.7
11 Corn	24.1	11 Tin	61.1
12 Tin	18.8	12 Soya oil	56.5
13 Oil[a]	16.8	13 Wheat	56.2
14 Palm oil	12.5	14 Palm oil	54.4
15 Soya oil	10.9	15 Rice	48.7
16 Wool (NZ)	8.6	16 Lamb	40.1
17 Hides	7.2	17 Beef (Aus)	38.7
18 Coffee	6.9	18 Coconut oil	32.2
19 Rice	6.8	19 Coffee	31.4
20 Wool (Aus)	5.8	20 Beef (US)	25.5
21 Cotton	5.7	21 Corn	24.5
22 Cocoa	3.2	22 Soyabeans	18.7
23 Beef (US)	0.0	23 Timber	9.1
24 Coconut oil	-0.7	24 Hides	7.6
25 Lamb	-1.6	25 Wool (Aus)	7.1
26 Beef (Aus)	-2.5	26 Soya meal	3.6

The Economist's house-price indicators

Q4 2006[b], % change on a year earlier		1997–2006, % change	
1 Denmark	23.3	1 South Africa	351
2 South Africa	14.7	2 Ireland	253
3 Belgium	11.8	3 United Kingdom	196
4 France	11.1	4 Spain	173
5 Canada	10.8	5 France	137
Spain	10.8	6 Australia	135
7 Ireland	10.6	7 Sweden	124
8 Sweden	10.5	8 Belgium	118
9 United Kingdom	10.2	9 Denmark	115
Singapore	10.2	10 New Zealand	105
11 New Zealand	8.8	11 United States	102
12 Australia	8.3	12 Netherlands	97
13 Italy	6.2	13 Italy	92
Netherlands	6.2	14 Canada	69
15 United States	5.9	15 Switzerland	17
16 China	5.6	16 Japan	-32
17 Hong Kong	3.0	17 Hong Kong	-43
18 Swizerland	1.8		
19 Germany	0.7		
20 Japan	-2.7		

a West Texas Intermediate.   b Or latest.

Debt

Highest foreign debt[a]

$bn

1	China	281.6	26	Pakistan	33.7
2	Russia	229.0	27	Ukraine	33.3
3	Brazil	188.0	28	South Africa	30.6
4	Turkey	171.1	29	Croatia	30.2
5	Mexico	167.2	30	Peru	28.7
6	South Korea	152.8	31	Singapore	23.8
7	Indonesia	138.3	32	Slovakia	23.7
8	India	123.1	33	Lebanon	22.4
9	Argentina	114.3		Qatar	22.4
10	Poland	98.8	35	Nigeria	22.2
11	Taiwan	90.8	36	Iran	21.3
12	Israel	76.4	37	Vietnam	19.3
13	Hong Kong	72.3	38	Bangladesh	18.9
14	Hungary	66.1	39	Sudan	18.5
15	Philippines	61.5	40	Slovenia	18.4
16	Thailand	52.3	41	Tunisia	17.8
17	Malaysia	51.0	42	Ecuador	17.1
18	Czech Republic	46.8	43	Kuwait	17.0
19	Chile	45.2	44	Algeria	16.9
20	Venezuela	44.2	45	Bulgaria	16.8
21	Kazakhstan	43.4		Morocco	16.8
22	Romania	38.7	47	Serbia	16.3
23	Colombia	37.7	48	Uruguay	14.6
24	United Arab Emirates	36.7	49	Cuba	14.5
25	Egypt	34.1	50	Latvia	14.3

Highest foreign debt

As % of exports of goods and services

1	Liberia	3,514	20	Kazakhstan	185
2	Somalia	1,137	21	Brazil	183
3	Burundi	1,072	22	Sierra Leone	178
4	Central African Rep	715	23	Cuba	174
5	Guinea-Bissau	660	24	Colombia	171
6	Congo-Kinshasa	383	25	Ecuador	166
7	Sudan	358	26	Gambia, The	162
8	Uruguay	332		Malawi	162
9	Madagascar	323		Togo	162
10	Mauritania	289	29	Croatia	159
11	Argentina	245		Indonesia	159
12	Zimbabwe	228	31	Rwanda	154
13	Eritrea	213	32	Myanmar	148
14	Latvia	211	33	Guinea	146
15	Serbia	202	34	Niger	142
16	Laos	200	35	Jamaica	141
17	Peru	198	36	Romania	137
18	Burkina Faso	196		Uganda	137
19	Turkey	195	38	Pakistan	134

a Foreign debt is debt owed to non-residents and repayable in foreign currency; the figures shown include liabilities of government, public and private sectors. Developed countries have been excluded.

Highest foreign debt burden
Foreign debt as % of GDP

1	Liberia	1,087		Hungary	69
2	Guinea-Bissau	290		Serbia	69
3	Congo-Brazzaville	124		Tunisia	69
4	Congo-Kinshasa	123	26	Bulgaria	68
5	Mauritania	117	27	Central African Rep	67
6	Uruguay	116		Philippines	67
7	Lebanon	114	29	Jordan	65
8	Burundi	110	30	Gabon	63
9	Kazakhstan	106		Laos	63
10	Latvia	104		Mongolia	63
11	Estonia	102	33	Slovakia	61
12	Gambia, The	99	34	Ecuador	60
13	Jamaica	93		Ireland	60
14	Panama	90	36	Angola	59
15	Croatia	89		Israel	59
16	Sudan	88		Turkey	59
17	Zimbabwe	85	39	Cambodia	58
18	Myanmar	75		Malawi	58
19	Togo	74	41	Eritrea	57
20	Argentina	73	42	Indonesia	55
21	Moldova	70	43	Papua New Guinea	55
22	Côte d'Ivoire	69			

Highest debt service ratios[b]
%, average

1	Brazil	45		Mexico	17
2	Kazakhstan	42		Philippines	17
3	Burundi	41	25	Jamaica	16
4	Turkey	39		Nigeria	16
	Uruguay	39	27	Bolivia	15
6	Latvia	37		Chile	15
7	Colombia	35		Russia	15
8	Bulgaria	32		Slovakia	15
9	Ecuador	31		Thailand	15
	Hungary	31	32	Cuba	14
11	Poland	29		Estonia	14
12	Peru	26	34	Tunisia	13
13	Croatia	24		Ukraine	13
14	Argentina	21		Zimbabwe	13
15	Namibia	19	37	Algeria	12
16	Lebanon	18		Czech Republic	12
	Panama	18		Gambia, The	12
	Romania	18		India	12
	Slovenia	18	41	Israel	11
20	Indonesia	17		Morocco	11
	Lithuania	17		Papua New Guinea	11
	Madagascar	17		Paraguay	11

b Debt service is the sum of interest and principal repayments (amortisation) due on outstanding foreign debt. The debt service ratio is debt service expressed as a percentage of the country's exports of goods and services.

Aid

Largest bilateral and multilateral donors[a]
$m

1	United States	27,622	14	Switzerland	1,767
2	Japan	13,147	15	Saudi Arabia[b]	1,734
3	United Kingdom	10,767	16	Australia	1,680
4	Germany	10,082	17	Austria	1,573
5	France	10,026	18	Finland	902
6	Netherlands	5,115	19	South Korea	752
7	Italy	5,091	20	Ireland	719
8	Canada	3,756	21	Turkey	601
9	Sweden	3,362	22	Kuwait	547
10	Spain	3,018	23	Taiwan	483
11	Norway	2,786	24	Greece	384
12	Denmark	2,109	25	Portugal	377
13	Belgium	1,963	26	New Zealand	274

Largest recipients of bilateral and multilateral aid
$m

1	Iraq	21,654	35	Malawi	575
2	Nigeria	6,437	36	Philippines	562
3	Afghanistan	2,775	37	Bosnia	546
4	Indonesia	2,524	38	Cambodia	538
5	Ethiopia	1,937	39	Haiti	515
6	Vietnam	1,905		Niger	515
7	Sudan	1,829	41	Colombia	511
8	Congo-Kinshasa	1,828	42	Turkey	464
9	China	1,757	43	Angola	442
10	India	1,724	44	Nepal	428
11	Pakistan	1,666	45	Cameroon	414
12	Tanzania	1,505	46	Ukraine	410
13	Congo	1,449	47	Peru	398
14	Bangladesh	1,321	48	Chad	380
15	Mozambique	1,286	49	Tunisia	376
16	Uganda	1,198	50	Algeria	371
17	Sri Lanka	1,189	51	Zimbabwe	368
18	Serbia	1,132	52	Burundi	365
19	Ghana	1,120	53	Eritrea	355
20	West Bank and Gaza	1,102	54	Benin	349
21	Zambia	945	55	Sierra Leone	343
22	Madagascar	929	56	Yemen	336
23	Egypt	926	57	Albania	319
24	Kenya	768	58	Georgia	310
25	Nicaragua	740	59	Laos	296
26	South Africa	700	60	Kyrgyzstan	268
27	Mali	691	61	Papua New Guinea	266
28	Senegal	689	62	Guatemala	254
29	Honduras	681	63	Lebanon	243
30	Burkina Faso	660	64	Tajikistan	241
31	Morocco	652	65	Liberia	236
32	Jordan	622		Somalia	236
33	Bolivia	583	67	Macedonia	230
34	Rwanda	576	68	Kazakhstan	229

Largest bilateral and multilateral donors[a]
% of GDP

#	Country	Value	#	Country	Value
1	Norway	0.94	17	Japan	0.28
	Sweden	0.94	18	New Zealand	0.27
3	Luxembourg	0.82		Spain	0.27
	Netherlands	0.82	20	Australia	0.25
5	Denmark	0.81	21	United States	0.22
6	Saudi Arabia[b]	0.69	22	Portugal	0.21
7	Belgium	0.53	23	Iceland	0.18
8	Austria	0.52	24	Greece	0.17
9	France	0.47		Turkey	0.17
	United Kingdom	0.47	26	Slovakia	0.12
11	Finland	0.46	27	Czech Republic	0.11
12	Switzerland	0.44		Hungary	0.11
13	Ireland	0.42	29	South Korea	0.10
14	Germany	0.36	30	Israel	0.07
15	Canada	0.34		Poland	0.07
16	Italy	0.29			

Largest recipients of bilateral and multilateral aid
$ per head

#	Country	Value	#	Country	Value
1	Congo-Brazzaville	362	31	Kyrgyzstan	52
2	West Bank and Gaza	303	32	Ghana	51
3	Timor-Leste	189		Mali	51
4	Bosnia	140	34	Burkina Faso	50
5	Serbia	139		Guinea-Bissau	50
6	Nicaragua	135		Laos	50
7	Jordan	115		Madagascar	50
8	Macedonia	113		Sudan	50
9	Albania	102	39	Nigeria	49
10	Bhutan	98	40	Burundi	48
	Suriname	98	41	Moldova	46
12	Honduras	95	42	Belize	45
13	Mongolia	83		Malawi	45
14	Eritrea	81		Papua New Guinea	45
	Zambia	81	45	Uganda	42
16	Equatorial Guinea	78	46	Benin	41
17	Fiji	75		Swaziland	41
18	Liberia	72	48	Botswana	40
19	Georgia	69	49	Chad	39
20	Lebanon	68		Gabon	39
21	Mozambique	65		Tanzania	39
22	Armenia	64	52	Cambodia	38
	Rwanda	64		Gambia	38
24	Bolivia	63		Lesotho	38
25	Mauritania	62		Tunisia	38
	Sierra Leone	62	56	Niger	37
27	Namibia	61		Tajikistan	37
	Sri Lanka	61	58	Congo-Kinshasa	32
29	Haiti	60	59	El Salvador	29
30	Senegal	59		Somalia	29

a China also provides aid, but does not disclose amounts.   b 2004

Industry and services

Largest industrial output
$bn

1	United States	2,732		25	Iran	85
2	Japan	1,360			Taiwan	85
3	China	1,072		27	Thailand	78
4	Germany	838		28	Ireland	75
5	United Kingdom	572		29	United Arab Emirates	73
6	Italy	476			Venezuela	73
7	France	447		31	South Africa	72
8	Spain	337		32	Malaysia	68
9	South Korea	315		33	Argentina	66
10	Russia	290		34	Denmark	65
11	Brazil	289		35	Algeria	63
12	India	218		36	Finland	58
13	Mexico	200		37	Nigeria	56
14	Australia	198		38	Chile	54
15	Saudi Arabia	183		39	Greece	47
16	Netherlands	150		40	Czech Republic	46
17	Indonesia	132			Portugal	46
18	Norway	127		42	Colombia	42
19	Switzerland	103		43	Kuwait	41
20	Sweden	100		44	Singapore	40
21	Austria	95		45	Hungary	34
22	Poland	94			Romania	34
23	Belgium	89		47	Egypt	32
24	Turkey	87			Philippines	32

Highest growth in industrial output
Average annual real % growth, 2000–2005

1	Chad	45.9		10	Kazakhstan	11.3
2	Afghanistan	21.1		11	Belarus	11.1
3	Armenia	16.8		12	China	10.9
4	Azerbaijan	16.7		13	Angola	10.5
5	Cambodia	14.2			Estonia	10.5
6	Trinidad and Tobago	12.7			Lithuania	10.5
7	Georgia	12.6		16	Mozambique	10.3
8	Laos	12.1		17	Vietnam	10.2
9	Tajikistan	11.6		18	Tanzania	9.7

Lowest growth in industrial output
Average annual real % growth, 2000–2005

1	Iraq	-17.0		10	Dominican Republic	-0.6
2	Zimbabwe	-10.0		11	Oman	-0.5
3	Burundi	-6.2		12	Italy	-0.2
4	Papua New Guinea	-3.6			Venezuela	-0.2
5	Hong Kong	-3.4		14	Netherlands	-0.1
6	Côte d'Ivoire	-1.8			United Kingdom	-0.1
7	Portugal	-1.1		16	Japan	0.0
8	Denmark	-0.9			Yemen	0.0
9	Syria	-0.7		18	Belgium	0.4

Largest manufacturing output
$bn

1	United States	1,738	21	Austria		61
2	Japan	952	22	Poland		55
3	China	760	23	Ireland		54
4	Germany	643	24	Turkey		51
5	United Kingdom	330	25	South Africa		46
6	Italy	317	26	Argentina		42
7	France	276		Finland		42
8	South Korea	221	28	Malaysia		40
9	Spain	180	29	Denmark		36
10	Mexico	138	30	Norway		33
11	Russia	137		Singapore		33
12	India	129	32	Czech Republic		31
13	Australia	88		Saudi Arabia		31
14	Netherlands	87	34	Portugal		29
15	Indonesia	80	35	Hungary		25
16	Switzerland	73		Venezuela		25
	Taiwan	73	37	Greece		25
18	Sweden	72	38	Romania		24
19	Belgium	63	39	Iran		23
20	Thailand	62		Philippines		23

Largest services output
$bn

1	United States	9,561	28	Portugal	134
2	Japan	3,083	29	Finland	131
3	Germany	1,928	30	Ireland	121
4	France	1,638	31	Indonesia	118
5	United Kingdom	1,605	32	Saudi Arabia	115
6	Italy	1,251	33	Argentina	101
7	China	894	34	Iran	85
8	Spain	754	35	Thailand	81
9	Mexico	538	36	Singapore	77
10	Australia	513	37	Czech Republic	75
11	Netherlands	462	38	Hungary	71
12	South Korea	441	39	Colombia	65
13	India	435	40	Venezuela	62
14	Russia	428	41	Pakistan	59
15	Brazil	410	42	Chile	55
16	Belgium	278	43	Romania	54
17	Switzerland	257		United Arab Emirates	54
18	Sweden	254	45	Malaysia	52
	Taiwan	254		Philippines	52
20	Turkey	236	47	Peru	46
21	Austria	208		Ukraine	46
22	Poland	197	49	Egypt	44
23	Denmark	191	50	Kuwait	40
24	Greece	167	51	Bangladesh	32
25	Norway	163	52	Algeria	31
26	Hong Kong	160		Kazakhstan	31
	South Africa	160		Slovakia	31

Agriculture

Most economically dependent on agriculture
% of GDP from agriculture

1	Liberia	63.6	24	Burkina Faso	30.6
2	Guinea-Bissau	61.8	25	Madagascar	28.1
3	Central African Rep	53.9		Uzbekistan	28.1
4	Ethiopia	47.7	27	Kenya	27.4
5	Sierra Leone	46.1	28	Paraguay	26.8
6	Congo-Kinshasa	46.0	29	Bhutan[b]	25.8
	Laos	46.0	30	Guinea	25.6
8	Tanzania	44.5	31	Albania[b]	25.2
9	Rwanda	42.2	32	Nigeria	23.7
10	Togo	41.8	33	Mozambique	23.2
11	Cameroon	40.8	34	Guatemala	22.9
12	Nepal	40.2	35	Chad	22.7
13	Niger[a]	39.9	36	Eritrea	22.6
14	Ghana	38.8	37	Zimbabwe	22.4
15	Mali	36.0	38	Mongolia	22.1
16	Burundi	34.9	39	Tajikistan	22.0
17	Malawi	34.7	40	Vietnam[b]	21.8
18	Kyrgyzstan	34.1	41	Côte d'Ivoire	21.7
19	Sudan	33.7	42	Pakistan	21.6
20	Uganda	33.5	43	Syria	21.4
21	Gambia	33.0	44	Moldova	21.3
22	Cambodia[b]	32.9	45	Armenia	20.5
23	Benin	32.2		Bangladesh	20.5

Least economically dependent on agriculture
% of GDP from agriculture

1	Hong Kong[b]	0.1	24	South Africa	3.1
	Singapore	0.1	25	Finland[b]	3.2
3	Kuwait[a]	0.5	26	Australia[a]	3.4
4	Luxembourg[b]	0.6		Czech Republic[b]	3.4
5	Puerto Rico[c]	0.7	28	Slovakia	3.5
6	Trinidad & Tobago[b]	0.9		Spain[b]	3.5
7	United Kingdom[b]	1.0	30	Portugal[b]	3.7
8	Germany[b]	1.1		South Korea[b]	3.7
9	Japan[a]	1.3	32	Hungary[b]	3.8
10	Belgium[b]	1.4		Mexico	3.8
11	Norway[b]	1.6	34	Saudi Arabia[b]	4.0
12	Sweden[b]	1.8	35	Latvia[b]	4.1
13	Austria[b]	1.9	36	Estonia[b]	4.3
	Oman[b]	1.9	37	Venezuela[a]	4.5
15	Denmark[b]	2.3	38	Poland	4.9
	Jordan	2.3	39	Barbados[a]	5.4
17	Netherlands[b]	2.4	40	Chile	5.5
18	France[b]	2.5		Jamaica[b]	5.5
	Slovenia[b]	2.5	42	Congo-Brazzaville	5.6
20	Botswana	2.6		Russia	5.6
	Italy[b]	2.6	44	Lithuania	5.9
22	Ireland[a]	2.7	45	Mauritius	6.1
	United Arab Emirates[b]	2.7	46	Ecuador	6.3

a 2003   b 2004   c 2001

Highest growth
Average annual real % growth, 1995–2005ᵃ

1	Sudan	10.9		Benin	5.6
2	Angola	10.3		Yemen	5.6
3	United Arab Emirates	8.6	12	Azerbaijan	5.3
4	Rwanda	7.5		Kyrgyzstan	5.3
5	Kuwait	6.3		United States	5.3
	Mozambique	6.3	15	Armenia	5.2
7	Tajikistan	5.8	16	Cameroon	5.1
8	Tunisia	5.7		Gambia, The	5.1
9	Belize	5.6	18	Algeria	5.0

Lowest growth
Average annual real % growth, 1995–2005ᵃ

1	West Bank and Gaza	-4.0	9	Congo-Kinshasa	-1.1
2	Jamaica	-3.3		Zimbabwe	-1.1
3	Luxembourg	-2.9	11	Burundi	-1.0
4	Japan	-2.5		Eritrea	-1.0
5	Switzerland	-2.1	13	Estonia	-0.8
6	Barbados	-1.6	14	Georgia	-0.3
7	Trinidad & Tobago	-1.5		Mongolia	-0.3
8	Fiji	-1.2	16	Slovenia	-0.2

Biggest producers
'000 tonnes

Cereals

1	China	429,374	6	Indonesia	64,224
2	United States	366,542	7	Brazil	55,689
3	India	242,284	8	Canada	53,086
4	Russia	76,564	9	Germany	45,980
5	France	65,998	10	Bangladesh	41,155

Meat

1	China	78,754	6	India	6,716
2	United States	39,530	7	Mexico	5,551
3	Brazil	19,966	8	Canada	5,547
4	Germany	7,077	9	Spain	5,254
5	France	6,824	10	Russia	4,881

Fruit

1	China	87,127	6	Spain	15,490
2	India	47,031	7	Mexico	14,888
3	Brazil	36,863	8	Indonesia	13,777
4	United States	26,977	9	Iran	13,193
5	Italy	18,015	10	Philippines	12,958

Vegetables

1	China	429,256	5	Italy	15,664
2	India	77,029	6	Egypt	15,475
3	United States	35,984	7	Russia	14,323
4	Turkey	25,064	8	Spain	12,788

a Or nearest available years.

Commodities

Wheat

Top 10 producers
'000 tonnes

1	EU27	133,800
2	China	97,500
3	India	68,600
4	United States	57,300
5	Russia	47,600
6	Canada	26,800
7	Australia	25,100
8	Pakistan	21,600
9	Ukraine	18,700
10	Turkey	18,000

Top 10 consumers
'000s tonnes

1	EU27	129,400
2	China	100,500
3	India	72,200
4	Russia	38,000
5	United States	31,200
6	Pakistan	21,100
7	Turkey	15,700
8	Egypt	15,600
9	Iran	14,800
10	Ukraine	12,000

Rice[a]

Top 10 producers
'000 tonnes

1	China	126,414
2	India	91,790
3	Indonesia	34,959
4	Bangladesh	28,758
5	Vietnam	22,772
6	Thailand	18,200
7	Myanmar	10,440
8	Philippines	9,820
9	Japan	8,257
10	Brazil	7,874

Top 10 consumers
'000 tonnes

1	China	128,000
2	India	85,220
3	Indonesia	35,800
4	Bangladesh	29,000
5	Vietnam	18,250
6	Philippines	11,000
7	Myanmar	10,400
8	Thailand	9,500
9	Brazil	8,974
10	Japan	8,250

Sugar[b]

Top 10 producers
'000 tonnes

1	Brazil	28,135
2	EU25	21,698
3	India	15,216
4	China	9,785
5	United States	6,784
6	Mexico	5,619
7	Australia	5,393
8	Thailand	4,589
9	Pakistan	2,839
10	Russia	2,719

Top 10 consumers
'000 tonnes

1	India	20,110
2	EU25	16,765
3	China	11,785
4	Brazil	10,950
5	United States	9,248
6	Russia	6,600
7	Mexico	4,877
8	Pakistan	4,075
9	Indonesia	4,052
10	Egypt	2,675

Coarse grains[c]

Top 5 producers
'000 tonnes

1	United States	298,700
2	China	149,000
3	EU27	148,300
4	Brazil	44,400
5	India	34,600

Top 5 consumers
'000 tonnes

1	United States	244,300
2	China	146,100
3	EU27	144,900
4	Brazil	41,700
5	Mexico	38,500

Tea

Top 10 producers		*Top 10 consumers*	
'000 tonnes		*'000 tonnes*	
1 China	935	1 India	757
2 India	928	2 China	587
3 Kenya	329	3 Russia	173
4 Sri Lanka	317	4 Japan	150
5 Indonesia	166	5 Pakistan	139
6 Turkey	135	6 Turkey	133
7 Vietnam	109	7 United Kingdom	128
8 Japan	100	8 United States	100
9 Argentina	73	9 Egypt	77
10 Bangladesh	59	10 Iran	62

Coffee

Top 10 producers		*Top 10 consumers*	
'000 tonnes		*'000s tonnes*	
1 Brazil	1,977	1 United States	1,246
2 Vietnam	810	2 Brazil	957
3 Colombia	718	3 Germany	501
4 Indonesia	520	4 Japan	433
5 India	277	5 Italy	328
6 Ethiopia	270	6 France	303
7 Mexico	240	7 Spain	186
8 Guatemala	221	8 United Kingdom	144
9 Honduras	192	9 Poland	131
10 Côte d'Ivoire	130	10 Indonesia	120

Cocoa

Top 10 producers		*Top 10 consumers*	
'000 tonnes		*'000 tonnes*	
1 Côte d'Ivoire	1,286	1 United States	781
2 Ghana	599	2 Germany	278
3 Indonesia	460	3 France	246
4 Nigeria	200	4 United Kingdom	220
5 Cameroon	184	5 Russia	184
6 Brazil	171	6 Japan	153
7 Ecuador	116	7 Italy	110
8 Papua New Guinea	48	8 Spain	90
9 Colombia	37	9 Brazil	88
10 Mexico	36	10 Poland	63

a Milled.
b Raw.
c Includes: maize (corn), barley, sorghum, rye, oats and millet.

Copper

Top 10 producers[a] '000 tonnes		*Top 10 consumers*[b] '000 tonnes	
1 Chile	5,321	1 China	3,656
2 United States	1,140	2 United States	2,270
3 Indonesia	1,064	3 Japan	1,229
4 Peru	1,010	4 Germany	1,115
5 Australia	930	5 South Korea	869
6 Russia	805	6 Russia	792
7 China	762	7 Italy	681
8 Canada	595	8 Taiwan	638
9 Poland	512	9 France	472
10 Zambia	441	10 Mexico	437

Lead

Top 10 producers[a] '000 tonnes		*Top 10 consumers*[b] '000 tonnes	
1 China	1,327	1 China	1,985
2 Australia	767	2 United States	1,460
3 United States	441	3 South Korea	353
4 Peru	319	4 Germany	330
5 Mexico	135	5 Japan	294
6 Canada	79	6 Mexico	289
7 Ireland	64	7 United Kingdom	282
8 India	60	8 Spain	279
Sweden	60	9 Italy	262
10 Poland	51	10 France	210

Zinc

Top 10 producers[a] '000 tonnes		*Top 10 consumers*[c] '000 tonnes	
1 China	2,548	1 China	2,989
2 Australia	1,367	2 United States	1,120
3 Peru	1,202	3 Japan	602
4 United States	748	4 Germany	514
5 Canada	667	5 South Korea	443
6 India	477	6 India	389
7 Mexico	473	7 Italy	373
8 Ireland	429	8 Belgium	345
9 Kazakhstan	364	9 Taiwan	306
10 Sweden	216	10 France	271

Tin

Top 5 producers[a] '000 tonnes		*Top 5 consumers*[b] '000 tonnes	
1 China	121.6	1 China	115.5
2 Indonesia	120.0	2 United States	42.1
3 Peru	42.1	3 Japan	33.2
4 Bolivia	18.7	4 Germany	19.1
5 Brazil	11.7	5 South Korea	17.9

Nickel

Top 10 producers[a]		*Top 10 consumers[b]*	
'000 tonnes		*'000 tonnes*	
1 Russia	289.2	1 China	200.7
2 Canada	199.9	2 Japan	171.0
3 Australia	186.0	3 United States	128.0
4 Indonesia	134.6	4 South Korea	117.7
5 New Caledonia	111.9	5 Germany	116.4
6 China	72.7	6 Taiwan	84.1
7 Cuba	72.0	7 Italy	60.0
8 Colombia	52.7	8 Finland	50.4
9 South Africa	42.4	9 Belgium	49.3
10 Brazil	36.6	10 Spain	48.0

Aluminium

Top 10 producers[d]		*Top 10 consumers[e]*	
'000 tonnes		*'000 tonnes*	
1 China	7,806	1 China	7,119
2 Russia	3,647	2 United States	6,114
3 Canada	2,894	3 Japan	2,276
4 United States	2,480	4 Germany	1,759
5 Australia	1,903	5 South Korea	1,201
6 Brazil	1,498	6 Russia	1,020
7 Norway	1,377	7 Italy	977
8 India	942	8 India	958
9 South Africa	851	9 Canada	803
10 United Arab Emirates	850	10 Brazil	759

Precious metals

Gold [a]		*Silver* [a]	
Top 10 producers		*Top 10 producers*	
tonnes		*tonnes*	
1 South Africa	297.3	1 Peru	3,193
2 Australia	263.0	2 Mexico	2,870
3 United States	255.0	3 Australia	2,417
4 China	208.8	4 China	2,000
5 Peru	207.8	5 Chile	1,400
6 Russia	156.6	6 Poland	1,263
7 Indonesia	138.7	7 United States	1,225
8 Canada	120.5	8 Canada	1,124
9 Uzbekistan	86.0	9 Kazakhstan	804
10 Papua New Guinea	68.7	10 Bolivia	420

Platinum		*Palladium*	
Top 3 producers		*Top 3 producers*	
tonnes		*tonnes*	
1 South Africa	159.1	1 Russia	143.7
2 Russia	27.7	2 South Africa	81.0
3 United States/Canada	11.4	3 United States/Canada	28.1

a Mine production. b Refined consumption. c Slab consumption.
d Primary refined production. e Primary refined consumption.

Rubber (natural and synthetic)

	Top 10 producers '000 tonnes			Top 10 consumers '000 tonnes	
1	Thailand	3,077	1	China	4,625
2	United States	2,366	2	United States	3,114
3	Indonesia	2,321	3	Japan	2,013
4	China	2,060	4	India	1,023
5	Japan	1,627	5	Germany	898
6	Russia	1,147	6	South Korea	714
7	Malaysia	1,082	7	Brazil	707
8	India	867	8	Russia	636
9	Germany	855	9	France	585
10	France	655	10	Malaysia	557

Raw wool

	Top 10 producers[a] '000 tonnes			Top 10 consumers[a] '000 tonnes	
1	Australia	335	1	China	358
2	China	171	2	India	120
3	New Zealand	167	3	Italy	110
4	Argentina	43	4	Turkey	69
5	India	38	5	United Kingdom	31
6	United Kingdom	31	6	Japan	30
7	Uruguay	29	7	Russia	29
8	South Africa	27	8	Iran	26
	Turkey	27	9	Belgium	25
10	Iran	24	10	New Zealand	23

Cotton

	Top 10 producers '000 tonnes			Top 10 consumers '000 tonnes	
1	China	5,714	1	China	9,617
2	United States	5,201	2	India	3,627
3	India	4,148	3	Pakistan	2,390
4	Pakistan	2,089	4	Turkey	1,500
5	Uzbekistan	1,210	5	United States	1,282
6	Brazil	1,038	6	Brazil	870
7	Turkey	800	7	Indonesia	470
8	Australia	598	8	Bangladesh	455
9	Greece	430	9	Mexico	455
10	Syria	330	10	Thailand	440

Major oil seeds[b]

	Top 5 producers '000 tonnes			Top 5 consumers '000 tonnes	
1	United States	94,841	1	China	78,526
2	Brazil	57,778	2	United States	63,566
3	China	51,818	3	Argentina	37,659
4	Argentina	45,469	4	EU25	37,385
5	India	28,370	5	Brazil	32,850

Oil[c]

Top 10 producers
'000 barrels per day

1	Saudi Arabia[d]	11,035
2	Russia	9,551
3	United States	6,830
4	Iran[d]	4,049
5	Mexico	3,759
6	China	3,627
7	Canada	3,047
8	Venezuela[d]	3,007
9	Norway	2,969
10	United Arab Emirates[d]	2,751

Top 10 consumers
'000 barrels per day

1	United States	20,655
2	China	6,988
3	Japan	5,360
4	Russia	2,753
5	Germany	2,586
6	India	2,485
7	South Korea	2,308
8	Canada	2,241
9	Mexico	1,978
10	France	1,961

Natural gas

Top 10 producers
Billion cubic metres

1	Russia	598.0
2	United States	525.7
3	Canada	185.5
4	United Kingdom	88.0
5	Algeria[d]	87.8
6	Iran[d]	87.0
7	Norway	85.0
8	Indonesia[d]	76.0
9	Saudi Arabia[d]	69.5
10	Netherlands	62.9

Top 10 consumers
Billion cubic metres

1	United States	633.5
2	Russia	405.1
3	United Kingdom	94.6
4	Canada	91.4
5	Iran[d]	88.5
6	Germany	85.9
7	Japan	81.1
8	Italy	79.0
9	Ukraine	72.9
10	Saudi Arabia[d]	69.5

Coal

Top 10 producers
Million tonnes oil equivalent

1	China	1107.7
2	United States	576.2
3	Australia	202.4
4	India	199.6
5	South Africa	138.9
6	Russia	137.0
7	Indonesia[d]	83.2
8	Poland	68.7
9	Germany	53.2
10	Kazakhstan	44.0

Top 10 consumers
Million tonnes oil equivalent

1	China	1081.9
2	United States	575.4
3	India	212.9
4	Japan	121.3
5	Russia	111.6
6	South Africa	91.9
7	Germany	82.1
8	Poland	56.7
9	South Korea	54.8
10	Australia	52.2

Oil[c]

Top proved reserves
% of world total

1	Saudi Arabia[d]	22.0	5	United Arab Emirates[d]	8.1
2	Iran[d]	11.5	6	Venezuela[d]	6.6
3	Iraq[d]	9.6	7	Russia	6.2
4	Kuwait[d]	8.5			

a Clean basis. b Soybeans, sunflower seed, cottonseed, groundnuts and rapeseed.
c Includes crude oil, shale oil, oil sands and natural gas liquids. d Opec members.

Energy

Largest producers
Million tonnnes oil equivalent, 2004

1	United States	1,641.0	16	Algeria	165.7
2	China	1,536.8	17	United Arab Emirates	164.0
3	Russia	1,158.5	18	South Africa	156.0
4	Saudi Arabia	556.2	19	France	137.4
5	India	466.9	20	Germany	136.0
6	Canada	397.5	21	Kuwait	132.8
7	Iran	278.0	22	Kazakhstan	118.6
8	Australia	261.8	23	Iraq	103.4
9	Indonesia	258.0	24	Japan	96.8
10	Mexico	253.9	25	Malaysia	88.5
11	Norway	238.6	26	Argentina	85.4
12	Nigeria	229.4		Libya	85.4
13	United Kingdom	225.2	28	Poland	78.8
14	Venezuela	196.1	29	Ukraine	76.3
15	Brazil	176.3	30	Colombia	76.2

Largest consumers
Million tonnnes oil equivalent, 2004

1	United States	2,325.9	16	Spain	142.2
2	China	1,609.3	17	Saudi Arabia	140.4
3	Russia	641.5	18	Ukraine	140.3
4	India	572.9	19	South Africa	131.1
5	Japan	533.2	20	Australia	115.8
6	Germany	348.0	21	Nigeria	99.0
7	France	275.2	22	Thailand	97.1
8	Canada	269.0	23	Poland	91.7
9	United Kingdom	233.7	24	Netherlands	82.1
10	South Korea	213.0	25	Turkey	81.9
11	Brazil	204.8	26	Pakistan	74.4
12	Italy	184.5	27	Argentina	63.7
13	Indonesia	174.0	28	Belgium	57.7
14	Mexico	165.5	29	Egypt	56.9
15	Iran	145.8	30	Malaysia	56.7

Energy efficiency[a]

Most efficient			Least efficient		
GDP per unit of energy use, 2004			*GDP per unit of energy use, 2003*		
1	Hong Kong	11.5	1	Uzbekistan	0.8
2	Colombia	10.9	2	Tanzania	1.3
	Peru	10.9		Trinidad & Tobago	1.3
4	Bangladesh	10.5	4	Nigeria	1.4
5	Uruguay	10.4	5	Zambia	1.5
6	Morocco	10.3	6	Kazakhstan	1.9
7	Namibia	10.2		Kuwait	1.9
8	Costa Rica	10.0	8	Moldova	2.0
9	Ireland	9.5		Russia	2.0
10	Botswana	8.6		Ukraine	2.0

a 2000 PPP$, per kg of oil equivalent.

Net energy importers
% of commercial energy use, 2004

Highest			Lowest		
1	Hong Kong	100	1	Congo-Brazzaville	-1084
2	Singapore	99	2	Norway	-763
3	Moldova	98	3	Gabon	-615
4	Jordan	96	4	Angola	-505
	Lebanon	96	5	Kuwait	-429
6	Morocco	94	6	Algeria	-404
7	Israel	92	7	Oman	-391
8	Jamaica	88	8	Libya	-369
9	Ireland	87	9	Saudi Arabia	-296
10	Belarus	86	10	Turkmenistan	-274
11	Portugal	85		United Arab Emirates	-274

Largest consumption per head
Kg of oil equivalent, 2004

1	Kuwait	10,212	12	Belgium	5,536
2	United Arab Emirates	10,142	13	Netherlands	5,045
3	Trinidad & Tobago	8,675	14	Oman	4,667
4	Canada	8,411	15	France	4,547
5	United States	7,921	16	Czech Republic	4,460
6	Finland	7,286		Russia	4,460
7	Saudi Arabia	6,233	18	South Korea	4,431
8	Singapore	6,034	19	New Zealand	4,344
9	Norway	6,024	20	Germany	4,218
10	Sweden	5,998	21	Japan	4,173
11	Australia	5,762	22	Austria	4,060

Sources of electricity
% of total, 2004

Oil			Gas		
1	Yemen	100.0	1	Turkmenistan	100.0
2	Benin	98.8	2	Trinidad & Tobago	99.5
3	Iraq	98.5	3	Moldova	97.9
4	Jamaica	96.5	4	United Arab Emirates	97.5
5	Cuba	95.3	5	Algeria	97.0

Hydropower			Nuclear power		
1	Congo-Brazzaville	100.0	1	Lithuania	80.5
	Paraguay	100.0	2	France	79.0
3	Nepal	99.8	3	Belgium	56.1
4	Congo-Kinshasa	99.7	4	Slovakia	55.9
	Mozambique	99.7	5	Sweden	51.1

Coal		
1	Botswana	95.7
2	Poland	94.1
3	South Africa	93.2
4	Estonia	92.4
5	Australia	79.3

Workers of the world[a]

Highest % of population in labour force

1	Cayman Islands	68.9	21	Slovenia	50.5
2	Bermuda	59.4	22	Czech Republic	50.3
3	China	57.8	23	United Kingdom	50.2
4	Switzerland	57.5	24	Finland	50.0
5	Thailand	55.7	25	Cyprus	49.9
6	Canada	55.4	26	South Korea	49.7
	Denmark	54.4	27	Slovakia	49.4
8	Iceland	54.0	28	Ecuador	49.3
9	Norway	52.9	29	United States	49.1
10	Netherlands	52.6	30	Latvia	49.0
11	Brazil	52.4	31	Brunei	48.8
	Portugal	52.4	32	Estonia	48.6
	Singapore	52.4	33	Austria	48.5
14	Hong Kong	52.0		Germany	48.5
	Japan	52.0	35	Ghana	47.8
16	Macau	51.8	36	Belgium	47.6
17	New Zealand	51.7		Spain	47.6
18	Australia	50.8	38	Ireland	47.5
19	Sweden	50.7	39	Bahrain	47.4
20	Russia	50.6	40	Lithuania	47.2

Most male workforce
Highest % men in workforce

1	Pakistan	83.9
2	West Bank and Gaza	83.4
3	Algeria	83.0
4	Oman	81.6
5	Syria	80.6
6	Bahrain	78.3
7	Egypt	78.1
8	Bangladesh	77.7
9	Guatemala	77.4
10	Tunisia	74.3
11	Turkey	73.7
12	Morocco	72.9
13	Malta	69.2
	Nicaragua	69.2
15	India	68.4
16	Sri Lanka	66.5
17	Honduras	66.3
18	Costa Rica	65.4
19	Malaysia	65.3
	Mauritius	65.3
21	Mexico	64.5
22	Chile	64.4
23	Suriname	63.1
24	Panama	62.7
25	Philippines	62.2

Most female workforce
Highest % women in workforce

1	Belarus	53.3
2	Benin	53.1
3	Moldova	51.0
	Mongolia	51.0
	Tanzania	51.0
6	Cayman Islands	49.7
7	Ghana	49.6
8	Armenia	49.5
	Madagascar	49.5
10	Bahamas	49.4
	Estonia	49.4
12	Guadeloupe	49.1
	Lithuania	49.1
	Russia	49.1
15	Kazakhstan	49.0
16	Ukraine	48.9
17	Barbados	48.7
	Latvia	48.7
19	Bermuda	48.5
20	Zimbabwe	48.2
21	Papua New Guinea	47.9
	Sweden	47.9
23	Ethiopia	47.8
24	Finland	47.7
	Azerbaijan	47.7

Lowest % of population in labour force

1	West Bank and Gaza	21.9		Mongolia	39.3
2	Algeria	27.6	22	Malta	39.5
3	Syria	29.3	23	Moldova	39.6
4	Pakistan	29.6	24	Chile	39.7
5	Egypt	30.5	25	Guinea-Bissau	39.9
6	Congo-Brazzaville	32.3	26	El Salvador	40.1
7	Armenia	32.4		Sri Lanka	40.1
8	Turkey	33.5	28	Croatia	40.8
9	Suriname	34.6	29	Honduras	40.9
10	Bangladesh	34.7		Macedonia	40.9
11	Botswana	35.0	31	Malaysia	41.3
	Guatemala	35.0	32	Zimbabwe	41.5
	Tunisia	35.0	33	Mexico	41.7
14	Nicaragua	36.5	34	Hungary	42.0
15	Puerto Rico	37.0	35	Israel	42.1
16	Oman	37.3	36	Italy	42.2
17	Morocco	37.4	37	Costa Rica	42.3
18	Panama	38.7	38	Albania	42.4
19	India	39.1	39	Bulgaria	42.7
20	Georgia	39.3		Greece	42.7

Highest rate of unemployment

% of labour force[b]

1	Macedonia	37.2	26	Lithuania	12.8
2	Namibia	33.8	27	Georgia	12.6
3	South Africa	27.1	28	Kyrgyzstan	12.5
4	West Bank and Gaza	26.7	29	Iran	12.3
5	Guinea-Bissau	26.3		Panama	12.3
6	Guadeloupe	24.7	31	Nicaragua	12.2
7	Ethiopia	22.9	32	Bulgaria	12.0
8	Martinique	22.4	33	Morocco	11.9
9	Botswana	19.6	34	Syria	11.7
10	Poland	19.0	35	Yemen	11.5
11	Dominican Republic	18.4	36	Jamaica	11.4
12	Slovakia	18.1	37	Germany	11.0
13	Algeria	17.7		Spain	11.0
14	Uruguay	16.9	39	Philippines	10.9
15	Venezuela	15.8	40	Bahamas	10.8
16	Argentina	15.6	41	Israel	10.7
17	Albania	15.2	42	Puerto Rico	10.6
	Serbia	15.2	43	Peru	10.5
19	Netherlands Antilles	15.1	44	Latvia	10.4
20	Tunisia	14.3		Trinidad & Tobago	10.4
21	Burundi	14.0	46	Turkey	10.3
	Suriname	14.0	47	France	9.9
23	Croatia	13.8	48	Barbados	9.8
24	Colombia	13.6	49	Brazil	9.7
25	Jordan	13.2		Estonia	9.7

a Latest available year.   b ILO definition.

The business world

Global competitiveness

	Overall	Government	Infrastructure
1	United States	Singapore	United States
2	Singapore	Hong Kong	Switzerland
3	Hong Kong	Switzerland	Singapore
4	Luxembourg	Denmark	Denmark
5	Denmark	Ireland	Sweden
6	Switzerland	New Zealand	Japan
7	Iceland	Australia	Germany
8	Netherlands	China	Iceland
9	Sweden	Luxembourg	Norway
10	Canada	Austria	Netherlands
11	Austria	Canada	Finland
12	Australia	Iceland	Canada
13	Norway	Estonia	Austria
14	Ireland	Sweden	Israel
15	China	Norway	Luxembourg
16	Germany	Chile	Australia
17	Finland	Finland	Belgium
18	Taiwan	Netherlands	France
19	New Zealand	United States	South Korea
20	United Kingdom	Taiwan	Hong Kong
21	Israel	Malaysia	Taiwan
22	Estonia	United Kingdom	United Kingdom
23	Malaysia	Germany	New Zealand
24	Japan	Portugal	Ireland
25	Belgium	Israel	Hungary
26	Chile	Lithuania	Malaysia
27	India	Thailand	Czech Republic
28	France	Belgium	China
29	South Korea	Spain	Spain
30	Spain	Greece	Lithuania
31	Lithuania	South Korea	Estonia
32	Czech Republic	Jordan	Portugal
33	Thailand	India	Slovenia
34	Slovakia	Japan	Greece
35	Hungary	South Africa	Italy
36	Greece	Colombia	Jordan
37	Jordan	Slovakia	Russia
38	Colombia	Bulgaria	Slovakia
39	Portugal	Russia	Chile
40	Slovenia	Hungary	Poland
41	Bulgaria	Czech Republic	Bulgaria
42	Italy	France	Romania
43	Russia	Slovenia	Croatia
44	Romania	Mexico	Argentina

Notes: Rankings reflect assessments for the ability of a country to achieve sustained high rates of GDP growth per head. Column 1 is based on 259 criteria covering: the openness of an economy, the role of the government, the development of financial markets, the quality of infrastructure, technology, business management and judicial and political institutions and labour-market flexibility. Column 2 looks at the extent to which government policies are conducive to competitiveness. Column 3 is based on the extent to which a country is integrated into regional trade blocks.

The business environment

		2007–11 score	2002–2006 score	2002–2006 ranking
1	Denmark	8.80	8.71	1
2	Singapore	8.77	8.69	2
3	Canada	8.74	8.63	4
	Finland	8.74	8.67	3
5	Hong Kong	8.73	8.57	7
6	United States	8.67	8.61	6
7	Netherlands	8.65	8.53	8
8	Switzerland	8.62	8.48	10
9	Sweden	8.60	8.29	11
10	United Kingdom	8.55	8.61	5
11	Ireland	8.48	8.51	9
12	Australia	8.45	8.17	13
13	Germany	8.43	7.98	15
14	New Zealand	8.30	8.19	12
15	Austria	8.28	7.87	17
16	Belgium	8.20	8.01	14
17	Norway	8.17	7.92	16
18	France	8.13	7.86	18
19	Taiwan	8.09	7.66	21
20	Chile	7.94	7.76	19
21	Estonia	7.86	7.68	20
22	Spain	7.83	7.44	22
23	Israel	7.68	6.99	29
24	United Arab Emirates	7.54	7.25	24
25	South Korea	7.53	7.13	25
26	Czech Republic	7.51	6.84	31
	Slovakia	7.51	7.02	28
28	Japan	7.48	7.01	28
29	Qatar	7.42	6.90	30
30	Portugal	7.41	6.70	35
31	Malaysia	7.40	7.29	23
32	Bahrain	7.39	6.70	34
	Slovenia	7.39	7.08	26
34	Hungary	7.25	6.79	32
35	Poland	7.16	6.68	37
36	Latvia	7.12	6.61	38
37	Cyprus	7.03	6.68	36
38	Lithuania	7.02	6.60	40
39	Italy	6.99	6.44	42
40	Mexico	6.96	6.60	39
41	South Africa	6.93	6.21	46
42	Thailand	6.84	6.72	33
43	Brazil	6.83	6.40	43
44	Greece	6.82	6.31	44
45	Bulgaria	6.76	5.89	50
50	Romania	6.75	5.89	49

Note: Scores reflect the opportunities for, and hindrances to, the conduct of business, measured by countries' rankings in ten categories including market potential, tax and labour-market policies, infrastructure, skills and the political environment. Scores reflect average and forecast average over given date range.

Business creativity and research

Innovation index[a]

1	United States	6.51	13	Iceland	4.32
2	Taiwan	6.32	14	Australia	4.20
3	Japan	5.86	15	Netherlands	4.12
4	Finland	5.85	16	Singapore	4.10
5	Sweden	5.57	17	Belgium	4.08
6	South Korea	5.19	18	United Kingdom	4.07
7	Israel	4.96	19	France	3.82
8	Switzerland	4.78	20	Austria	3.81
9	Denmark	4.62		Ireland	3.81
10	Norway	4.55	22	New Zealand	3.76
11	Germany	4.53	23	Slovenia	3.69
12	Canada	4.35	24	Greece	3.63

Information and communications technology index[b]

1	Sweden	5.89	13	Singapore	5.17
2	Iceland	5.87		South Korea	5.17
3	Denmark	5.69	15	United Kingdom	5.14
4	Netherlands	5.63	16	Austria	5.11
5	United States	5.59	17	Canada	5.08
6	Luxembourg	5.54	18	Israel	4.98
7	Australia	5.48	19	Japan	4.89
8	Finland	5.47	20	New Zealand	4.65
9	Switzerland	5.29	21	Estonia	4.64
10	Hong Kong	5.24		Germany	4.64
	Taiwan	5.24	23	Malta	4.56
12	Norway	5.18	24	France	4.43

Brain drain[c]

Highest			*Lowest*		
1	Guyana	0.5	1	United States	6.1
2	Lesotho	1.6	2	Japan	5.7
3	Zimbabwe	1.7		Qatar	5.7
4	Zambia	1.9	4	Norway	5.6
5	Bulgaria	2.0	5	Ireland	5.5
6	Albania	2.1		United Arab Emirates	5.5
	Ethiopia	2.1	7	Finland	5.4
	Kenya	2.1		Iceland	5.4
	Kyrgyzstan	2.1		Kuwait	5.4
	Moldova	2.1	10	Chile	5.3
	Nepal	2.1	11	Switzerland	5.2
	Philippines	2.1	12	Netherlands	5.0
	Romania	2.1			
	Serbia	2.1			
15	Bosnia	2.2			

a The innovation index is a measure of the adoption of new technology, and the interaction between business and the scientific sector. It includes measures of the number of patents granted and higher education enrolment rates.
b The information and communications technology (ICT) index is a measure of ICT usage and includes per capita measures of telephone lines, internet usage, personal computers and mobile phone users.
c Talented people: 1=normally leave for other countries, 7=almost always remain in home country.

Total expenditure on R&D

% of GDP, 2004

1	Israel	4.55	26	New Zealand	1.22
2	Sweden	3.95	27	Ireland	1.19
3	Finland	3.48	28	Russia	1.17
4	Japan	3.20	29	Italy	1.13
5	Iceland	2.87	30	Spain	1.05
6	United States	2.66	31	Brazil	0.93
7	South Korea	2.63	32	Estonia	0.91
8	Denmark	2.61	33	Hungary	0.88
9	Switzerland	2.57	34	India	0.84
10	Germany	2.49	35	Jordan	0.81
11	Taiwan	2.42	36	Portugal	0.74
12	Austria	2.26	37	South Africa	0.73
13	Singapore	2.24	38	Hong Kong	0.69
14	France	2.16	39	Turkey	0.66
15	Canada	1.90	40	Chile	0.65
16	United Kingdom	1.88	41	Malaysia	0.63
17	Belgium	1.85	42	Greece	0.62
18	Luxembourg	1.78	43	Poland	0.54
19	Norway	1.75	44	Slovakia	0.53
20	Netherlands	1.72	45	Bulgaria	0.50
21	Australia	1.69	46	Venezuela	0.46
22	Slovenia	1.47	47	Argentina	0.44
23	Czech Republic	1.27	48	Mexico	0.39
24	Croatia	1.25	49	Romania	0.39
25	China	1.23	50	Thailand	0.28

Patents

No. of patents granted to residents			*No. of patents in force*		
Total, average 2002–04			*Per 100,000 people*		
1	Japan	109,823	1	Luxembourg	5,804
2	United States	84,958	2	Switzerland	1,152
3	South Korea	31,915	3	Sweden	1,144
4	Taiwan	29,773	4	Taiwan	1,094
5	Russia	18,264	5	Singapore	932
6	Germany	12,804	6	Japan	865
7	France	9,023	7	Belgium	851
8	China	5,913	8	Ireland	831
9	United Kingdom	3,430	9	United Kingdom	792
10	Italy	2,298	10	Netherlands	776
11	Sweden	2,276	11	Finland	714
12	Netherlands	1,887	12	Denmark	701
13	Spain	1,432	13	South Korea	689
14	Finland	1,150	14	France	644
15	Canada	1,057	15	United States	556
16	Austria	1,029	16	Germany	498
17	Poland	742	17	Australia	481
18	Romania	709	18	Canada	457
19	India	695	19	Portugal	349
20	Brazil	676	20	Slovenia	314

Business costs and FDI

Office rents
Occupation cost[a], $ per square metre, November 2006

1	London (West End), UK	2,282	15	Leeds, UK		774
2	Tokyo (Inner Central), Japan	1,568	16	Seoul, South Korea		769
3	London (City), UK	1,558	17	Birmingham, UK		754
4	Tokyo (Outer Central), Japan	1,437	18	Glasgow, UK		739
5	Hong Kong	1,251	19	Bristol, UK		734
6	Moscow, Russia	1,176	20	Madrid, Spain		714
7	Mumbai, India	1,142	21	Milan, Italy		689
8	Paris, France	1,136	22	Aberdeen, UK		679
9	Dublin, Ireland	996	23	Zurich, Switzerland		670
10	Dubai, UAE	938	24	New York, Midtown Manhattan, US		668
11	New Delhi, India	881	25	Stockholm, Sweden		631
12	Edinburgh, UK	845	26	Jersey, UK		623
	Manchester, UK	845	27	Luxembourg City, Luxembourg		617
14	Paris La Défense, France	831	28	Geneva, Switzerland		614

Employment costs
Pay, social security and other benefits, $ per hr. worked for a production worker

1	Denmark	39.29	11	Canada	26.67
2	Norway	39.15	12	Australia	25.86
3	Germany	33.50	13	France	25.58
4	Finland	33.14	14	United States	24.71
5	Netherlands	32.09	15	Ireland	23.99
6	Belgium	31.71	16	Italy	21.80
7	Switzerland	30.98	17	Japan	20.88
8	Austria	30.38	18	Spain	18.50
9	Sweden	29.96	19	New Zealand	14.45
10	United Kingdom	27.25	20	Singapore	8.63

Foreign direct investment[b]

	Inflow, $m			*Outflow, $m*	
1	United Kingdom	164,530	1	Netherlands	119,454
2	United States	99,443	2	France	115,668
3	China	72,406	3	United Kingdom	101,099
4	France	63,576	4	Japan	45,781
5	Netherlands	43,630	5	Germany	45,634
6	Hong Kong	35,897	6	Switzerland	42,858
7	Canada	33,822	7	Italy	39,671
8	Germany	32,663	8	Spain	38,772
9	Belgium	23,691	9	Canada	34,083
10	Spain	22,987	10	Hong Kong	32,560
11	Singapore	20,083	11	Sweden	25,938
12	Italy	19,971	12	Belgium	22,925
13	Mexico	18,055	13	Norway	14,461
14	Brazil	15,066	14	Russia	13,126
15	Russia	14,600	15	Ireland	12,938
16	Bermuda	13,615	16	China	11,306
17	Sweden	13,389	17	Denmark	9,328
18	UAE	12,000	18	Austria	9,293

Business burdens and corruption

Number of days taken to register a new company

Highest			Lowest		
1	Suriname	694	1	Australia	2
2	Guinea-Bissau	233	2	Canada	3
3	Haiti	203	3	Denmark	5
4	Laos	163		Iceland	5
5	Congo	155		United States	5
6	Brazil	152	6	Singapore	6
7	Venezuela	141	7	Puerto Rico	7
8	Equatorial Guinea	136	8	Afghanistan	8
9	Angola	124		France	8
10	Mozambique	113		Jamaica	8
11	Botswana	108		Portugal	8
12	Indonesia	97	12	Turkey	9
13	Zimbabwe	96	13	Netherlands	10
14	Namibia	95	14	Hong Kong	11
15	West Bank and Gaza	93		Romania	11
16	Cambodia	86		Tunisia	11

Corruption perceptions index[c]

2006, 10 = least corrupt

Lowest			Highest		
1	Finland	9.6	1	Haiti	1.8
	Iceland	9.6	2	Guinea	1.9
	New Zealand	9.6		Iraq	1.9
4	Denmark	9.5		Myanmar	1.9
5	Singapore	9.4	5	Bangladesh	2.0
6	Sweden	9.2		Chad	2.0
7	Switzerland	9.1		Congo-Kinshasa	2.0
8	Norway	8.8		Sudan	2.0
9	Australia	8.7	9	Belarus	2.1
	Netherlands	8.7		Cambodia	2.1
11	Austria	8.6		Equatorial Guinea	2.1
	Luxembourg	8.6		Côte d'Ivoire	2.1
	United Kingdom	8.6		Uzbekistan	2.1
14	Canada	8.5			
15	Hong Kong	8.3			
16	Germany	8.0			

Business software piracy

% of software that is pirated

1	Vietnam	90	8	Cameroon	84
	Zimbabwe	90	9	Algeria	83
3	Indonesia	87		Bolivia	83
4	China	86		Paraguay	83
	Pakistan	86		Russia	83
6	Kazakhstan	85		Zambia	83
	Ukraine	85			

a Total rent, taxes and operating expenses.
b Investment in companies in a foreign country.
c This index ranks countries based on how much corruption is perceived by business
  people, academics and risk analysts to exist among politicians and public officials.

Businesses and banks

Largest businesses

By sales, $bn

1	Exxon Mobil	United States	339.9
2	Wal-Mart Stores	United States	315.7
3	Royal Dutch Shell Group	United Kingdom/Netherlands	306.7
4	BP	United Kingdom	267.6
5	General Motors	United States	192.6
6	Chevron	United States	189.5
7	DaimlerChrysler	United States	186.1
8	Toyota Motor	Japan	185.8
9	Ford Motor	United States	177.2
10	ConocoPhillips	United States	166.7
11	General Electric	United States	157.2
12	Total Fina Elf	France	152.4
13	ING Group	Netherlands	138.2
14	Citigroup	United States	131.0
15	AXA	France	129.8
16	Allianz	Germany	121.4
17	Volkswagen	Germany	118.4
18	Fortis	Netherlands	112.4
19	Crédit Agricole Group	France	110.8
20	American Intl. Group	United States	108.9
21	Assicurazioni Generali	Italy	101.4
22	Siemens	Germany	100.1
23	Sinopec	China	98.8
24	Nippon Telegraph & Telephone	Japan	94.9
25	Carrefour	France	94.5
26	HSBC Holdings	United Kingdom	93.5
27	Aviva	United Kingdom	92.6
	ENI	Italy	92.6
29	IBM	United States	91.1
30	McKesson	United States	88.1
31	Honda Motor	Japan	87.5
32	State Grid	China	87.0
33	Hewlett-Packard	United States	86.7
34	BNP Paribas	France	85.7
35	PDVSA	Venezuela	85.6
36	UBS	Switzerland	84.7
37	Bank of America Corp	United States	84.0
38	China National Petroleum	China	83.6
	Hitachi	Japan	83.6
40	Pemex	Mexico	83.4
41	Nissan Motor	Japan	83.3
42	Berkshire Hathaway	United States	81.7
43	Home Depot	United States	81.5
44	Valero Energy	United States	81.4

Notes: Industrial and service corporations. Figures refer to the year ended December 31, 2005, except for Japanese companies, where figures refer to year ended March 31, 2006. They include sales of consolidated subsidiaries but exclude excise taxes, thus differing, in some instances, from figures published by the companies themselves.

Largest banks

By capital, $m

1	Citigroup	United States	79,407
2	HSBC Holdings	United Kingdom	74,403
3	Bank of America Corp	United States	74,027
4	JPMorgan Chase	United States	72,474
5	Mitsubishi UFJ Financial Group	Japan	63,898
6	Crédit Agricole Groupe	France	60,599
7	Royal Bank of Scotland	United Kingdom	48,585
8	Sumitomo Mitsui Financial Group	Japan	39,573
9	Mizuho Financial Group	Japan	38,807
10	Santander Central Hispano	Spain	38,377
11	China Construction Bank	China	35,647
12	HBOS	United Kingdom	35,584
13	UniCredit	Italy	34,030
14	Barclays Bank	United Kingdom	32,533
15	ABN-AMRO Bank	Netherlands	32,302
16	Industrial and Commercial Bank of China	China	31,670
17	Bank of China	China	31,346
18	UBS	Switzerland	30,391
19	Wells Fargo & Co.	United States	29,873
20	Rabobank Group	Netherlands	29,326
21	Wachovia Corporation	United States	28,654
22	ING Bank	Netherlands	27,614
23	Deutsche Bank	Germany	25,832
24	BNP Paribas	France	25,146
25	Crédit Mutuel	France	23,130
26	Société Générale	France	22,750
27	Groupe Caisse d'Epargne	France	22,407
28	Credit Suisse Group	Switzerland	20,047
29	Lloyds TSB Group	United Kingdom	19,762
30	Washington Mutual	United States	19,661
31	Banco Bilbao Vizcaya Argentaria	Spain	19,204
32	Norinchukin Bank	Japan	18,996
33	Fortis Bank	Belgium	18,515
34	Banca Intesa	Italy	17,808
35	National Australia Bank	Australia	17,346
36	Groupe Banques Populaires	France	17,263
37	Royal Bank of Canada	Canada	16,016
38	Scotiabank	Canada	15,372
39	US Bancorp	United States	15,145
40	Commerzbank	Germany	14,346
41	Dexia	Belgium	14,031
42	MBNA Corporation	United States	13,804
43	Nordea Group	Sweden	13,493
44	Dresdner Bank	Germany	13,125
45	KBC Group	Belgium	13,053
46	Sanpaolo IMI	Italy	12.903

Notes: Capital (tier one) is essentially equity and reserves.
Figures for Japanese banks refer to the year ended March 31, 2006. Figures for all other
countries refer to the year ended December 31, 2005.

Stockmarkets

Largest market capitalisation
$m, end 2006

1	United States	19,426	27	Malaysia	235
2	Japan	4,726	28	Denmark	231
3	United Kingdom	3,794	29	Greece	208
4	France	2,429	30	Austria	191
5	China	2,426	31	Chile	175
6	Hong Kong	1,715	32	Israel	173
7	Canada	1,701	33	Ireland	163
8	Germany	1,638	34	Turkey	162
9	Spain	1,323	35	Poland	149
10	Switzerland	1,213	36	Thailand	141
11	Australia	1,096	37	Indonesia	139
12	Russia	1,057		United Arab Emirates	139
13	Italy	1,027	39	Kuwait	129
14	South Korea	835	40	Portugal	104
15	India	819	41	Egypt	93
16	Netherlands	780	42	Argentina	80
17	South Africa	715		Luxembourg	80
18	Brazil	711	44	Philippines	68
19	Taiwan	655	45	Qatar	62
20	Sweden	573	46	Peru	60
21	Belgium	396	47	Colombia	56
22	Mexico	348	48	Czech Republic	49
23	Saudi Arabia	327		Morocco	49
24	Norway	281	50	Pakistan	46
25	Singapore	276	51	New Zealand	45
26	Finland	265	52	Kazakhstan	44

Highest growth in market capitalisation, $ terms
% increase, 2001–06

1	Vietnam[a]	5,805	21	Malawia	583
2	Kazakhstan	3,529	22	Lebanon	566
3	Ukraine	3,041	23	Oman	520
4	Amenia	2,900	24	Ghana	512
5	Uzbekistan	2,454	25	Nigeria	507
6	United Arab Emirates	2,299	26	Indonesia	504
7	Macedonia	2,287	27	Sri Lanka	483
8	Kyrgyzstan	2,225	28	Poland	473
9	Bulgaria	1,945	29	Kuwait	456
10	Romania	1,444	30	Morocco	443
11	Serbia[b]	1,397	31	Peru	436
12	Russia	1,287	32	Slovenia	435
13	Kenya	984	33	Fiji	426
14	Pakistan	821	34	Czech Republic	421
15	Croatia	774	35	South Africa	412
16	Iceland	768	36	Montenegro[c]	394
17	Lithuania	750	37	Jordan	371
18	Austria	680	38	Zambia	367
19	Georgia	651	39	China	363
20	India	642	40	Saudi Arabia	347

Highest growth in value traded
$ terms, % increase, 2001–06

1	Serbia	133,900		23	Austria	998
2	United Arab Emirates	77,834		24	Pakistan	916
3	Barbados	10,260		25	Lithuania	897
4	Vietnam[a]	6,588		26	Czech Republic	882
5	Saudi Arabia	6,213		27	Montenegro[a]	860
6	Kazakhstan	5,151		28	Oman	651
7	Lebanon	3,470		29	Poland	641
8	Kenya	3,150		30	Bahrain	631
9	Colombia	3,090		31	El Salvador	630
10	Ecuador	2,800		32	Nigeria	618
11	Iceland	2,212		33	Chile	581
12	Russia	2,145		34	Norway	571
13	Bulgaria	2,056		35	Sri Lanka	556
14	Jordan	2,049		36	Hungary	547
15	Romania	1,564		37	Mongolia	450
16	Georgia	1,483		38	Malta	443
17	Croatia	1,458		39	Ukraine	431
18	West Bank and Gaza	1,323		40	Kyrgyzstan	426
19	Morocco	1,286		41	Indonesia	405
20	Côte d'Ivoire	1,238		42	Peru	404
21	Papua New Guinea[b]	1,150		43	Kuwait	388
22	Egypt	1,118		44	South Africa	348

Highest growth in number of listed companies
% increase, 2001–06

1	Serbia	15,771			Oman	36
2	Macedonia	2,050		26	Thailand	35
3	Uzbekistan	1,800		27	Australia	31
4	United Arab Emirates	575			Russia	31
5	Vietnam[a]	364		29	Papua New Guinea	29
6	Croatia	195		30	Malaysia	27
7	Canada	192		31	Netherlands	26
8	Slovenia	163		32	China	24
9	Uganda	150			Qatar[c]	24
10	Spain	129		34	Bolivia	21
11	Kazakhstan	116		35	South Korea	20
12	Kuwait	109		36	Swaziland	20
	Taiwan	109		37	Singapore	19
14	Ukraine	90		38	Trinidad & Tobago	19
15	Montenegro[a]	60		39	Morocco	18
16	Zambia	56		40	Bangladesh	17
17	United Kingdom	51			Bahrain	17
18	El Salvador	50			New Zealand	17
	Tanzania	50			Malta	17
20	Ghana	45		44	Poland	16
21	Jordan	41		45	Nepal	14
22	West Bank and Gaza	38		46	Botswana	13
23	Hong Kong	36			Saudi Arabia	13
	Japan	36			Sweden	13

a 2003–06   b 2002–06   c 2004–06

Transport: roads and cars

Longest road networks
Km, 2004 or latest

1	United States	6,433,272	21	Germany	231,420
2	India	3,383,344	22	Argentina	231,374
3	China	1,870,661	23	Vietnam	222,179
4	Brazil	1,751,868	24	Philippines	200,037
5	Canada	1,408,900	25	Romania	198,817
6	Japan	1,177,278	26	Nigeria	193,200
7	France	951,220	27	Iran	179,388
8	Australia	810,200	28	Ukraine	169,739
9	Spain	666,292	29	Hungary	159,568
10	Russia	537,289	30	Congo-Kinshasa	153,497
11	Italy	484,688	31	Saudi Arabia	152,044
12	Turkey	426,906	32	Belgium	150,567
13	Sweden	424,947	33	Austria	133,901
14	Poland	423,997	34	Czech Republic	127,672
15	United Kingdom	387,674	35	Netherlands	126,100
16	Indonesia	368,360	36	Greece	114,931
17	South Africa	364,131	37	Colombia	112,988
18	Pakistan	258,340	38	Algeria	108,302
19	Bangladesh	239,226	39	South Korea	100,279
20	Mexico	235,670	40	Malaysia	98,721

Densest road networks
Km of road per km² land area, 2004 or latest

1	Macau	21.3		Trinidad & Tobago	1.6
2	Malta	7.1		United Kingdom	1.6
3	Bahrain	5.1	24	Sri Lanka	1.5
4	Singapore	5.0	25	Ireland	1.4
5	Belgium	4.9		Poland	1.4
6	Barbados	3.7	27	Cyprus	1.3
7	Japan	3.1		Estonia	1.3
8	Netherlands	3.0		Spain	1.3
9	Puerto Rico	2.8	30	Lithuania	1.2
10	Luxembourg	2.0	31	Latvia	1.1
11	Jamaica	1.9		Netherlands Antilles	1.1
	Slovenia	1.9	33	India	1.0
13	Hong Kong	1.8		Mauritius	1.0
14	Bangladesh	1.7		South Korea	1.0
	Denmark	1.7	36	Greece	0.9
	France	1.7		Portugal	0.9
	Hungary	1.7		Slovakia	0.9
	Switzerland	1.7		Sweden	0.9
19	Austria	1.6	40	Israel	0.8
	Czech Republic	1.6		Romania	0.8
	Italy	1.6			

Most crowded road networks
Number of vehicles per km of road network, 2004 or latest

1	Qatar	283.6	26	Switzerland	58.0
2	Hong Kong	254.1	27	Croatia	57.7
3	Germany	206.9	28	Netherlands	53.9
4	Macau	185.5	29	Guatemala	52.7
5	Kuwait	180.7	30	Tunisia	49.1
6	Singapore	178.8	31	Russia	47.3
7	South Korea	144.7	32	Greece	45.8
8	Malta	113.2	33	Ukraine	38.5
9	Brunei	112.7	34	Cyprus	37.9
10	Israel	112.4		France	37.9
11	Serbia	102.1	36	United States	36.9
12	Mexico	92.8	37	Belgium	36.6
13	Netherlands Antilles	84.7	38	Austria	36.5
14	Mauritius	79.4	39	Spain	34.7
15	United Kingdom	78.7	40	Finland	34.5
16	Bahrain	77.2	41	Poland	32.2
17	Jordan	77.0	42	Slovakia	32.1
18	Italy	72.7	43	Denmark	31.7
19	Portugal	67.4	44	Czech Republic	31.5
	Malaysia	67.4	45	Honduras	30.7
21	Japan	63.6	46	New Zealand	30.6
22	Bulgaria	63.4	47	Moldova	28.9
23	Luxembourg	63.3	48	Morocco	28.6
24	Barbados	63.1	49	Chile	27.1
25	Indonesia	62.4		Panama	27.1

Most used road networks
'000 vehicle-km per year per km of road network, 2004 or latest

1	Hong Kong	5,565.6	21	Norway	381.3
2	Singapore	4,049.6	22	Mexico	381.2
3	Germany	2,761.6	23	Austria	357.1
4	Israel	2,242.2	24	Ireland	351.1
5	Bahrain	1,528.0	25	Romania	341.2
6	South Korea	1,314.5	26	Spain	336.7
7	United Kingdom	1,272.8	27	Poland	325.7
8	Switzerland	831.5	28	Guatemala	322.6
9	Cyprus	783.5	29	Ghana	320.6
10	Luxembourg	778.5		Suriname	320.6
11	United States	738.6	31	Egypt	310.6
12	Greece	690.3	32	Morocco	310.3
13	Japan	664.0	33	Slovenia	281.2
14	Denmark	647.5	34	Slovakia	255.6
15	Finland	637.0	35	Australia	247.0
16	Croatia	635.9	36	Tanzania	243.8
17	Peru	633.6	37	Pakistan	192.4
18	Belgium	621.0	38	Cambodia	188.5
19	France	580.8	39	Sweden	173.3
20	Ecuador	568.1	40	India	168.3

Highest car ownership
Number of cars per 1,000 population, 2004 or latest

1	Luxembourg	647	26	Ireland	382
2	Iceland	601	27	Greece	368
3	New Zealand	592	28	Denmark	360
4	Italy	590	29	Czech Republic	358
5	Canada	561	30	Estonia	349
6	Germany	546		Kuwait	349
7	Australia	524	32	Barbados	343
8	Malta	523	33	Qatar	335
9	Switzerland	516	34	Bahrain	325
10	Austria	503	35	Netherlands Antilles	321
11	France	495	36	Bulgaria	314
12	Portugal	471	37	Croatia	302
13	Belgium	468	38	Latvia	297
14	United States	465	39	Poland	294
15	Sweden	457	40	Hungary	274
16	Slovenia	456	41	Israel	234
17	United Kingdom	451	42	Malaysia	225
18	Finland	446	43	Slovakia	222
19	Spain	445	44	South Korea	218
20	Japan	441	45	Serbia	181
21	Netherlands	429	46	Belarus	174
22	Norway	422	47	Suriname	171
23	Cyprus	406	48	Romania	149
24	Brunei	397	49	Costa Rica	146
25	Lithuania	383	50	Mexico	142

Lowest car ownership
Number of cars per 1,000 population, 2004 or latest

1	Ethiopia	1	21	Ecuador	32
	Rwanda	1	22	Kyrgyzstan	39
3	Sierra Leone	2	23	Swaziland	40
4	Gambia, The	5	24	Botswana	42
5	Cameroon	8		Namibia	42
	Guinea	8	26	Colombia	44
	India	8	27	Zimbabwe	45
8	Kenya	9	28	Morocco	47
9	China	10	29	Albania	48
	Pakistan	10	30	Honduras	52
	Philippines	10	31	Azerbaijan	53
12	Bhutan	12		Guatemala	53
	Syria	12		Hong Kong	53
14	Sri Lanka	13	34	Georgia	56
15	Bolivia	15	35	Moldova	65
16	Nigeria	17	36	Jordan	71
17	Nicaragua	18	37	Panama	73
18	Cambodia	25	38	Turkey	75
19	Mongolia	26	39	Kazakhstan	80
20	Peru	30	40	Tunisia	83

Most injured in road accidents
Number of people injured per 100,000 population, 2004 or latest

1	Qatar	9,989	26	Croatia	386
2	Kuwait	2,231	27	United Kingdom	346
3	Mauritius	1,580	28	Switzerland	310
4	Saudi Arabia	1,305	29	Malta	298
5	Costa Rica	1,231	30	Sri Lanka	290
6	Malaysia	1,222	31	Chile	287
7	Panama	1,212	32	Iceland	277
8	Botswana	1,025	33	Mongolia	275
9	Jordan	1,023	34	Peru	271
10	Suriname	913	35	Israel	261
11	Barbados	769	36	Czech Republic	260
12	Japan	745	37	New Zealand	255
13	Brunei	734	38	Cyprus	252
14	United States	647	39	Nicaragua	245
15	Slovenia	637	40	Bahrain	237
16	Austria	522	41	Bolivia	230
17	Swaziland	501	42	Latvia	220
18	Canada	473		Spain	220
19	Belgium	467	44	Hong Kong	218
20	South Korea	459	45	Lesotho	215
21	Namibia	440	46	Hungary	207
22	Germany	411	47	Sweden	201
23	Oman	406	48	Lithuania	185
24	Italy	390	49	United Arab Emirates	183
25	Portugal	387	50	Norway	178

Most deaths in road accidents
Number of people killed per 100,000 population, 2004 or latest

1	Botswana	30		Namibia	17
2	South Africa	28	20	Kuwait	16
3	Malaysia	25		Lesotho	16
4	Russia	24	22	Greece	15
	Swaziland	24		Jordan	15
6	Gabon	23		Poland	15
	Oman	23		Suriname	15
	Thailand	23		Tunisia	15
9	Latvia	22		Ukraine	15
	Lithuania	22		United States	15
	United Arab Emirates	22	29	Croatia	14
12	Kazakhstan	21		Cyprus	14
	Qatar	21		Czech Republic	14
	Saudi Arabia	21		Jamaica	14
15	Kyrgyzstan	18		Slovenia	14
16	Belarus	17		South Korea	14
	Colombia	17		Vietnam	14
	Mongolia	17			

Transport: planes and trains

Most air travel
Million passenger-km[a] per year

1	United States	1,238,952		16	Russia	48,828
2	China	201,948		17	Brazil	48,779
3	United Kingdom	196,488		18	Malaysia	47,304
4	Germany	152,909		19	Thailand	41,570
5	Japan	151,080		20	India	34,092
6	France	115,116		21	South Africa	33,103
7	Australia	77,112		22	Belgium	32,650
8	Canada	70,956		23	Saudi Arabia	30,183
9	South Korea	69,276		24	Switzerland	28,488
10	Singapore	69,084		25	Mexico	27,864
11	Netherlands	68,316		26	New Zealand	24,942
12	Hong Kong	66,168		27	Ireland	20,796
13	Spain	66,084		28	Turkey	20,328
14	United Arab Emirates	59,292		29	Indonesia	19,917
15	Italy	56,650		30	Austria	18,828

Busiest airports

Total passengers, m

1	Atlanta, Hartsfield	84.8
2	Chicago, O'Hare	76.2
3	London, Heathrow	67.5
4	Tokyo, Haneda	65.2
5	Los Angeles, Intl.	61.0
6	Dallas, Ft. Worth	60.1
7	Paris, Charles de Gaulle	56.8
8	Frankfurt, Main	52.8
9	Beijing, Capital	48.5
10	Denver, Intl.	47.3
11	Las Vegas, McCarran Intl.	46.2
12	Amsterdam, Schipol	46.1

Total cargo, m tonnes

1	Memphis, Intl.	3.69
2	Hong Kong, Intl.	3.61
3	Anchorage, Intl.	2.80
4	Seoul, Inchon	2.34
5	Tokyo, Narita	2.28
6	Shanghai, Pudong Intl.	2.16
7	Frankfurt, Main	2.13
8	Louisville, Standiford Fd.	1.98
9	Paris, Charles de Gaulle	1.95
10	Singapore, Changi	1.93
11	Los Angeles, Intl.	1.91
12	Miami, Intl.	1.83

Average daily aircraft movements, take-offs and landings

1	Atlanta, Hartsfield	2,675
2	Chicago, O'Hare	2,626
3	Dallas, Ft. Worth	1,919
4	Los Angeles, Intl.	1,800
5	Las Vegas, McCarran Intl.	1,697
6	Houston, George Bush Intercont.	1,651
7	Denver, Intl.	1,636
8	Phoenix, Skyharbor Intl.	1,483
9	Philadelphia, Intl.	1,413
10	Minneapolis, St Paul	1,303
11	Paris, Charles de Gaulle	1,484
12	Detroit, Metro	1,320
13	Charlotte/Douglas, Intl.	1,396
14	Toronto, Pearson Intl.	1,146
15	Madrid	1,192
16	Frankfurt, Main	1,341
17	London, Heathrow	1,307
18	Salt Lake City	1,152
19	Newark	1,217
20	Amsterdam, Schipol	1,206

a Air passenger–km data refer to the distance travelled by each aircraft of national origin.

Longest railway networks
'000 km

1	United States	229.0		Czech Republic	9.5
2	Russia	85.5	23	Turkey	8.7
3	India	63.5	24	Hungary	8.0
4	China	62.2	25	Chile	7.9
5	Canada	57.7	26	Pakistan	7.8
6	Argentina	35.8	27	Iran	7.1
7	Germany	34.2	28	Austria	5.8
8	Brazil	29.3	29	Finland	5.7
	France	29.3	30	Belarus	5.5
10	Mexico	26.7		Sudan	5.5
11	Ukraine	22.0	32	Egypt	5.2
12	Japan	20.1	33	Bulgaria	4.2
13	South Africa	20.0	34	Norway	4.1
14	Poland	19.6		Serbia	4.1
15	Italy	16.7	36	Uzbekistan	4.0
16	United Kingdom	16.2	37	Slovakia	3.7
17	Spain	14.5	38	Algeria	3.6
18	Kazakhstan	14.2		Congo-Brazzaville	3.6
19	Romania	10.8	40	Belgium	3.5
20	Sweden	9.9		Nigeria	3.5
21	Australia	9.5			

Most rail passengers
Km per person per year

1	Switzerland	2,040	10	Germany	874
2	Japan	1,922	11	Belgium	832
3	Belarus	1,357	12	Kazakhstan	809
4	France	1,284	13	Italy	803
5	Russia	1,149	14	United Kingdom	734
6	Ukraine	1,120	15	Hungary	714
7	Denmark	1,092	16	Finland	696
8	Austria	1,073	17	Czech Republic	663
9	Netherlands	921			

Most rail freight
Million tonnes-km per year

1	United States	2,717,513	10	Germany	88,022
2	China	1,934,612	11	Mexico	54,387
3	Russia	1,801,601	12	Australia	46,164
4	India	407,398	13	Poland	46,060
5	Canada	338,661	14	Belarus	43,559
6	Ukraine	223,980	15	France	41,898
7	Brazil	221,600	16	Japan	22,632
8	Kazakhstan	171,855	17	United Kingdom	22,110
9	South Africa	108,513			

Transport: shipping

Merchant fleets
Number of vessels, by country of domicile

1	Japan	3,091	11	Singapore	754
2	Greece	3,027	12	Denmark	744
3	China	2,893	13	Netherlands	722
4	Germany	2,786	14	Indonesia	711
5	Russia	2,157	15	Italy	702
6	United States	1,679	16	Hong Kong	663
7	Norway	1,665	17	Taiwan	553
8	South Korea	993	18	India	406
9	Turkey	801	19	Switzerland	372
10	United Kingdom	779	20	Canada	356

By country of domicile, deadweight tonnage, m

1	Greece	163.4	11	United Kingdom	21.3
2	Japan	131.7	12	Denmark	19.6
3	Germany	71.5	13	Russia	16.7
4	China	65.5	14	Italy	14.5
5	United States	46.9	15	India	13.8
6	Norway	45.4	16	Switzerland	11.8
7	Hong Kong	43.8	17	Belgium	11.6
8	South Korea	29.7	18	Saudi Arabia	11.4
9	Taiwan	24.4	19	Turkey	10.3
10	Singapore	23.0	20	Iran	9.8

Maritime trading
% of value of world trade generated

1	United States	12.5	14	Mexico	2.1
2	Germany	8.3	15	Singapore	2.0
3	China	6.7	16	Russia	1.8
4	Japan	5.3		Taiwan	1.8
5	France	4.5	18	Austria	1.2
6	United Kingdom	4.2		Malaysia	1.2
7	Netherlands	3.6		Switzerland	1.2
8	Italy	3.5	21	Australia	1.1
9	Canada	3.2		Sweden	1.1
10	Belgium	3.1		Thailand	1.1
11	Hong Kong	2.8	24	India	1.0
12	South Korea	2.6	25	Brazil	0.9
13	Spain	2.2			

% of world fleet deadweight tonnage, by country of ownership

1	Japan	14.1	11	Italy	1.7
2	United States	10.1	12	India	1.5
3	Hong Kong	7.9	13	Belgium	1.3
4	Germany	7.5	14	Malaysia	1.2
5	China	7.1		Netherlands	1.2
6	Singapore	5.9		Switzerland	1.2
7	United Kingdom	3.9	17	France	1.0
8	South Korea	3.3	18	Canada	0.7
9	Taiwan	2.5		Sweden	0.7
10	Russia	1.9	20	Brazil	0.6

Tourism

Most tourist arrivals
Number of arrivals, '000

1	France	76,001	21	Saudi Arabia	9,100
2	Spain	55,577	22	Croatia	8,467
3	United States	46,085	23	Macau	8,324
4	China	41,761	24	Egypt	8,244
5	Italy	36,513	25	South Africa	7,518
6	United Kingdom	29,970	26	Ireland	7,333
7	Germany	21,500	27	Switzerland	7,229
8	Mexico	20,617	28	Belgium	6,747
9	Turkey	20,273	29	Tunisia	6,378
10	Austria	19,952	30	Czech Republic	6,336
11	Russia	19,940	31	Japan	6,138
12	Canada	19,152	32	Morocco	5,843
13	Malaysia	15,703	33	South Korea	5,818
14	Poland	15,200	34	Indonesia	5,321
15	Greece	14,276	35	Bulgaria	4,837
16	Hong Kong	13,655	36	Brazil	4,794
17	Thailand	11,737	37	Australia	4,774
18	Portugal	11,617	38	Denmark	4,562
19	Hungary	10,048	39	Norway	3,859
20	Netherlands	10,012	40	Puerto Rico	3,541

Biggest tourist spenders
$m

1	Germany	78,530	11	Belgium	14,250
2	United States	66,733	12	South Korea	12,638
3	United Kingdom	61,070	13	Spain	12,545
4	Japan	40,587	14	Austria	12,136
5	France	30,527	15	Hong Kong	11,446
6	Italy	21,981	16	Sweden	10,568
7	China	21,135	17	Australia	10,166
8	Netherlands	17,928	18	Switzerland	9,285
9	Russia	16,923	19	Norway	9,081
10	Canada	16,584	20	Taiwan	8,764

Largest tourist receipts
$m

1	United States	81,680	11	Greece	13,731
2	Spain	47,891	12	Canada	13,584
3	France	42,276	13	Japan	12,439
4	Italy	35,398	14	Mexico	11,803
5	United Kingdom	30,669	15	Switzerland	11,040
6	China	29,296	16	Netherlands	10,475
7	Germany	29,204	17	Hong Kong	10,286
8	Turkey	18,152	18	Thailand	10,108
9	Australia	16,866	19	Belgium	9,863
10	Austria	15,467	20	Malaysia	8,543

Education

Highest primary enrolment
Number enrolled as % of relevant age group

1	Sierra Leone	155		15	China	118
2	Brazil	141			Mongolia	118
3	Madagascar	138			Uganda	118
4	Cambodia	134		18	Cameroon	117
5	Lesotho	132			Ecuador	117
6	Gabon	130			Indonesia	117
7	Netherlands Antilles	126		21	India	116
8	Belize	124			Laos	116
	Syria	124			Portugal	116
10	Russia	123		24	Aruba	114
11	Malawi	122			Equatorial Guinea	114
12	Rwanda	120			Guatemala	114
	Suriname	120			Kenya	114
14	Argentina	119			Peru	114

Lowest primary enrolment
Number enrolled as % of relevant age group

1	Somalia	17		15	Oman	84
2	Niger	47		16	Burundi	85
3	Central African Rep	56		17	Afghanistan	87
4	Burkina Faso	58			Andorra	87
5	Sudan	60			Pakistan	87
6	Congo-Brazzaville	62			Yemen	87
7	Eritrea	64		21	Congo	88
8	Mali	66			Ghana	88
9	Côte d'Ivoire	72			Senegal	88
10	Papua New Guinea	75		24	West Bank and Gaza	89
11	Chad	77		25	Cayman Islands	90
12	Gambia, The	81		26	Saudi Arabia	91
	Guinea	81		27	Moldova	92
14	United Arab Emirates	83				

Highest tertiary enrolment[a]
Number enrolled as % of relevant age group

1	Finland	90		13	Ukraine	69
	South Korea	90		14	Iceland	68
3	New Zealand	86			Russia	68
4	Sweden	84		16	Spain	66
5	United States	82		17	Estonia	65
6	Norway	80		18	Argentina	64
7	Greece	79		19	Belgium	63
8	Denmark	74			Italy	63
	Latvia	74		21	Belarus	62
	Slovenia	74		22	Cuba	61
11	Lithuania	73			Macau	61
12	Australia	72			Poland	61

Notes: Latest available year 2000–04. The gross enrolment ratios shown are the actual number enrolled as a percentage of the number of children in the official primary age group. They may exceed 100 when children outside the primary age group are receiving primary education.

Least literate
% adult literacy rate

1	Mali	19.0		17	Papua New Guinea	57.3
2	Burkina Faso	21.8		18	Ghana	57.9
3	Chad	25.7		19	Burundi	59.3
4	Afghanistan	28.1		20	Bhutan	59.5
5	Niger	28.7		21	Sudan	60.9
6	Guinea	29.5		22	India	61.0
7	Bermuda	34.7		23	Malawi	64.1
8	Sierra Leone	35.1		24	Rwanda	64.9
9	Senegal	39.3		25	Uganda	66.8
10	Central African Rep	48.6		26	Congo-Brazzaville	67.2
	Nepal	48.6		27	Angola	67.4
12	Côte d'Ivoire	48.7		28	Cameroon	67.9
13	Pakistan	49.9		29	Zambia	68.0
14	Mauritania	51.2		30	Laos	68.7
15	Morocco	52.3		31	Guatemala	69.1
16	Togo	53.2		32	Tanzania	69.4

Highest education spending
% of GDP

1	Cuba	9.8		12	Barbados	6.9
2	Yemen	9.6			Namibia	6.9
3	Lesotho	9.0		14	New Zealand	6.8
4	Denmark	8.4			Saudi Arabia	6.8
5	Iceland	8.1		16	Kenya	6.7
	Tunisia	8.1			Morocco	6.7
7	Malaysia	8.0		18	Finland	6.5
8	Norway	7.7		19	Bolivia	6.4
9	Sweden	7.5			Fiji	6.4
10	Cyprus	7.4			Ukraine	6.4
11	Israel	7.3				

Lowest education spending
% of GDP

1	Equatorial Guinea	0.6			Zambia	2.0
2	Indonesia	0.9		13	Chad	2.1
3	Myanmar	1.3		14	Botswana	2.2
	United Arab Emirates	1.3			Congo	2.2
5	Qatar	1.6			Uruguay	2.2
6	Cameroon	1.8		17	Kazakhstan	2.3
	Dominican Republic	1.8			Laos	2.3
8	Bermuda	1.9			Macau	2.3
	Cambodia	1.9			Mauritania	2.3
10	Gambia, The	2.0			Niger	2.3
	Guinea	2.0			Pakistan	2.3

a Tertiary education includes all levels of post-secondary education including courses
leading to awards not equivalent to a university degree, courses leading to a first
university degree and postgraduate courses.

Life expectancy

Highest life expectancy
Years, 2005–10

1	Andorra[a]	83.5		Malta	79.4
2	Japan	82.6		United Kingdom	79.4
3	Hong Kong	82.2		Virgin Islands (US)	79.4
4	Iceland	81.8	28	Finland	79.3
5	Switzerland	81.7	29	Guadeloupe	79.2
6	Australia	81.2	30	Channel Islands	79.0
7	Spain	80.9		Cyprus	79.0
	Sweden	80.9	32	Ireland	78.9
9	Canada	80.7	33	Costa Rica	78.8
	France	80.7	34	Luxembourg	78.7
	Israel	80.7		Puerto Rico	78.7
	Macau	80.7		United Arab Emirates	78.7
13	Italy	80.5	37	Chile	78.6
14	New Zealand	80.2		South Korea	78.6
	Norway	80.2	39	Cuba	78.3
16	Cayman Islands[a]	80.1		Denmark	78.3
17	Singapore	80.0	41	United States	78.2
18	Austria	79.8	42	Portugal	78.1
	Netherlands	79.8	43	Bermuda[a]	78.0
20	Greece	79.5	44	Slovenia	77.9
	Martinique	79.5	45	Kuwait	77.6
22	Belgium	79.4	46	Taiwan[a]	77.4
	Faroe Islands[a]	79.4	47	Barbados	77.3
	Germany	79.4	48	Brunei	77.1

Highest male life expectancy
Years, 2005–10

1	Andorra[a]	80.6	10	Canada	78.3
2	Iceland	80.2	11	New Zealand	78.2
3	Hong Kong	79.4	12	Singapore	78.0
4	Japan	79.0	13	Norway	77.8
	Switzerland	79.0	14	Spain	77.7
6	Australia	78.9	15	Cayman Islands[a]	77.5
7	Sweden	78.7		Italy	77.5
8	Israel	78.6		Netherlands	77.5
9	Macau	78.5	18	Malta	77.3

Highest female life expectancy
Years, 2005–10

1	Andorra[a]	86.6		Virgin Islands (US)	83.3
2	Japan	86.1	11	Sweden	83.0
3	Hong Kong	85.1	12	Canada	82.9
4	Spain	84.2	13	Faroe Islands[a]	82.8
	Switzerland	84.2		Israel	82.8
6	France	84.1		Macau	82.8
7	Australia	83.6	16	Cayman Islands[a]	82.7
8	Italy	83.5		Puerto Rico	82.7
9	Iceland	83.3	18	Austria	82.6

a 2006 estimate.

Lowest life expectancy
Years, 2005–10

1	Swaziland	39.6	26	Tanzania	52.5
2	Mozambique	42.1	27	Ethiopia	52.9
3	Zambia	42.4		Namibia	52.9
4	Lesotho	42.6	29	Kenya	54.1
	Sierra Leone	42.6	30	Mali	54.5
6	Angola	42.7	31	Congo-Brazzaville	55.3
7	Zimbabwe	43.5	32	Guinea	56.0
8	Afghanistan	43.8	33	Benin	56.7
9	Central African Rep	44.7		Gabon	56.7
10	Liberia	45.7	35	Niger	56.9
11	Rwanda	46.2	36	Papua New Guinea	57.2
12	Guinea-Bissau	46.4	37	Eritrea	58.0
13	Congo-Kinshasa	46.5	38	Togo	58.4
14	Nigeria	46.9	39	Sudan	58.6
15	Somalia	48.2	40	Gambia, The	59.4
16	Côte d'Ivoire	48.3		Madagascar	59.4
	Malawi	48.3	42	Iraq	59.5
18	South Africa	49.3	43	Cambodia	59.7
19	Burundi	49.6	44	Ghana	60.0
20	Cameroon	50.4	45	Haiti	60.9
21	Botswana	50.7	46	Myanmar	62.1
	Chad	50.7	47	Yemen	62.7
23	Uganda	51.5	48	Senegal	63.1
24	Equatorial Guinea	51.6	49	Turkmenistan	63.2
25	Burkina Faso	52.3	50	Nepal	63.8

Lowest male life expectancy
Years, 2005–10

1	Swaziland	39.8	11	Liberia	44.8
2	Sierra Leone	41.0	12	Guinea-Bissau	44.9
3	Angola	41.2	13	Congo-Kinshasa	45.2
4	Mozambique	41.7	14	Nigeria	46.4
5	Zambia	42.1	15	Somalia	46.9
6	Lesotho	42.9	16	Côte d'Ivoire	47.5
7	Central African Rep	43.3	17	Burundi	48.1
8	Afghanistan	43.9		Malawi	48.1
9	Zimbabwe	44.1	19	South Africa	48.8
10	Rwanda	44.6	20	Chad	49.3

Lowest female life expectancy
Years, 2005–10

1	Swaziland	39.4	10	Liberia	46.6
2	Lesotho	42.3	11	Nigeria	47.3
3	Mozambique	42.4	12	Congo-Kinshasa	47.7
4	Zambia	42.5	13	Rwanda	47.8
5	Zimbabwe	42.7	14	Guinea-Bissau	47.9
6	Afghanistan	43.8	15	Malawi	48.4
7	Sierra Leone	44.2	16	Côte d'Ivoire	49.3
8	Angola	44.3	17	Somalia	49.4
9	Central African Rep	46.1	18	South Africa	49.7

Death rates and infant mortality

Highest death rates
Number of deaths per 1,000 population, 2005–10

#	Country	Rate	#	Country	Rate
1	Sierra Leone	22.1	49	Czech Republic	10.9
2	Swaziland	21.2	50	Germany	10.7
3	Angola	20.5	51	Portugal	10.6
4	Afghanistan	19.9	52	Italy	10.5
5	Mozambique	19.8	53	Gambia, The	10.4
6	Lesotho	19.2	54	Denmark	10.3
7	Zambia	18.8	55	Kazakhstan	10.1
8	Guinea-Bissau	18.4		Sudan	10.1
9	Liberia	18.3		Sweden	10.1
10	Central African Rep	18.1		Togo	10.1
	Congo-Kinshasa	18.1	59	Belgium	10.0
12	Zimbabwe	17.9		Poland	10.0
13	Rwanda	17.2		Slovakia	10.0
14	South Africa	17.0	62	Greece	9.9
15	Nigeria	16.8		North Korea	9.9
16	Somalia	16.6		Slovenia	9.9
17	Ukraine	16.4		United Kingdom	9.9
18	Russia	16.2	66	Finland	9.7
19	Burundi	15.6		Madagascar	9.7
20	Chad	15.4		Myanmar	9.7
	Côte d'Ivoire	15.4	69	Armenia	9.6
22	Bulgaria	14.8		Papua New Guinea	9.6
	Equatorial Guinea	14.8	71	Bosnia	9.5
	Malawi	14.8		Channel Islands	9.5
25	Belarus	14.7	73	Austria	9.4
	Mali	14.7	74	Ghana	9.3
27	Burkina Faso	14.4	75	Eritrea	9.2
	Cameroon	14.4		Haiti	9.2
29	Estonia	14.3		Macedonia	9.2
30	Botswana	14.1		Uruguay	9.2
31	Niger	13.8	79	Iraq	9.1
32	Latvia	13.6		Norway	9.1
33	Uganda	13.4	81	Cambodia	9.0
34	Hungary	13.2		Japan	9.0
35	Ethiopia	13.0		Senegal	9.0
36	Tanzania	12.9	84	France	8.9
37	Moldova	12.5	85	Spain	8.8
38	Namibia	12.4	86	Faroe Islands [a]	8.7
	Romania	12.4		Luxembourg	8.7
40	Lithuania	12.3	88	Netherlands	8.6
41	Croatia	12.1	89	Thailand	8.5
42	Guinea	11.9	90	India	8.2
43	Georgia	11.8		Turkmenistan	8.2
	Kenya	11.8		United States	8.2
45	Gabon	11.7	93	Kyrgyzstan	8.1
46	Serbia	11.6		Switzerland	8.1
47	Congo-Brazzaville	11.4		Trinidad & Tobago	8.1
48	Benin	11.2	96	Malta	8.0

Note: Both death and, in particular, infant mortality rates can be underestimated in certain countries where not all deaths are officially recorded.   a 2006 estimate.

Highest infant mortality
Number of deaths per 1,000 live births, 2005–10

1	Sierra Leone	160.3	21	Equatorial Guinea	92.3
2	Afghanistan	157.0	22	Malawi	89.4
3	Liberia	132.5	23	Togo	88.6
4	Angola	131.9	24	Cameroon	87.5
5	Mali	128.5	25	Ethiopia	86.9
6	Chad	119.2	26	Iraq	81.5
7	Côte d'Ivoire	116.9	27	Uganda	76.9
8	Somalia	116.3	28	Turkmenistan	74.7
9	Congo-Kinshasa	113.5	29	Gambia, The	74.2
10	Guinea-Bissau	112.7	30	Tanzania	72.6
11	Rwanda	112.4	31	Azerbaijan	72.3
12	Niger	110.8	32	Swaziland	71.0
13	Nigeria	109.5	33	Congo-Brazzaville	70.3
14	Burkina Faso	104.4	34	Pakistan	67.5
15	Guinea	102.5	35	Myanmar	66.0
16	Burundi	99.4	36	Senegal	65.7
17	Benin	98.0	37	Madagascar	65.5
18	Central African Rep	96.8	38	Sudan	64.9
19	Mozambique	95.9	39	Lesotho	64.6
20	Zambia	92.7	40	Kenya	64.4

Lowest death rates
No. deaths per 1,000 pop., 2005–10

1	United Arab Emirates	1.4
2	Kuwait	1.9
3	Qatar	2.4
4	Oman	2.7
5	Brunei	2.8
6	Bahrain	3.2
7	Syria	3.4
8	Saudi Arabia	3.7
	West Bank and Gaza	3.7
10	Belize	3.8
11	Jordan	3.9
12	Costa Rica	4.1
	Libya	4.1
14	Malaysia	4.5
15	Macau	4.7
	Nicaragua	4.7
17	Mexico	4.8
	Philippines	4.8
19	Algeria	4.9
	Cayman Islands[a]	4.9
21	Panama	5.0
22	Ecuador	5.1
	Venezuela	5.1
	Vietnam	5.1
25	French Polynesia	5.2

Lowest infant mortality
No. deaths per 1,000 live births, 2005–10

1	Iceland	2.9
2	Singapore	3.0
3	Japan	3.2
	Sweden	3.2
5	Norway	3.3
6	Finland	3.7
	Hong Kong	3.7
8	Czech Republic	3.8
9	Andorra[a]	4.0
10	South Korea	4.1
	Switzerland	4.1
12	Belgium	4.2
	France	4.2
	Spain	4.2
15	Germany	4.3
16	Australia	4.4
	Austria	4.4
	Denmark	4.4
19	Luxembourg	4.5
20	Israel	4.7
	Netherlands	4.7
22	Canada	4.8
	Slovenia	4.8
	United Kingdom	4.8
25	Ireland	4.9

a 2006 estimate.

Death and disease

Diabetes
% of population aged 20–79, 2007

1	United Arab Emirates	19.5
2	Saudi Arabia	16.7
3	Kuwait	14.4
4	Oman	13.1
5	Trinidad & Tobago	11.5
6	Mauritius	11.1
7	Egypt	11.0
8	Malaysia	10.7
	Puerto Rico	10.7
10	Mexico	10.6
	Syria	10.6
12	Jamaica	10.3
13	Nicaragua	10.1
	Singapore	10.1
15	Iraq	10.0
16	Jordan	9.8
17	Afghanistan	9.7
	Panama	9.7
19	Pakistan	9.6

Cardiovascular disease
Deaths per 100,000 population, age standardised, 2002

1	Turkmenistan	844
2	Tajikistan	753
3	Kazakhstan	713
4	Afghanistan	706
5	Russia	688
6	Uzbekistan	663
7	Ukraine	637
8	Moldova	619
9	Azerbaijan	613
10	Kyrgyzstan	602
11	Belarus	592
12	Georgia	584
13	Somalia	580
14	Albania	573
15	Egypt	560
16	Bulgaria	554
17	Yemen	553
18	Turkey	542
19	Sierra Leone	515

Cancer
Deaths per 100,000 population, age standardised, 2000

1	Mongolia	306
2	Bolivia	256
3	Hungary	201
4	Sierra Leone	181
5	Poland	180
6	Angola	179
7	Czech Republic	177
8	Peru	175
9	Slovakia	170
	Uruguay	170
11	Liberia	169
	Niger	169
	South Korea	169
14	Croatia	167
	Denmark	167
	Kazakhstan	167
17	Mali	166
18	Burkina Faso	162
	Swaziland	162
20	Congo-Kinshasa	161
	Lithuania	161
22	Côte d'Ivoire	160
	Slovenia	160

Tuberculosis
Incidence per 100,000 population, 2005

1	Swaziland	1,262
2	Namibia	697
3	Lesotho	696
4	Botswana	654
5	Kenya	641
6	Zimbabwe	601
7	South Africa	600
	Zambia	600
9	Cambodia	506
10	Sierra Leone	475
11	Mozambique	447
12	Malawi	409
13	Côte d'Ivoire	382
14	Togo	373
15	Uganda	369
16	Congo-Brazzaville	367
17	Rwanda	361
18	Congo-Kinshasa	356
19	Ethiopia	344
20	Tanzania	342
21	Burundi	334
22	Central African Rep	314
23	Gabon	308

Note: Statistics are not available for all countries. The number of cases diagnosed and reported depends on the quality of medical practice and administration and can be under-reported in a number of countries.

Measles immunisation

*Lowest % of children aged
12–23 months, 2005*

1	Chad	23
2	Central African Rep	35
	Nigeria	35
	Somalia	35
5	Laos	41
6	Angola	45
7	Côte d'Ivoire	51
8	Haiti	54
9	Gabon	55
10	Congo-Brazzaville	56
11	India	58
12	Ethiopia	59
	Guinea	59
	Madagascar	59
15	Papua New Guinea	60
	Sudan	60
	Swaziland	60
18	Mauritania	61
19	Afghanistan	64
	Bolivia	64

DPT[a] immunisation

*Lowest % of children aged
12–23 months, 2005*

1	Chad	20
2	Nigeria	25
3	Somalia	35
4	Gabon	38
5	Central African Rep	40
6	Haiti	43
7	Angola	47
8	Laos	49
9	Côte d'Ivoire	56
10	Ethiopia	59
	India	59
	Sudan	59
13	Madagascar	61
	Papua New Guinea	61
15	Sierra Leone	64
16	Congo-Brazzaville	65
17	Guinea	69
18	Indonesia	70
19	Mauritania	71
	Swaziland	71

HIV/AIDS

*Prevalence among population
aged 15–49, %, 2005*

1	Swaziland	33.4
2	Botswana	24.1
3	Lesotho	23.2
4	Zimbabwe	20.1
5	Namibia	19.6
6	South Africa	18.8
7	Zambia	17.0
8	Mozambique	16.1
9	Malawi	14.1
10	Central African Rep	10.7
11	Gabon	7.9
12	Côte d'Ivoire	7.1
13	Uganda	6.7
14	Tanzania	6.5
15	Kenya	6.1
16	Cameroon	5.4
17	Congo-Brazzaville	5.3
18	Nigeria	3.9
19	Guinea-Bissau	3.8
	Haiti	3.8
21	Angola	3.7
22	Chad	3.5
23	Bahamas	3.3
	Burundi	3.3

AIDS

*Estimated deaths per 100,000
pop., 2005*

1	Swaziland	1,455
2	Zimbabwe	1,395
3	Lesotho	1,278
4	Botswana	1,000
5	Zambia	899
6	Namibia	850
7	Mozambique	729
8	South Africa	708
9	Malawi	634
10	Central African Rep	615
11	Kenya	432
12	Côte d'Ivoire	385
13	Tanzania	371
14	Uganda	341
15	Gabon	336
16	Congo-Brazzaville	289
17	Cameroon	282
18	Rwanda	247
19	Angola	213
20	Equatorial Guinea	197
21	Belize	192
22	Haiti	190
23	Barbados	185
24	Burundi	183

a Diptheria, pertussis and tetanus

Health

Highest health spending
As % of GDP

1	United States	15.4
2	West Bank and Gaza	13.0
3	Malawi	12.9
4	Lebanon	11.6
5	Switzerland	11.5
6	Germany	10.6
7	France	10.5
8	Austria	10.3
9	Serbia	10.1
10	Iceland	9.9
11	Canada	9.8
	Jordan	9.8
	Portugal	9.8
14	Belgium	9.7
	Norway	9.7
16	Argentina	9.6
	Australia	9.6
18	Malta	9.2
	Netherlands	9.2
20	Sweden	9.1
21	Brazil	8.8
22	Israel	8.7
	Italy	8.7
	Slovenia	8.7
25	Denmark	8.6
	South Africa	8.6
27	New Zealand	8.4
28	Bosnia	8.3
29	Nicaragua	8.2
	Uruguay	8.2

Lowest health spending
As % of GDP

1	Equatorial Guinea	1.6
2	Angola	1.9
3	Myanmar	2.2
	Pakistan	2.2
5	Qatar	2.4
6	Congo-Kinshasa	2.5
7	Indonesia	2.8
	Kuwait	2.8
9	Mauritania	2.9
	United Arab Emirates	2.9
11	Madagascar	3.0
	Oman	3.0
13	Bangladesh	3.1
14	Brunei	3.2
	Burundi	3.2
16	Saudi Arabia	3.3
	Sierra Leone	3.3
18	Philippines	3.4
19	North Korea	3.5
	Thailand	3.5
	Trinidad & Tobago	3.5
22	Algeria	3.6
	Azerbaijan	3.6
	Papua New Guinea	3.6
25	Singapore	3.7
26	Côte d'Ivoire	3.8
	Kazakhstan	3.8
	Libya	3.8
	Malaysia	3.8
30	Laos	3.9

Highest pop. per doctor

1	Niger	56,278
2	Malawi	52,374
3	Tanzania	50,834
4	Burundi	35,434
5	Sierra Leone	35,420
6	Mozambique	34,362
7	Ethiopia	32,807
8	Liberia	31,269
9	Togo	30,725
10	Benin	30,576
11	Chad	27,385
12	Botswana	24,513
13	Rwanda	21,265
14	Eritrea	20,471
15	Papua New Guinea	20,300
16	Lesotho	19,942
17	Burkina Faso	19,743
18	Senegal	18,864

Lowest pop. per doctor

1	Cuba	169
2	Georgia	215
3	Belarus	217
4	Belgium	227
5	Greece	230
6	Estonia	231
7	Russia	236
	Turkmenistan	236
9	Italy	244
10	Lithuania	253
11	Andorra	256
12	Armenia	271
13	Israel	275
14	Kazakhstan	278
15	Bulgaria	279
	Uruguay	279
17	Azerbaijan	281
	Iceland	281

Most hospital beds
Beds per 1,000 pop.

1	Japan	14.3	22	Romania	6.6
2	North Korea	13.2		South Korea	6.6
3	Belarus	11.1	24	Bulgaria	6.4
4	Russia	9.7		Moldova	6.4
5	Ukraine	8.7	26	Israel	6.3
6	Czech Republic	8.4		Luxembourg	6.3
	Germany	8.4	28	Tajikistan	6.2
8	Azerbaijan	8.2	29	New Zealand	6.0
9	Lithuania	8.1	30	Serbia	5.9
10	Hungary	7.9	31	Estonia	5.8
11	Kazakhstan	7.8	32	Ireland	5.7
12	Austria	7.7		Switzerland	5.7
	Latvia	7.7	34	Croatia	5.5
14	France	7.5	35	Belgium	5.3
	Iceland	7.5		Poland	5.3
	Malta	7.5	37	Uzbekistan	5.2
	Mongolia	7.5	38	Kyrgyzstan	5.1
18	Australia	7.4	39	Netherlands	5.0
19	Barbados	7.3	40	Cuba	4.9
20	Finland	7.0		Turkmenistan	4.9
21	Slovakia	6.9			

Child well-being
Ranking[a]

		Average rank[b]	Material well-being	Health/ safety	Educational well-being	Family/ friends relationships
1	Netherlands	4.2	10	2	6	3
2	Sweden	5.0	1	1	5	15
3	Denmark	7.2	4	4	8	9
4	Finland	7.5	3	3	4	17
5	Spain	8.0	12	6	15	8
6	Switzerland	8.3	5	9	14	4
7	Norway	8.7	2	8	11	10
8	Italy	10.0	14	5	20	1
9	Ireland	10.2	19	19	7	7
10	Belgium	10.7	7	16	1	5
11	Germany	11.2	13	11	10	13
12	Canada	11.8	6	13	2	18
13	Greece	11.8	15	18	16	11
14	Poland	12.3	21	15	3	14
15	Czech Republic	12.5	11	10	9	19
16	France	13.0	9	7	18	12
17	Portugal	13.7	16	14	21	2
18	Austria	13.8	8	20	19	16
19	Hungary	14.5	20	17	13	6
20	United States	18.0	17	21	12	20
21	United Kingdom	18.2	18	12	17	21

Note: Data for these health rankings refer to the latest year available, 1999–2005.
a Comparing 21 OECD countries.   b Average of six measures.

Marriage and divorce

Highest marriage rates
Number of marriages per 1,000 population, 2005 or latest available year

1	Bermuda	13.8		South Korea	6.5
2	Barbados	13.1		Turkey	6.5
3	Aruba	12.1	33	Singapore	6.3
	Vietnam	12.1	34	Belize	6.1
5	Jordan	9.7		Romania	6.1
6	Iran	8.9	36	Costa Rica	6.0
7	Mauritius	8.8		Hong Kong	6.0
8	Algeria	8.7		Malta	6.0
9	Jamaica	8.3		Tajikistan	6.0
10	Guam	8.2		Tunisia	6.0
11	United States	8.0	41	China	5.9
12	Azerbaijan	7.6		Malaysia	5.9
	West Bank and Gaza	7.6		Ukraine	5.9
14	Taiwan	7.5	44	Bahamas	5.8
15	Belarus	7.3		Lithuania	5.8
	Cyprus	7.3		Mongolia	5.8
	Indonesia	7.3		Trinidad & Tobago	5.8
	Iraq	7.3	48	Channel Islands[a]	5.7
19	Denmark	7.1		Finland	5.7
20	Kazakhstan	7.0		Serbia	5.7
	Moldova	7.0	51	Bosnia	5.6
22	Macedonia	6.9		Greece	5.6
23	Kyrgyzstan	6.8		Japan	5.6
	Philippines	6.8	54	Australia	5.5
	Russia	6.8	55	Armenia	5.3
	Uzbekistan	6.8		Israel	5.3
27	Albania	6.7		Mexico	5.3
	Egypt	6.7		Spain	5.3
29	Turkmenistan	6.6		Switzerland	5.3
30	Puerto Rico	6.5			

Lowest marriage rates
Number of marriages per 1,000 population, 2005 or latest available year

1	Colombia	1.7	13	Martinique	3.6
2	Dominican Republic	2.8	14	El Salvador	3.8
3	Venezuela	2.8		Macau	3.8
4	Andorra	2.9		South Africa	3.8
	Peru	2.9	17	Guadeloupe	3.9
6	United Arab Emirates	3.1		Netherlands Antilles	3.9
7	Argentina	3.2		Nicaragua	3.9
	Slovenia	3.2	20	Bulgaria	4.0
9	Panama	3.3		New Caledonia	4.0
10	Chile	3.4		Portugal	4.0
	Georgia	3.4		Suriname	4.0
12	Qatar	3.5		Uruguay	4.0

a Guernsey only
Note: The data are based on latest available figures and hence will be affected by the population age structure at the time. Marriage rates refer to registered marriages only and, therefore, reflect the customs surrounding registry and efficiency of administration.

Highest divorce rates
Number of divorces per 1,000 population, 2005 or latest available year

1	Aruba	5.0		Portugal	2.3
2	Russia	4.4	34	Canada	2.2
3	Uruguay	4.3		Cyprus	2.2
4	Moldova	4.1		France	2.2
5	South Korea	3.9		Sweden	2.2
6	Puerto Rico	3.7	38	Guadeloupe	2.1
	Ukraine	3.7		Singapore	2.1
	United States	3.7		Slovakia	2.1
9	Czech Republic	3.3	41	Bulgaria	2.0
	Lithuania	3.3		Japan	2.0
11	Cuba	3.2	43	Iceland	1.8
12	Estonia	3.1		Kuwait	1.8
	Taiwan	3.1		Netherlands	1.8
14	Belgium	3.0	46	Bahamas	1.7
	Bermuda	3.0		Jordan	1.7
	Denmark	3.0	48	Israel	1.6
17	Belarus	2.9		Romania	1.6
	Channel Islands[a]	2.9	50	Poland	1.5
	United Kingdom	2.9	51	China	1.3
20	Netherlands Antilles	2.8		Suriname	1.3
21	Germany	2.7	53	Croatia	1.2
	New Zealand	2.7		Greece	1.2
23	Australia	2.5		Slovenia	1.2
	Finland	2.5		Trinidad & Tobago	1.2
	Switzerland	2.5		Turkmenistan	1.2
26	Hungary	2.4	58	New Caledonia	1.1
	Norway	2.4		Réunion	1.1
28	Austria	2.3		Serbia	1.1
	Hong Kong	2.3		Spain	1.1
	Kazakhstan	2.3		Thailand	1.1
	Latvia	2.3		Tunisia	1.1
	Luxembourg	2.3		West Bank and Gaza	1.1

Lowest divorce rates
Number of divorces per 1,000 population, 2005 or latest available year

1	Colombia	0.2		Uzbekistan	0.6
2	Libya	0.3	13	Ireland	0.7
3	Bosnia	0.4		Jamaica	0.7
	Georgia	0.4		Turkey	0.7
	Mongolia	0.4	16	Azerbaijan	0.8
	Tajikistan	0.4		Brazil	0.8
7	Chile	0.5		Egypt	0.8
	Vietnam	0.5		Indonesia	0.8
9	Armenia	0.6		Italy	0.8
	El Salvador	0.6		Macedonia	0.8
	Mexico	0.6		Venezuela	0.8

a Guernsey only

Households and living costs

Biggest number of households[a]

m

1	China	372.1	15	Italy	22.4
2	India	206.3	16	Pakistan	22.1
3	United States	112.7	17	Ukraine	19.8
4	Indonesia	58.6	18	Congo-Kinshasa	17.3
5	Russia	53.0		South Korea	17.3
6	Brazil	50.0	20	Thailand	17.2
7	Japan	48.5	21	Philippines	17.1
8	Germany	39.3	22	Egypt	16.0
9	Nigeria	26.8	23	Turkey	15.4
10	United Kingdom	26.1	24	Spain	15.2
11	Bangladesh	25.5	25	Ethiopia	14.7
12	France	25.3	26	Poland	13.6
13	Vietnam	25.2	27	Myanmar	13.5
14	Mexico	24.6			

Biggest households[a]

Population per dwelling

1	Congo-Brazzaville	8.2		Sudan	6.1
2	Pakistan	7.2	11	Algeria	6.0
3	Papua New Guinea	6.8	12	Bangladesh	5.9
4	United Arab Emirates	6.5		Saudi Arabia	5.9
5	Gabon	6.3		Uzbekistan	5.9
	Guinea	6.3	15	French Polynesia	5.8
	Kuwait	6.3		Kyrgyzstan	5.8
8	Cambodia	6.2	17	Guinea-Bissau	5.7
9	Réunion	6.1		Jordan	5.7

Highest cost of living[b]

End 2006, USA=100

1	Norway	132		New Caledonia	104
2	France	130		Sweden	104
3	Denmark	126	19	Netherlands	101
4	United Kingdom	125		Russia	101
5	Japan	124	21	Italy	98
6	Iceland	118	22	Spain	97
7	Finland	116	23	Canada	96
8	South Korea	115	24	Luxembourg	95
9	Austria	112	25	Cote d'Ivoire	89
	Switzerland	112	26	Israel	88
11	Singapore	108	27	New Zealand	86
12	Hong Kong	107	28	Taiwan	85
13	Australia	106		Turkey	85
	Germany	106	30	Czech Republic	84
15	Belgium	104		Greece	84
	Ireland	104			

a Latest available year.
b The cost of living index shown is compiled by the Economist Intelligence Unit for use
by companies in determining expatriate compensation: it is a comparison of the cost
of maintaining a typical international lifestyle in the country rather than a
comparison of the purchasing power of a citizen of the country. The index is based on
typical urban prices an international executive and family will face abroad. The prices

Smallest number of households[a]

m

1	Cayman Islands	0.01	16	Malta	0.12
	Virgin Islands	0.01	17	Equatorial Guinea	0.13
3	Bermuda	0.02		Iceland	0.13
4	Aruba	0.03		Réunion	0.13
	Guam	0.03	20	Macau	0.15
6	French Polynesia	0.04	21	Fiji	0.16
	New Caledonia	0.04		Luxembourg	0.16
8	Netherlands Antilles	0.05		Qatar	0.16
9	Barbados	0.06	24	Bahrain	0.19
10	Bahamas	0.07	25	Swaziland	0.20
	Brunei	0.07	26	Gabon	0.22
12	Suriname	0.09	27	Mauritius	0.23
13	Martinique	0.10	28	Cyprus	0.27
14	Belize	0.11	29	Guinea-Bissau	0.28
	Guadeloupe	0.11		Trinidad & Tobago	0.28

Smallest households[a]

Population per dwelling

1	Finland	2.1		Netherlands	2.3
	Germany	2.1		Norway	2.3
	Sweden	2.1		United Kingdom	2.3
4	Denmark	2.2	11	Belgium	2.4
	Switzerland	2.2		Estonia	2.4
6	Austria	2.3		France	2.4
	Iceland	2.3		Ukraine	2.4

Lowest cost of living[b]

End 2006, USA=100

1	Iran	34	17	Cambodia	59
2	Philippines	43	18	Bulgaria	60
3	Pakistan	44		Kazakhstan	60
4	India	45		Peru	60
	Libya	45	21	Panama	61
	Nepal	45	22	Ecuador	62
7	Bangladesh	46		Uruguay	62
8	Paraguay	51		Vietnam	62
9	Algeria	52	25	Brunei	63
10	Costa Rica	53		Kuwait	63
11	Argentina	54		Oman	63
	Uzbekistan	54	28	South Africa	64
13	Syria	57	29	Saudi Arabia	65
	Venezuela	57	30	Bahrain	66
15	Egypt	58		Romania	66
	Sri Lanka	58			

are for products of international comparable quality found in a supermarket or
department store. Prices found in local markets and bazaars are not used unless the
available merchandise is of the specified quality and the shopping area itself is safe
for executive and family members. New York City prices are used as the base, so United
States = 100.

Consumer goods ownership

TV

Colour TVs per 100 households

1	Belgium	99.8	17	Germany	97.4
2	United States	99.7	18	United Arab Emirates	97.3
3	Ireland	99.4	19	Sweden	97.0
4	Taiwan	99.3	20	Israel	96.9
5	Hong Kong	99.1	21	Switzerland	96.8
	Saudi Arabia	99.1	22	Venezuela	96.3
7	Japan	99.0	23	Italy	96.0
8	Canada	98.8	24	France	95.9
9	Finland	98.7	25	Norway	94.0
	Netherlands	98.7	26	South Korea	93.8
	Singapore	98.7	27	Jordan	93.4
	Spain	98.7	28	Slovenia	92.8
13	Portugal	98.3	29	Hungary	92.7
	United Kingdom	98.3	30	Denmark	92.6
15	New Zealand	98.2	31	Kuwait	92.2
16	Austria	97.9	32	Argentina	92.1

Telephone

Telephone lines per 100 people

1	Bermuda	86.2	18	Faroe Islands	50.7
2	Switzerland	69.0	19	Malta	50.4
3	Germany	66.6	20	Cyprus	50.3
4	Iceland	65.9	21	Australia	50.2
5	Canada	64.1	22	Ireland	49.5
6	Virgin Islands (US)	63.9	23	South Korea	49.2
7	Denmark	61.7	24	Guadeloupe	48.7
8	Taiwan	59.8	25	Netherlands	46.6
9	United States	58.8	26	Austria	45.7
10	Sweden	58.2		Greenland	45.7
11	Greece	56.8		Norway	45.7
12	France	55.7	29	Belgium	45.4
13	Hong Kong	53.9	30	Japan	45.3
14	United Kingdom	53.3	31	Martinique	44.5
15	Andorra	52.8	32	Bahamas	43.9
16	Luxembourg	52.6	33	Italy	43.1
17	Guam	50.9	34	New Zealand	42.9

CD player

CD players per 100 households

1	Norway	89.5	12	Austria	69.7
2	Denmark	89.1	13	Belgium	66.3
3	New Zealand	88.5	14	Finland	64.1
4	Netherlands	87.7	15	United States	61.3
5	United Kingdom	87.1	16	Switzerland	59.2
6	Australia	85.5	17	Hong Kong	58.4
7	Germany	85.2	18	Singapore	56.0
8	Sweden	83.4	19	Portugal	43.1
9	Canada	81.5	20	Spain	42.4
10	Taiwan	70.6	21	Ireland	41.1
11	Japan	69.8	22	Peru	36.3

Computer
Computers per 100 people

1	Switzerland	86.2		New Zealand	48.2
2	United States	76.2	26	Slovenia	41.1
3	Sweden	76.1	27	Italy	37.0
4	Israel	73.4	28	Réunion	36.3
5	Canada	69.8	29	Slovakia	35.7
6	Australia	68.9	30	Saudi Arabia	35.4
7	Netherlands	68.5	31	Macau	34.8
8	Denmark	65.5	32	Belgium	34.7
9	Luxembourg	62.4	33	Cyprus	30.9
10	Singapore	62.2	34	Spain	28.1
11	Austria	61.1	35	Czech Republic	24.0
12	United Kingdom	60.0	36	Costa Rica	23.1
13	Hong Kong	59.3	37	Kuwait	22.3
14	France	57.9	38	Macedonia	22.2
15	Taiwan	57.5	39	Latvia	21.9
16	Norway	57.2	40	Martinique	20.8
17	Germany	54.5	41	Guadeloupe	20.3
18	Japan	54.2	42	United Arab Emirates	19.8
19	South Korea	53.2	43	Malaysia	19.2
20	Bermuda	52.3	44	Croatia	19.1
21	Ireland	49.7		Poland	19.1
22	Estonia	48.9	46	Qatar	17.9
23	Iceland	48.3	47	Bahrain	16.9
24	Finland	48.2	48	Malta	16.6

Mobile telephone
Subscribers per 100 people

1	Luxembourg	154.8	24	Netherlands	97.2
2	Aruba	135.1	25	Spain	96.8
3	Lithuania	127.1	26	Andorra	96.1
4	Italy	124.3	27	Germany	95.8
5	Hong Kong	123.5	28	Greece	92.3
6	Macau	115.9		Hungary	92.3
7	Czech Republic	115.2	30	Qatar	92.2
8	Israel	112.4	31	Switzerland	91.6
9	United Kingdom	109.8	32	Australia	91.4
10	Portugal	109.1	33	Netherlands Antilles	90.1
11	Estonia	108.8	34	Belgium	90.0
12	Austria	105.8	35	Faroe Islands	89.4
	Jamaica	105.8	36	Nepal	85.9
14	Iceland	103.4	37	Ukraine	83.9
15	Bahrain	103.0	38	Cuba	83.4
16	Ireland	102.9	39	Armenia	78.9
	Norway	102.9	40	Bosnia	76.4
18	United Arab Emirates	100.9	41	Réunion	75.5
19	Singapore	100.8	42	Thailand	73.0
20	Sweden	100.5	43	South Africa	71.6
21	Finland	100.4	44	Uzbekistan	68.4
22	Denmark	100.3	45	Ecuador	66.9
23	Taiwan	97.4			

Cinema and newspapers

Cinema attendances

Total visits, m			Visits per head		
1	India	1,618.7	1	New Zealand	7.7
2	United States	1,422.2	2	Australia	6.3
3	China	1,420.7	3	United States	4.8
4	Indonesia	272.0	4	Ireland	4.2
5	France	204.8	5	Canada	4.0
6	United Kingdom	178.8	6	France	3.4
7	Japan	176.3		Spain	3.4
8	Mexico	159.7	8	United Kingdom	3.0
9	Germany	159.0	9	Norway	2.6
10	Spain	146.7	10	Austria	2.5
11	Canada	130.7	11	Denmark	2.4
12	Australia	127.9		Singapore	2.4
13	Italy	119.2		Switzerland	2.4
14	Russia	113.7	14	Belgium	2.2
15	Philippines	94.2	15	Italy	2.1
16	South Africa	61.3	16	Venezuela	2.0
17	Venezuela	53.1	17	Germany	1.9
18	Brazil	49.0		Sweden	1.9
19	South Korea	47.8	19	Portugal	1.6
20	Argentina	44.7		Slovenia	1.6
21	Poland	36.2	21	India	1.5
22	Turkey	31.2		Netherlands	1.5
23	New Zealand	30.7		Mexico	1.5
24	Netherlands	24.1	24	Ecuador	1.4
25	Belgium	23.3		Greece	1.4
26	Austria	20.5		Japan	1.4
27	Taiwan	19.0	27	Czech Republic	1.3
28	Ecuador	18.9		Finland	1.3
29	Switzerland	17.6		Hungary	1.3
30	Ireland	17.1		Israel	1.3
31	Sweden	16.8		South Africa	1.3
32	Portugal	16.3			

Daily newspapers

Copies per '000 population, latest year					
1	Japan	546	16	Estonia	190
2	Norway	514	17	New Zealand	183
3	Sweden	488		Slovenia	183
4	Finland	436	19	United States	182
5	Singapore	380	20	Hong Kong	181
6	Denmark	368	21	Canada	180
7	Austria	339	22	Latvia	157
8	Switzerland	334	23	Belgium	144
9	United Kingdom	284	24	Australia	143
10	Germany	262	25	Hungary	139
11	Bulgaria	253	26	Italy	134
12	Netherlands	243	27	Ireland	131
13	Luxembourg	240	28	France	129
14	Iceland	217	29	Poland	116
15	Czech Republic	204	30	Malaysia	106

Music and the internet

Music sales

Total including downloads, $m

1	United States	7,011.9
2	Japan	3,718.4
3	United Kingdom	2,162.2
4	Germany	1,457.5
5	France	1,248.3
6	Canada	544.3
7	Australia	440.0
8	Italy	428.5
9	Spain	368.9
10	Brazil	265.4
11	Mexico	262.7
12	Netherlands	246.3
13	Switzerland	205.9
14	Russia	193.7
15	Belgium	161.8
16	South Africa	158.8
17	Sweden	148.2
18	Austria	138.7
19	Norway	133.1
20	Denmark	113.1

$ per head

1	United Kingdom	36.2
2	Japan	29.0
3	Norway	28.9
4	Switzerland	28.2
5	United States	23.5
6	Ireland	22.2
7	Australia	21.8
8	Denmark	20.9
9	France	20.6
10	New Zealand	19.4
11	Germany	17.6
12	Austria	16.9
	Canada	16.9
14	Sweden	16.5
15	Belgium	15.6
	Finland	15.6
17	Netherlands	15.1
18	Hong Kong	9.5
19	Spain	8.6

Internet hosts

By country, January 2007

1	United States	245,327,938
2	Japan	30,841,523
3	Italy	13,853,673
4	Germany	13,093,255
5	France	10,335,974
6	Netherlands	9,014,103
7	Australia	8,529,020
8	Brazil	7,422,440
9	Mexico	6,697,570
10	United Kingdom	6,650,334
11	Poland	5,001,786
12	Taiwan	4,418,705
13	Canada	4,257,825
14	Finland	3,187,643
15	Belgium	3,150,856
16	Sweden	3,039,770
17	Spain	2,929,627
18	Denmark	2,807,348
19	Switzerland	2,570,891
20	Norway	2,370,078
21	Russia	2,353,171
22	Austria	2,330,325
23	China	1,933,919
24	Argentina	1,837,050
25	India	1,684,958

Per 1,000 pop., January 2007

1	United States	822.7
2	Iceland	696.9
3	Finland	613.0
4	Netherlands	553.0
5	Denmark	519.9
6	Norway	515.2
7	Australia	422.2
8	Switzerland	352.2
9	Estonia	345.4
10	New Zealand	338.9
11	Sweden	337.8
12	Belgium	303.0
13	Ireland	294.7
14	Austria	284.2
15	Japan	240.8
16	Italy	238.4
17	Greenland	235.5
18	Singapore	211.5
19	Israel	195.8
20	Taiwan	193.0
21	Luxembourg	191.4
22	Cayman Islands	172.9
23	France	170.8
24	Germany	158.3
25	Czech Republic	147.3

Nobel prize winners: 1901–2006

Peace (two or more)

1	United States	17
2	United Kingdom	11
3	France	9
4	Sweden	5
5	Belgium	4
	Germany	4
7	Austria	3
	Norway	3
	South Africa	3
10	Argentina	2
	Egypt	2
	Israel	2
	Russia	2
	Switzerland	2

Economics[a]

1	United States	30
2	United Kingdom	8
3	Norway	2
	Sweden	2
5	France	1
	Germany	1
	Israel	1
	Netherlands	1
	Russia	1

Literature (three or more)

1	France	14
2	United States	12
3	United Kingdom	10
4	Germany	7
5	Sweden	6
6	Italy	5
	Spain	5
8	Norway	3
	Poland	3
	Russia	3

Medicine (three or more)

1	United States	50
2	United Kingdom	21
3	Germany	14
4	Sweden	7
5	France	6
	Switzerland	6
7	Austria	5
	Denmark	5
9	Australia	3
	Belgium	3
	Italy	3

Physics

1	United States	48
2	United Kingdom	19
3	Germany	18
4	France	8
5	Netherlands	6
	Russia	6
7	Japan	4
	Sweden	4
	Switzerland	4
10	Austria	3
	Italy	3
12	Canada	2
	Denmark	2
14	Colombia	1
	India	1
	Ireland	1
	Pakistan	1
	Poland	1

Chemistry

1	United States	42
2	United Kingdom	22
3	Germany	14
4	France	7
5	Switzerland	6
6	Sweden	5
7	Canada	4
	Japan	4
9	Argentina	1
	Austria	1
	Belgium	1
	Czech Republic	1
	Denmark	1
	Finland	1
	Israel	1
	Italy	1
	Netherlands	1
	Norway	1
	Russia	1

a Since 1969.

Notes: Prizes by country of residence at time awarded. When prizes have been shared in the same field, one credit given to each country. Only top rankings in each field are included.

Olympic medal winners

Summer games, 1896–2004

		Gold	Silver	Bronze
1	United States	895	690	604
2	Soviet Union[a]	440	357	325
3	United Kingdom	180	233	225
4	France	173	187	203
5	Italy	172	136	153
6	Germany[b]	162	191	205
7	Germany (East)	153	129	127
8	Hungary	148	130	154
9	Sweden	138	154	171
10	China	112	96	78
11	Australia	100	106	131
12	Finland	100	80	113
13	Japan	98	97	103
14	Romania	74	86	106
15	Netherlands	60	65	84
16	Russia[c]	59	53	47
17	Poland	56	72	113
18	Germany (West)	56	67	81
19	Cuba	56	46	41
20	Canada	52	79	99

Winter games, 1924–2006

		Gold	Silver	Bronze
1	Germany[b]	129	117	93
2	Norway	96	102	75
3	Soviet Union[a]	87	63	67
4	United States	78	81	59
5	Austria	50	64	70
6	Sweden	46	32	34
7	Finland	42	57	52
8	Canada	38	38	44
9	Switzerland	37	37	43
10	Italy	36	31	33
11	Russia	35	26	21
12	France	25	24	32
13	Netherlands	25	30	23
14	South Korea	17	8	6
15	Japan	9	10	13
16	United Kingdom	8	5	15
17	China	4	16	13
18	Croatia	4	3	0
19	Estonia	4	1	1
20	Australia	3	0	2

a 1952–1992.
b Germany 1896–1936, unified teams in 1956–64, then since 1992.
c Russia 1896–1912, then since 1996.
Note: Figures exclude mixed teams in 1896, 1900 and 1904 and Australasia teams in 1908 and 1912.

Drinking and smoking

Beer drinkers
Off-trade sales, litres per head of pop.

1	Czech Republic	82.4
2	Venezuela	71.6
3	Australia	68.7
4	Germany	67.5
5	Austria	66.6
6	Finland	64.6
7	United States	61.7
8	Slovakia	60.6
9	Hungary	56.7
10	Russia	55.5
11	Netherlands	54.4
12	New Zealand	53.9
13	Canada	51.6
14	Denmark	50.9
	Poland	50.9
16	Romania	49.7
17	Belgium	45.7
18	Bulgaria	43.7
19	Mexico	42.5
20	Norway	41.5
21	Sweden	38.4
22	Japan	38.1
23	South Africa	38.0

Wine drinkers
Off-trade sales, litres per head of pop.

1	Portugal	32.1
2	Switzerland	29.5
3	Italy	29.4
4	France	27.4
5	Denmark	24.5
6	Argentina	24.0
7	Hungary	23.9
8	Germany	21.9
9	Netherlands	21.8
10	Belgium	19.0
11	Australia	18.7
12	United Kingdom	17.5
13	New Zealand	17.2
14	Austria	17.0
15	Sweden	15.6
16	Ireland	14.4
17	Chile	13.7
18	Spain	13.0
19	Norway	11.7
20	Czech Republic	10.4
21	Finland	9.6
22	Canada	9.5

Alcoholic drinks
Off-trade sales, litres per head of pop.

1	Australia	99.2
2	Czech Republic	98.2
3	Germany	96.2
4	Finland	92.0
5	Austria	87.8
6	Hungary	84.9
7	Russia	80.6
8	Netherlands	79.8
9	New Zealand	78.7
10	Denmark	78.2
11	Venezuela	75.2
12	United States	73.8
13	Slovakia	73.1
14	Belgium	68.0
15	Canada	67.1
16	Portugal	66.9
17	Poland	66.2
18	United Kingdom	64.7
19	Switzerland	61.5
20	Argentina	60.5
21	Sweden	60.4
22	Romania	60.3
23	Norway	57.2
24	France	54.7

Smokers
Av. ann. consumption of cigarettes per head per day

1	Greece	8.4
2	Macedonia	7.1
3	Russia	6.8
4	Czech Republic	6.4
5	Slovenia	6.2
6	Spain	6.1
7	Japan	6.0
8	Ukraine	5.9
9	Bulgaria	5.8
	Latvia	5.8
	Moldova	5.8
	Serbia	5.8
13	Bosnia	5.2
14	Cyprus	5.1
15	Albania	5.0
	Kazakhstan	5.0
	Poland	5.0
	Taiwan	5.0
19	South Korea	4.9
20	Armenia	4.8
21	Belgium	4.7
22	Austria	4.6
	Lebanon	4.6

Crime and punishment

Murders
Per 100,000 pop.

1	Ecuador	18.3
2	Swaziland	13.6
3	Mongolia	12.8
4	Suriname	10.3
5	Lithuania	9.4
6	Latvia	8.5
7	Zimbabwe	8.4
8	Belarus	8.3
9	Kyrgyzstan	8.0
10	Uganda	7.4
	Ukraine	7.4
12	Estonia	6.8
13	Moldova	6.7
	Sri Lanka	6.7
15	Costa Rica	6.2
	Georgia	6.2
17	Uruguay	5.6
18	Peru	5.5
	United States	5.5
20	Philippines	4.3

Death penalty
Executions, 2004

1	China[a]	3,400
2	Iran	159
3	Vietnam[a]	64
4	Uzbekistan	62
5	United States	52
6	North Korea	40
7	Saudi Arabia	33
8	Pakistan	15
9	Kuwait	9
10	Bangladesh	7
11	Egypt	6
	Yemen	6
13	Belarus	5
14	Somalia	4
15	Indonesia	3
	Lebanon	3
	Taiwan	3
18	Japan	2
	Sudan	2

Prisoners
Total prison pop., latest available year

1	United States	2,193,798
2	China	1,548,498
3	Russia	871,693
4	Brazil	385,317
5	India	332,112
6	Mexico	214,452
7	Thailand	164,443
8	Ukraine	162,602
9	South Africa	160,198
10	Iran	147,926
11	Indonesia	99,946
12	Poland	90,268
13	Philippines	89,639
14	Pakistan	89,370
15	Vietnam	88,414
16	United Kingdom	88,197
17	Japan	79,052
18	Germany	77,166
19	Bangladesh[a]	71,200
20	Rwanda[a]	67,000
21	Turkey	65,458
22	Ethiopia[a]	65,000
23	Spain	64,721
24	Argentina	63,357

Per 100,000 pop., latest available year

1	United States	737
2	Russia	613
3	Virgin Islands (US)	549
4	Belize	505
5	Turkmenistan	489
6	Cuba	487
7	Bermuda	464
8	Bahamas	462
9	Cayman Islands	453
10	Belarus	426
11	Barbados	367
12	Netherlands Antilles	364
	Panama	364
14	Puerto Rico	356
	Suriname	356
16	Singapore	350
	Ukraine	350
18	Botswana	348
19	Guam	345
20	Kazakhstan	340
21	South Africa	336
22	Estonia	333
23	Aruba	324
24	Trinidad & Tobago	296

a Estimate.

Stars...

Space missions

Firsts and selected events

1957 Man-made satellite Dog in space, Laika

1961 Human in space, Yuri Gagarin
Entire day in space, Gherman Titov

1963 Woman in space, Valentina Tereshkova

1964 Space crew, one pilot and two passengers

1965 Space walk, Alexei Leonov
Computer guidance system
Eight days in space achieved (needed to travel to moon and back)

1966 Docking between space craft and target vehicle
Autopilot re-entry and landing

1968 Live television broadcast from space
Moon orbit

1969 Astronaut transfer from one craft to another in space
Moon landing

1971 Space station, Salyut
Drive on the moon

1973 Space laboratory, Skylab

1978 Non-Amercian, non-Soviet, Vladimir Remek (Czechoslovakia)

1982 Space shuttle, Columbia (first craft to carry four crew members)

1983 Five crew mission

1984 Space walk, untethered
Capture, repair and redeployment of satellite in space
Seven crew mission

1985 Classified US Defence Department mission

1986 Space shuttle explosion, Challenger
Mir space station activated

1990 Hubble telescope deployed

2001 Dennis Tito, first paying space tourist

2003 Space shuttle explosion, Columbia. Shuttle programme suspended
China's first manned space flight, Yang Liwei

2004 SpaceShipOne, first successful private manned space flight

2005 Space shuttle, resumption of flights

Space vehicle launches

By host country

2003

1	United States	24
2	Russia	19
3	China	6
4	France	4
5	India	2
	Japan	2

2004

1	United States	21
2	Russia	17
3	China	2
	France	2
5	India	1
	Sweden	1

2005

1	Russia	21
2	United States	15
3	France	5
4	China	3
5	Japan	2
6	India	1
	Sweden	1

2006

1	United States	20
2	Russia	19
3	Japan	7
4	France	5
5	China	4
6	Sweden	3

...and Wars

Defence spending
As % of GDP

1	Oman	12.3	16	Singapore		4.8
2	Myanmar	9.0	17	Uzbekistan		4.6
3	Saudi Arabia	8.8	18	Egypt		4.1
4	Israel	8.0		Guinea-Bissau		4.1
5	Jordan	7.6	20	Colombia		4.0
6	Kuwait	6.6		Cuba		4.0
7	Eritrea	6.3		United States		4.0
8	Burundi	6.1		Zimbabwe		4.0
9	Vietnam	6.0	24	Morocco		3.9
10	Syria	5.8	25	Bahrain		3.8
11	Armenia	5.6	26	Pakistan		3.7
12	Brunei	5.5		Russia		3.7
13	Madagascar	5.3		Yemen		3.7
14	Qatar	5.2	29	Chile		3.6
15	Angola	4.9	30	Belarus		3.5

Defence spending
$bn

1	United States	495.3	16	Netherlands	9.9
2	China	104.0	17	Israel	9.8
3	France	53.1	18	Indonesia	8.4
4	United Kingdom	51.7	19	Taiwan	8.0
5	Japan	43.9	20	Greece	6.9
6	Germany	38.0		Myanmar	6.9
7	Italy	31.4	22	Ukraine	6.0
8	Saudi Arabia	25.4	23	Sweden	5.9
9	India	21.7	24	Poland	5.6
10	South Korea	20.3		Singapore	5.6
11	Australia	15.6	26	Iran	5.2
12	Brazil	13.3	27	Colombia	4.9
13	Spain	13.2		Norway	4.9
14	Canada	12.8	29	Belgium	4.6
15	Turkey	11.7	30	Kuwait	4.4

Armed forces
'000

		Regulars	Reserves			Regulars	Reserves
1	China	2,255	800	14	Thailand	307	200
2	US	1,506	973	15	Indonesia	302	400
3	India	1,316	1,155	16	Taiwan	290	1,657
4	North Korea	1,106	4,700	17	Brazil	288	1,340
5	Russia	1,027	20,000	18	France	255	22
6	South Korea	687	4,500	19	Japan	239	44
7	Pakistan	619		20	Mexico	238	40
8	Iran	545	350	21	Saudi Arabia	225	
9	Turkey	515	379	22	Colombia	209	62
10	Myanmar	482		23	Eritrea	202	120
11	Egypt	469	479	24	Morocco	201	150
12	Vietnam	455	5,000	25	Italy	191	57
13	Syria	308	354	26	UK	191	199

Environment

Biggest emitters of carbon dioxide
Tonnes, m, 2003

1	United States	4,816.2	27	Egypt	139.6
2	China	4,143.5	28	Uzbekistan	129.2
3	Russia	1,493.0	29	Argentina	127.5
4	India	1,273.2	30	Venezuela	117.3
5	Japan	1,231.3	31	Czech Republic	116.3
6	Germany	805.0	32	Pakistan	114.1
7	Ukraine	684.0	33	Belgium	102.8
8	United Kingdom	569.1	34	Greece	96.2
9	Canada	565.5	35	Thailand	95.7
10	South Korea	455.9	36	Romania	91.1
11	Italy	445.5	37	Kuwait	78.5
12	Mexico	415.9	38	North Korea	77.5
13	Iran	381.4	39	Philippines	76.9
14	France	373.9	40	Iraq	72.9
15	Australia	354.1	41	Austria	70.3
16	Poland	304.5	42	Israel	68.3
17	Saudi Arabia	302.3	43	Finland	67.8
18	Brazil	298.3	44	Serbia	65.4
19	Indonesia	295.0	45	Belarus	62.5
20	South Africa	285.4	46	Chile	58.5
21	Spain	211.8	47	Hungary	58.2
22	Algeria	163.6	48	Portugal	57.5
23	Kazakhstan	159.2	49	Colombia	55.5
24	Malaysia	156.4	50	Denmark	54.2
25	Turkey	146.2		United Arab Emirates	54.2
26	Netherlands	140.9			

Carbon dioxide emissions
Average annual % change, 1990–2003

Biggest increase			Biggest fall		
1	Laos	16.7	1	Tajikistan	-12.5
2	Bosnia	15.3	2	North Korea	-11.9
3	Swaziland	12.0	3	Georgia	-11.3
4	Vietnam	11.5	4	Moldova	-10.1
5	Nepal	11.4	5	Gabon	-9.1
6	Kuwait	11.0	6	Afghanistan	-9.0
7	Sri Lanka	8.8	7	Kyrgyzstan	-7.5
8	Oman	8.7	8	Latvia	-6.9
9	Madagascar	8.5	9	Ukraine	-6.6
10	Ethiopia	8.0	10	Congo-Kinshasa	-6.5
11	Algeria	7.8	11	Kazakhstan	-6.0
	Togo	7.8	12	Lithuania	-5.2
13	Honduras	7.5	13	Azerbaijan	-5.1
14	Benin	7.4	14	Belarus	-4.4
15	Haiti	7.2	15	Puerto Rico	-4.1
	Uganda	7.2	16	Romania	-4.0
17	Bangladesh	6.9	17	Estonia	-3.9
18	Dominican Republic	6.8	18	Albania	-3.7
	Malaysia	6.8	19	Bulgaria	-3.6
20	Guatemala	6.7	20	Russia	-3.3

Largest amount of carbon dioxide emissions per person
Tonnes, 2003

1	United Arab Emirates	33.4		26	Austria	8.7
2	Kuwait	32.7			Greece	8.7
3	Trinidad & Tobago	22.1			Netherlands	8.7
4	United States	19.9			New Zealand	8.7
5	Canada	17.9		30	Poland	8.0
6	Australia	17.8		31	South Africa	7.9
7	Senegal	13.7		32	Italy	7.7
8	Estonia	13.5			Slovenia	7.7
9	Finland	13.0		34	Spain	7.4
10	Oman	12.8		35	Slovakia	7.0
11	Czech Republic	11.4		36	Ukraine	6.6
	Singapore	11.4		37	Malaysia	6.4
13	Kazakhstan	10.7		38	Belarus	6.3
14	Ireland	10.4		39	France	6.2
15	Russia	10.3			Serbia a	6.2
16	Israel	10.2		41	Sweden	5.9
17	Denmark	10.1		42	Hungary	5.7
18	Belgium	9.9			Iran	5.7
	Norway	9.9		44	Bulgaria	5.6
20	Germany	9.8			Hong Kong	5.6
21	Japan	9.6			Venezuela	5.6
22	South Korea	9.5		47	Portugal	5.5
23	United Kingdom	9.4			Switzerland	5.5
24	Turkmenistan	9.2		49	Croatia	5.4
25	Libya	8.9			Lebanon	5.4

Carbon dioxide emissions relative to GDP
Kg per $PPP of GDP [b], 2003

1	Uzbekistan	2.8			Saudi Arabia	0.9
2	Mongolia	1.8		19	Algeria	0.8
	Trinidad & Tobago	1.8			Iran	0.8
4	Kazakhstan	1.7			Macedonia	0.8
5	United Arab Emirates	1.5			South Africa	0.8
6	Kuwait	1.4			Syria	0.8
7	Russia	1.2		24	Bulgaria	0.7
	Ukraine	1.2			Jordan	0.7
9	Estonia	1.1			Malaysia	0.7
	Lebanon	1.1			Poland	0.7
	Venezuela	1.1			Tajikistan	0.7
12	Azerbaijan	1.0		29	Australia	0.6
	Belarus	1.0			Canada	0.6
	Jamaica	1.0			China	0.6
	Moldova	1.0			Czech Republic	0.6
	Yemen	1.0			Kyrgyzstan	0.6
17	Oman	0.9			Romania	0.6

a Includes Montenegro.
b Constant (2000) $.

Population using improved sanitation facilities[a]

Lowest, %, 2004

1	Chad	9		Sudan	34
	Eritrea	9	25	Guinea-Bissau	35
3	Burkina Faso	13		Nepal	35
	Ethiopia	13		Togo	35
	Niger	13	28	Burundi	36
6	Cambodia	17		Gabon	36
7	Ghana	18	30	Côte d'Ivoire	37
	Guinea	18		Lesotho	37
9	Namibia	25	32	Bangladesh	39
10	Somalia	26		Sierra Leone	39
11	Central African Rep	27	34	Botswana	42
	Congo-Brazzaville	27		Rwanda	42
	Liberia	27	36	Kenya	43
14	Congo-Kinshasa	30		Uganda	43
	Haiti	30		Yemen	43
	Laos	30	39	China	44
17	Angola	31		Nigeria	44
18	Mozambique	32		Papua New Guinea	44
19	Benin	33	42	Bolivia	46
	India	33		Mali	46
21	Afghanistan	34	44	Belize	47
	Madagascar	34		Nicaragua	47
	Mauritania	34		Tanzania	47

City health and sanitation index

New York, November 2006=100[b]

Highest			Lowest		
1	Calgary, Canada	131.7	1	Baku, Azerbaijan	27.6
2	Honolulu, US	130.3	2	Dhaka, Bangladesh	29.6
3	Helsinki, Finland	128.5	3	Antananarivo, Madag.	30.1
4	Ottawa, Canada	127.2	4	Port au Prince, Haiti	34.0
5	Minneapolis, US	125.7	5	Mexico City, Mexico	37.7
6	Oslo, Norway	125.0	6	Addis Ababa, Ethiopia	37.9
	Stockholm, Sweden	125.0	7	Mumbai, India	38.2
	Zurich, Switzerland	125.0	8	Baghdad, Iraq	39.0
9	Katsuyama, Japan	123.8	9	Brazzaville, Congo-Braz.	39.1
10	Bern, Switzerland	123.7		Almaty, Kazakhstan	39.1
	Boston, United States	123.7	11	Ndjamena, Chad	39.7
	Geneva, Switzerland	123.7	12	Dar es Salaam, Tanzania	40.4
	Lexington, US[c]	123.7	13	Bangui, Central Afr. Rep.	42.1
	Montreal, Canada	123.7	14	Moscow, Russia	43.4
	Nuremberg, Germany	123.7		Ouagadougou, B. Faso	43.4
	Pittsburgh, US	123.7	16	Bamako, Mali	43.7
	Vancouver, Canada	123.7	17	Pointe Noire, Congo-Braz.	43.8
18	Auckland, N. Zealand	123.1	18	Lomé, Togo	44.1
	Wellington, N. Zealand	123.1	19	Conakry, Guinea	44.2

a Mostly some type of flush-to-sewage system.
b Based on a range of factors, including: hospital care; pollution; sewage systems; waste removal; water potability.
c Kentucky.

Organic cropland[a]
% of total agricultural land, 2003

1	Austria	11.60	26	Belize	1.30
2	Switzerland	10.00		Canada	1.30
3	Italy	8.00	28	Bolivia	1.04
4	Finland	7.00	29	Israel	0.90
5	Denmark	6.65	30	Greece	0.86
6	Sweden	6.09	31	Latvia	0.81
7	Czech Republic	5.09	32	Ecuador	0.74
8	United Kingdom	4.22	33	Iceland	0.70
9	Germany	4.10		Ireland	0.70
10	Uruguay	4.00	35	Sri Lanka	0.65
11	Norway	3.13	36	Ukraine	0.58
12	Costa Rica	3.11	37	Peru	0.42
13	Estonia	3.00	38	Papua New Guinea	0.41
14	Spain	2.28	39	Dominican Republic	0.40
15	Australia	2.20	40	Paraguay	0.38
	Portugal	2.20	41	Poland	0.36
	Slovakia	2.20		Tunisia	0.36
18	Netherlands	2.19	43	Guatemala	0.33
19	Slovenia	1.91		New Zealand	0.33
20	Argentina	1.70	45	El Salvador	0.31
	France	1.70	46	Serbia	0.30
	Hungary	1.70	47	Suriname	0.28
23	Chile	1.50	48	Romania	0.27
24	Belgium	1.45	49	Jamaica	0.26
25	Uganda	1.39	50	Lithuania	0.25

Intensity of fertilisers used in agriculture[b]
Kgs per hectare, 2002

1	Iceland	2,555.4	18	Germany	216.2
2	Singapore	1,209.0	19	Switzerland	214.9
3	Martinique	842.9	20	Norway	211.3
4	Guadeloupe	740.0	21	France	202.6
5	Ireland	522.7	22	Virgin Islands (US)	200.0
6	Egypt	370.8	23	Chile	197.2
7	South Korea	370.3	24	Israel	190.4
8	Netherlands	354.1	25	Colombia	179.6
9	Slovenia	353.0	26	Bangladesh	168.9
10	Belgium[c]	340.4	27	Malaysia	162.2
11	United Kingdom	308.7	28	Oman	151.0
12	Costa Rica	288.7	29	Uzbekistan	148.8
13	Japan	269.6	30	Sri Lanka	148.3
14	China	256.6	31	Austria	142.5
15	New Zealand	252.9	32	Pakistan	133.0
16	Mauritius	235.8	33	Finland	132.6
17	Vietnam	224.1	34	United Arab Emirates	131.6

a Converted or in the process of conversion to certified organic agriculture. Definitions
of organic vary among countries.
b Fertiliser use intensity is the amount of fertiliser consumed for agriculture per hectare
of arable and permanent cropland.
c 1999, includes Luxembourg.

Protected areas as % of total land area[a]

2004

1	Venezuela	34.2	16	Tanzania	14.6
2	Bhutan	29.6	17	Slovenia	14.4
3	Germany	29.3	18	Congo-Brazzaville	14.1
4	Switzerland	28.7	19	Mongolia	13.5
5	Belize	28.6	20	Latvia	12.7
6	Austria	28.0		Suriname	12.7
7	New Zealand	24.0		Thailand	12.7
8	Dominican Republic	22.9	23	Central African Rep	11.8
9	Denmark	21.8	24	Burkina Faso	11.5
10	Cambodia	20.5	25	China	11.3
11	Israel	18.4	26	Bolivia	11.1
12	Tajikistan	18.3	27	Poland	11.0
13	Botswana	18.1	28	Senegal	10.7
14	Equatorial Guinea	16.8	29	Jordan	10.2
15	United Kingdom	15.3	30	Armenia	10.1

National parks and nature reserves[ab]

'000 hectares, 2004

1	United States	54,312	16	Tanzania	4,100
2	Australia	48,473	17	Sweden	3,928
3	Canada	45,636	18	Argentina	3,893
4	Russia	25,203	19	South Africa	3,889
5	Brazil	20,973	20	Peru	3,664
6	Mongolia	19,052	21	India	3,562
7	Venezuela	12,462	22	Congo-Brazzaville	3,534
8	Algeria	11,821	23	Thailand	3,486
9	Congo-Kinshasa	11,264	24	Kenya	3,432
10	Bolivia	10,865	25	Central African Rep	3,304
11	Sudan	8,473	26	Namibia	3,159
12	Colombia	7,490	27	Ethiopia	3,036
13	Zambia	6,359	28	Angola	2,958
14	Indonesia	5,668	29	Zimbabwe	2,717
15	Botswana	4,551	30	Nigeria	2,509

Largest number of national parks and nature reserves[ab]

2004

1	Australia	2,537	12	Russia	108
2	Canada	1,814	13	Argentina	91
3	United States	803	14	India	83
4	Sweden	750	15	Mexico	81
5	Slovakia	590	16	Thailand	59
6	Brazil	311	17	Finland	55
7	Estonia	281	18	Bulgaria	54
8	New Zealand	131	19	Japan	53
9	Indonesia	122	20	Sri Lanka	48
10	Malaysia	114	21	Philippines	47
11	Norway	110	22	South Africa	44

a As recognised by the UN Environment Programme. Includes nature reserves, natural
  monuments and areas managed for sustainable use.
b Including protected wilderness areas.

Country
profiles

ALGERIA

Area	2,381,741 sq km	Capital	Algiers
Arable as % of total land	3	Currency	Algerian dinar (AD)

People

Population	32.9m	Life expectancy: men	70.9 yrs
Pop. per sq km	13.8	women	73.7 yrs
Av. ann. growth		Adult literacy	69.9%
in pop. 2005–10	1.51%	Fertility rate (per woman)	2.4
Pop. under 15	29.6%	Urban population	63.3%
Pop. over 60	12.3%		per 1,000 pop.
No. of men per 100 women	102	Crude birth rate	20.8
Human Development Index	72.8	Crude death rate	4.9

The economy

GDP	AD7,493bn	GDP per head	$3,110
GDP	$102bn	GDP per head in purchasing	
Av. ann. growth in real		power parity (USA=100)	16.9
GDP 1995–2005	4.0%	Economic freedom index	52.2

Origins of GDP		Components of GDP	
	% of total		% of total
Agriculture	9	Private consumption	33.6
Industry, of which:	62	Public consumption	11.8
manufacturing	6	Investment	22.1
Services	30	Exports	45.2
		Imports	-20.7

Structure of employment

	% of total		% of labour force
Agriculture	21	Unemployed 2004	20.1
Industry	24	Av. ann. rate 1995–2004	27.0
Services	55		

Energy

	m TOE		
Total output	165.7	Net energy imports as %	
Total consumption	32.9	of energy use	-404
Consumption per head,			
kg oil equivalent	1,017		

Inflation and finance

Consumer price		av. ann. increase 2000–05	
inflation 2006	2.5%	Narrow money (M1)	18.3%
Av. ann. inflation 2001–06	2.3%	Broad money	19.4%
Money market rate, 2006	2.34%		

Exchange rates

	end 2006		December 2006
AD per $	71.16	Effective rates	2000 = 100
AD per SDR	107.05	– nominal	85.25
AD per €	93.93	– real	83.09

Trade

Principal exports		Principal imports	
	$bn fob		*$bn cif*
Crude oil	19.3	Capital goods	7.9
Natural gas	7.3	Semi-finished goods	3.7
Condensate	6.3	Food	3.4
Total incl. others	**46.5**	Total incl. others	**20.0**

Main export destinations		Main origins of imports	
	% of total		*% of total*
United States	21.2	France	31.3
Italy	15.4	Italy	8.6
Spain	9.7	Spain	7.9
France	9.3	Germany	7.4

Balance of payments[a], reserves and debt, $bn

Visible exports fob	32.2	Change in reserves	13.5
Visible imports fob	-18.0	Level of reserves	
Trade balance	14.3	end Dec.	59.2
Invisibles inflows	2.9	No. months of import cover	23.1
Invisibles outflows	-8.5	Official gold holdings, m oz	5.6
Net transfers	1.5	Foreign debt	16.9
Current account balance	11.1	– as % of GDP	21
– as % of GDP	20.7	– as % of total exports	45
Capital balance[b]	-2.0	Debt service ratio	12
Overall balance[b]	5.0		

Health and education

Health spending, % of GDP	3.6	Education spending, % of GDP	...
Doctors per 1,000 pop.	1.1	Enrolment, %: primary	114
Hospital beds per 1,000 pop.	1.7	secondary	81
Improved-water source access,		tertiary	15
% of pop.	85		

Society

No. of households	5.4m	Colour TVs per 100 households	75.6
Av. no. per household	6.0	Telephone lines per 100 pop.	78.2
Marriages per 1,000 pop.	8.7	Mobile telephone subscribers	
Divorces per 1,000 pop.	...	per 100 pop.	41.5
Cost of living, Dec. 2006		Computers per 100 pop.	1.1
New York = 100	52	Internet hosts per 1,000 pop.	...

a 2004
b 2001

ARGENTINA

Area	2,766,889 sq km	Capital	Buenos Aires
Arable as % of total land	10	Currency	Peso (P)

People

Population	38.7m	Life expectancy: men	71.6 yrs
Pop. per sq km	14.0	women	79.1 yrs
Av. ann. growth		Adult literacy	97.2%
in pop. 2005–10	1.00%	Fertility rate (per woman)	2.3
Pop. under 15	26.4%	Urban population	90.1%
Pop. over 60	13.9%		per 1,000 pop.
No. of men per 100 women	96	Crude birth rate	17.5
Human Development Index	86.3	Crude death rate	7.7

The economy

GDP	P532bn	GDP per head	$4,730
GDP	$183bn	GDP per head in purchasing	
Av. ann. growth in real		power parity (USA=100)	34.1
GDP 1995–2005	2.3%	Economic freedom index	57.5

Origins of GDP		Components of GDP	
	% of total		% of total
Agriculture	9.5	Private consumption	61.3
Industry, of which:	35.8	Public consumption	11.9
manufacturing	23.3	Investment	21.5
Services	54.7	Exports	25.1
		Imports	-19.2

Structure of employment

	% of total		% of labour force
Agricultural	1	Unemployed 2003	15.6
Industry	24	Av. ann. rate 1995–2003	16.2
Services	75		

Energy

	m TOE		
Total output	85.4	Net energy imports as %	
Total consumption	63.7	of energy use	-34
Consumption per head			
kg oil equivalent	1,661		

Inflation and finance

Consumer price		av. ann. increase 2000–05	
inflation 2006	10.9%	Narrow money (M1)	29.1%
Av. ann. inflation 2001–06	12.6%	Broad money	13.0%
Money market rate, 2006	7.2%		

Exchange rates

	end 2006		December 2006
P per $	3.04	Effective rates	2000 = 100
P per SDR	4.58	– nominal	...
P per €	4.01	– real	...

Trade

Principal exports		Principal imports	
	$bn fob		*$bn cif*
Agricultural products	13.2	Intermediate goods	10.4
Manufactures	11.9	Capital goods	7.1
Primary products	7.9	Consumer goods	3.2
Fuels	7.0	Fuels	1.5
Total incl. others	**40.1**	**Total incl. others**	**28.7**

Main export destinations		Main origins of imports	
	% of total		*% of total*
Brazil	16.6	Brazil	33.8
United States	11.2	United States	15.7
Chile	10.9	China	5.1
China	8.6	Germany	5.0

Balance of payments, reserves and debt, $bn

Visible exports fob	40.1	Change in reserves	8.4
Visible imports fob	-27.3	Level of reserves	
Trade balance	12.8	end Dec.	28.1
Invisibles inflows	10.4	No. months of import cover	7.4
Invisibles outflows	-18.3	Official gold holdings, m oz	1.8
Net transfers	0.6	Foreign debt	114.3
Current account balance	5.4	– as % of GDP	73
– as % of GDP	2.9	– as % of total exports	245
Capital balance	1.6	Debt service ratio	21
Overall balance	7.6		

Health and education

Health spending, % of GDP	9.6	Education spending, % of GDP	3.5
Doctors per 1,000 pop.	2.8	Enrolment, %: primary	119
Hospital beds per 1,000 pop.	4.1	secondary	86
Improved-water source access,		tertiary	48
% of pop.	96		

Society

No. of households	10.5m	Colour TVs per 100 households	92.1
Av. no. per household	3.6	Telephone lines per 100 pop.	24.5
Marriages per 1,000 pop.	3.2	Mobile telephone subscribers	
Divorces per 1,000 pop.	...	per 100 pop.	57.4
Cost of living, Dec. 2006		Computers per 100 pop.	8.4
New York = 100	54	Internet hosts per 1,000 pop.	47.5

AUSTRALIA

Area	7,682,300 sq km	Capital	Canberra
Arable as % of total land	6	Currency	Australian dollar (A$)

People

Population	20.2m	Life expectancy: men		78.9 yrs
Pop. per sq km	2.6		women	83.6 yrs
Av. ann. growth		Adult literacy		...
in pop. 2005–10	1.01%	Fertility rate (per woman)		1.8
Pop. under 15	19.5%	Urban population		88.2%
Pop. over 60	17.8%			per 1,000 pop.
No. of men per 100 women	99	Crude birth rate		12.4
Human Development Index	95.7	Crude death rate		7.1

The economy

GDP	A$959bn	GDP per head	$36,260
GDP	$733bn	GDP per head in purchasing	
Av. ann. growth in real		power parity (USA=100)	75.9
GDP 1995–2005	3.6%	Economic freedom index	82.7

Origins of GDP		Components of GDP	
	% of total		% of total
Agriculture & mining	7.9	Private consumption	59.9
Manufacturing	12.2	Public consumption	18.1
Other	79.9	Investment	27.0
		Exports	17.2
		Imports	-22.4

Structure of employment

	% of total		% of labour force
Agriculture	4	Unemployed 2004	5.6
Industry	21	Av. ann. rate 1995–2004	7.1
Services	75		

Energy

	m TOE		
Total output	261.8	Net energy imports as %	
Total consumption	115.8	of energy use	-126
Consumption per head,			
kg oil equivalent	5,762		

Inflation and finance

Consumer price		av. ann. increase 2000–05	
inflation 2006	3.5%	Narrow money (M1)	14.3%
Av. ann. inflation 2001–06	2.9%	Broad money	10.3%
Money market, 2006	5.81%	Household saving rate, 2006	-1.7%

Exchange rates

	end 2006		December 2006
A$ per $	1.26	Effective rates	2000 = 100
A$ per SDR	1.90	– nominal	118.6
A$ per €	1.66	– real	127.4

Trade

Principal exports		Principal imports	
	$bn fob		*$bn cif*
Minerals & metals	56.0	Intermediate & other goods	37.7
Manufacturing goods	21.1	Consumption goods	37.2
Rural goods	18.8	Capital goods	28.1
Other goods	10.0	Fuels and lubricants	12.9
Total incl. others	**105.9**	Total incl. others	**118.6**

Main export destinations		Main origins of imports	
	% of total		*% of total*
Japan	20.4	United States	13.9
China	11.5	China	13.7
South Korea	7.9	Japan	11.0
United States	6.7	Singapore	5.6
EU25	10.7	EU25	23.2

Balance of payments, reserves and aid, $bn

Visible exports fob	107.0	Overall balance	7.3
Visible imports fob	-120.4	Change in reserves	6.3
Trade balance	-13.4	Level of reserves	
Invisibles inflows	47.4	end Dec.	43.3
Invisibles outflows	-74.7	No. months of import cover	2.7
Net transfers	-0.3	Official gold holdings, m oz	2.6
Current account balance	-41.0	Aid given	1.68
– as % of GDP	-5.8	– as % of GDP	0.25
Capital balance	48.6		

Health and education

Health spending, % of GDP	9.6	Education spending, % of GDP	4.8
Doctors per 1,000 pop.	2.5	Enrolment, %: primary	101
Hospital beds per 1,000 pop.	7.4	secondary	149
Improved-water source access,		tertiary	63
% of pop.	100		

Society

No. of households	7.5m	Colour TVs per 100 households	92.1
Av. no. per household	2.7	Telephone lines per 100 pop.	50.2
Marriages per 1,000 pop.	5.5	Mobile telephone subscribers	
Divorces per 1,000 pop.	2.5	per 100 pop.	91.4
Cost of living, Dec. 2006		Computers per 100 pop.	68.9
New York = 100	106	Internet hosts per 1,000 pop.	422.3

AUSTRIA

Area	83,855 sq km	Capital	Vienna
Arable as % of total land	17	Currency	Euro (€)

People

Population	8.2m	Life expectancy:	men	76.9 yrs
Pop. per sq km	97.8		women	82.6 yrs
Av. ann. growth		Adult literacy		...
in pop. 2005–10	0.36%	Fertility rate (per woman)		1.4
Pop. under 15	15.8%	Urban population		66.0%
Pop. over 60	21.9%			per 1,000 pop.
No. of men per 100 women	96	Crude birth rate		9.2
Human Development Index	94.4	Crude death rate		9.4

The economy

GDP	€246bn	GDP per head	$37,330
GDP	$306bn	GDP per head in purchasing	
Av. ann. growth in real		power parity (USA=100)	80.4
GDP 1995–2005	2.1%	Economic freedom index	71.3

Origins of GDP		**Components of GDP**	
	% of total		% of total
Agriculture	1.6	Private consumption	56.1
Industry, of which:	29.7	Public consumption	18.1
manufacturing	...	Investment	20.5
Services	68.6	Exports	54.3
		Imports	-49.5

Structure of employment

	% of total		% of labour force
Agriculture	6	Unemployed 2004	4.9
Industry	28	Av. ann. rate 1995–2004	4.0
Services	66		

Energy

	m TOE		
Total output	9.9	Net energy imports as %	
Total consumption	33.2	of energy use	70
Consumption per head,			
kg oil equivalent	4,060		

Inflation and finance

Consumer price		av. ann. increase 2000–05	
inflation 2006	1.7%	Euro area:	
Av. ann. inflation 2001–06	1.8%	Narrow money (M1)	10.8%
Deposit rate, h'holds, 2006	2.15%	Broad money	7.7%
		Household saving rate, 2006	9.7%

Exchange rates

	end 2006		December 2006
€ per $	0.76	Effective rates	2000 = 100
€ per SDR	1.14	– nominal	106.4
		– real	101.5

Trade

Principal exports		Principal imports	
	$bn fob		*$bn cif*
Consumer goods	54.4	Consumer goods	51.0
Investment goods	30.5	Investment goods	26.8
Intermediate goods	16.6	Raw materials (incl. fuels)	19.9
Raw materials (incl. fuels)	9.1	Intermediate goods	15.5
Food & beverages	7.0	Food & beverages	6.8
Total incl. others	**117.9**	Total incl. others	**120.1**

Main export destinations		Main origins of imports	
	% of total		*% of total*
Germany	32.8	Germany	48.4
Eastern Europe	19.1	Eastern Europe	14.8
Italy	9.2	Italy	7.0
United States	6.2	Switzerland	4.5
EU25	71.1	EU25	75.0

Balance of payments, reserves and aid, $bn

Visible exports fob	117.2	Overall balance	-0.8
Visible imports fob	-113.8	Change in reserves	-0.4
Trade balance	3.4	Level of reserves	
Invisibles inflows	78.1	end Dec.	11.8
Invisibles outflows	-74.6	No. months of import cover	0.8
Net transfers	-2.6	Official gold holdings, m oz	9.7
Current account balance	4.3	Aid given	1.57
– as % of GDP	1.4	– as % of GDP	0.52
Capital balance	-1.9		

Health and education

Health spending, % of GDP	10.3	Education spending, % of GDP	5.5
Doctors per 1,000 pop.	3.4	Enrolment, %: primary	103
Hospital beds per 1,000 pop.	7.7	secondary	101
Improved-water source access,		tertiary	56
% of pop.	100		

Society

No. of households	3.4m	Colour TVs per 100 households	97.4
Av. no. per household	2.3	Telephone lines per 100 pop.	45.7
Marriages per 1,000 pop.	4.8	Mobile telephone subscribers	
Divorces per 1,000 pop.	2.3	per 100 pop.	105.8
Cost of living, Dec. 2006		Computers per 100 pop.	61.1
New York = 100	112	Internet hosts per 1,000 pop.	284.2

BANGLADESH

Area	143,998 sq km	Capital	Dhaka
Arable as % of total land	61	Currency	Taka (Tk)

People

Population	141.8m	Life expectancy:	men	63.2 yrs
Pop. per sq km	984.7		women	65.0 yrs
Av. ann. growth		Adult literacy		...
in pop. 2005–10	1.67%	Fertility rate (per woman)		2.8
Pop. under 15	35.2%	Urban population		25.1%
Pop. over 60	5.7%			per 1,000 pop.
No. of men per 100 women	105	Crude birth rate		24.8
Human Development Index	53.0	Crude death rate		7.5

The economy

GDP	Tk3,707bn	GDP per head	$420
GDP	$60.0bn	GDP per head in purchasing	
Av. ann. growth in real		power parity (USA=100)	4.9
GDP 1995–2005	5.3%	Economic freedom index	47.8

Origins of GDP[a]		Components of GDP[a]	
	% of total		% of total
Agriculture	22.3	Private consumption	74.2
Industry, of which:	28.3	Public consumption	5.6
manufacturing	16.5	Investment	24.4
Services	49.4	Exports	15.4
		Imports	-22.6

Structure of employment

	% of total		% of labour force
Agriculture	66	Unemployed 2003	4.3
Industry	10	Av. ann. rate 1995–2003	2.7
Services	24		

Energy

			m TOE
Total output	18.4	Net energy imports as %	
Total consumption	22.8	of energy use	19
Consumption per head,			
kg oil equivalent	164		

Inflation and finance

Consumer price		av. ann. increase 2000–05	
inflation 2006	6.3%	Narrow money (M1)	11.8%
Av. ann. inflation 2001–06	5.7%	Broad money	14.9%
Deposit rate, 2006	9.11%		

Exchange rates

	end 2006		December 2006
Tk per $	69.07	Effective rates	2000 = 100
Tk per SDR	103.90	– nominal	...
Tk per €	91.17	– real	...

Trade

Principal exports[a]

	$bn fob
Clothing	5.4
Fish & fish products	0.4
Jute goods	0.3
Leather	0.3
Total incl. others	**7.2**

Principal imports[a]

	$bn cif
Capital goods	3.4
Textiles & yarn	2.8
Fuels	1.6
Cereal & dairy products	0.5
Total incl. others	**12.9**

Main export destinations

	% of total
United States	24.2
Germany	13.2
United Kingdom	10.6
France	6.0
Italy	3.8

Main origins of imports

	% of total
India	14.7
China	14.6
Kuwait	8.0
Singapore	6.0
Japan	4.1

Balance of payments, reserves and debt, $bn

Visible exports fob	9.2	Change in reserves	-0.4
Visible imports fob	-12.3	Level of reserves	
Trade balance	-3.1	end Dec.	2.8
Invisibles inflows	1.4	No. months of import cover	2.2
Invisibles outflows	-3.1	Official gold holdings, m oz	0.1
Net transfers	4.7	Foreign debt	18.9
Current account balance	-0.1	– as % of GDP	22
– as % of GDP	-0.2	– as % of total exports	102
Capital balance	0.2	Debt service ratio	5
Overall balance	-0.5		

Health and education

Health spending, % of GDP	3.1	Education spending, % of GDP	2.5
Doctors per 1,000 pop.	0.3	Enrolment, %: primary	106
Hospital beds per 1,000 pop.	3.0	secondary	51
Improved-water source access,		tertiary	5
% of pop.	74		

Society

No. of households	25.5m	Colour TVs per 100 households	2.7
Av. no. per household	5.9	Telephone lines per 100 pop.	0.8
Marriages per 1,000 pop.	...	Mobile telephone subscribers	
Divorces per 1,000 pop.	...	per 100 pop.	6.4
Cost of living, Dec. 2006		Computers per 100 pop.	1.2
New York = 100	46	Internet hosts per 1,000 pop.	...

a Fiscal year ending June 30 2005.

BELGIUM

Area	30,520 sq km	Capital	Brussels
Arable as % of total land	28	Currency	Euro (€)

People

Population	10.4m	Life expectancy: men	76.5 yrs
Pop. per sq km	340.8	women	82.7 yrs
Av. ann. growth		Adult literacy	...
in pop. 2005–10	0.24%	Fertility rate (per woman)	1.7
Pop. under 15	17.0%	Urban population	97.2%
Pop. over 60	22.1%		*per 1,000 pop.*
No. of men per 100 women	96	Crude birth rate	10.4
Human Development Index	94.5	Crude death rate	10.0

The economy

GDP	€298bn	GDP per head	$35,660
GDP	$371bn	GDP per head in purchasing	
Av. ann. growth in real		power parity (USA=100)	76.7
GDP 1995–2005	2.1%	Economic freedom index	74.5

Origins of GDP		**Components of GDP**	
	% of total		*% of total*
Agriculture	1.1	Private consumption	53.3
Industry, of which:	24.0	Public consumption	23.1
manufacturing	...	Investment	19.9
Services	74.9	Exports	87.2
		Imports	-84.9

Structure of employment

	% of total		*% of labour force*
Agriculture	2	Unemployed 2004	7.4
Industry	25	Av. ann. rate 1995–2004	8.2
Services	73		

Energy

	m TOE		
Total output	13.5	Net energy imports as %	
Total consumption	57.7	of energy use	77
Consumption per head,			
kg oil equivalent	5,536		

Inflation and finance

Consumer price		*av. ann. increase 2000–05*	
inflation 2006	2.3%	Euro area:	
Av. ann. inflation 2001–06	2.0%	Narrow money (M1)	10.8%
Treasury bill rate, 2006	2.73%	Broad money	7.7%
		Household saving rate, 2006	11.5%

Exchange rates

	end 2006		*December 2006*
€ per $	0.76	Effective rates	*2000 = 100*
€ per SDR	1.14	– nominal	108.2
		– real	116.9

Trade

Principal exports		Principal imports	
	$bn fob		*$bn cif*
Chemicals	44.1	Chemicals	40.5
Transport equipment	36.1	Machinery	38.7
Machinery	35.9	Transport equipment	31.2
Food, drink & tobacco	25.0	Agriculture, food & drink	22.3
Total incl. others	**335.8**	**Total incl. others**	**318.7**

Main export destinations		Main origins of imports	
	% of total		*% of total*
France	17.6	Netherlands	21.1
Germany	17.0	Germany	15.8
Netherlands	12.4	France	12.8
United Kingdom	8.1	United Kingdom	7.1
EU25	76.3	EU25	73.4

Balance of payments, reserves and aid, $bn

Visible exports fob	263.0	Overall balance	-2.2
Visible imports fob	-257.1	Change in reserves	-2.0
Trade balance	5.9	Level of reserves	
Invisibles inflows	113.7	end Dec.	12.0
Invisibles outflows	-103.7	No. months of import cover	0.4
Net transfers	-6.4	Official gold holdings, m oz	7.3
Current account balance	9.3	Aid given	1.96
– as % of GDP	2.6	– as % of GDP	0.53
Capital balance	-11.5		

Health and education

Health spending, % of GDP	9.7	Education spending, % of GDP	6.2
Doctors per 1,000 pop.	4.5	Enrolment, %: primary	105
Hospital beds per 1,000 pop.	5.3	secondary	109
Improved-water source access,		tertiary	57
% of pop.	...		

Society

No. of households	4.4m	Colour TVs per 100 households	99.8
Av. no. per household	2.4	Telephone lines per 100 pop.	45.4
Marriages per 1,000 pop.	4.2	Mobile telephone subscribers	
Divorces per 1,000 pop.	3.0	per 100 pop.	100.0
Cost of living, Dec. 2006		Computers per 100 pop.	34.7
New York = 100	104	Internet hosts per 1,000 pop.	303.0

BRAZIL

Area	8,511,965 sq km	Capital	Brasilia
Arable as % of total land	7	Currency	Real (R)

People

Population	186.4m	Life expectancy: men	68.8 yrs
Pop. per sq km	21.9	women	76.1 yrs
Av. ann. growth		Adult literacy	88.6%
in pop. 2005–10	1.26%	Fertility rate (per woman)	2.3
Pop. under 15	27.8%	Urban population	84.2%
Pop. over 60	8.8%		per 1,000 pop.
No. of men per 100 women	97	Crude birth rate	19.2
Human Development Index	79.2	Crude death rate	6.3

The economy

GDP	R1,938bn	GDP per head	$4,270
GDP	$796bn	GDP per head in purchasing	
Av. ann. growth in real		power parity (USA=100)	20.1
GDP 1995–2005	2.2%	Economic freedom index	60.9

Origins of GDP		**Components of GDP**	
	% of total		% of total
Agriculture	8.0	Private consumption	55.5
Industry, of which:	37.9	Public consumption	19.5
manufacturing	...	Investment	20.6
Services	54.1	Exports	16.8
		Imports	-12.4

Structure of employment

	% of total		% of labour force
Agriculture	20	Unemployed 2003	9.7
Industry	22	Av. ann. rate 1995–2003	8.5
Services	58		

Energy

			m TOE
Total output	176.3	Net energy imports as %	
Total consumption	204.8	of energy use	14
Consumption per head,			
kg oil equivalent	1,114		

Inflation and finance

Consumer price		av. ann. increase 2000–05	
inflation 2006	4.2%	Narrow money (M1)	14.2%
Av. ann. inflation 2001–06	8.1%	Broad money	14.2%
Money market rate, 2006	15.28%		

Exchange rates

	end 2006		December 2006
R per $	2.14	Effective rates	2000 = 100
R per sdr	3.22	– nominal	...
R per €	2.82	– real	...

Trade

Principal exports		Principal imports	
	$bn fob		*$bn cif*
Transport equipment & parts	17.8	Machines & electrical	
Metal goods	13.1	equipment	18.2
Soyabeans etc.	8.7	Chemical products	12.4
Chemical products	2.4	Oil & derivatives	11.9
		Transport equipment & parts	8.3
Total incl. others	**118.3**	Total incl. others	**77.6**

Main export destinations		Main origins of imports	
	% of total		*% of total*
United States	19.2	United States	17.5
Argentina	8.4	Argentina	8.5
China	5.8	Germany	8.4
Netherlands	4.5	China	7.3

Balance of payments, reserves and debt, $bn

Visible exports fob	118.3	Change in reserves	0.9
Visible imports fob	-73.6	Level of reserves	
Trade balance	44.8	end Dec.	53.8
Invisibles inflows	19.3	No. months of import cover	5.1
Invisibles outflows	-53.4	Official gold holdings, m oz	0.4
Net transfers	3.6	Foreign debt	188.0
Current account balance	14.2	– as % of GDP	34
– as % of GDP	1.8	– as % of total exports	183
Capital balance	14.5	Debt service ratio	45
Overall balance	27.6		

Health and education

Health spending, % of GDP	8.8	Education spending, % of GDP	4.1
Doctors per 1,000 pop.	1.2	Enrolment, %: primary	166
Hospital beds per 1,000 pop.	2.7	secondary	102
Improved-water source access,		tertiary	15
% of pop.	90		

Society

No. of households	50.0m	Colour TVs per 100 households	87.9
Av. no. per household	3.6	Telephone lines per 100 pop.	21.4
Marriages per 1,000 pop.	4.2	Mobile telephone subscribers	
Divorces per 1,000 pop.	0.8	per 100 pop.	46.3
Cost of living, Dec. 2006		Computers per 100 pop.	16.1
New York = 100	72	Internet hosts per 1,000 pop.	39.8

BULGARIA

Area	110,994 sq km	Capital	Sofia
Arable as % of total land	29	Currency	Lev (BGL)

People

Population	7.7m	Life expectancy: men	69.5 yrs
Pop. per sq km	69.4	women	76.7 yrs
Av. ann. growth		Adult literacy	98.2%
in pop. 2005–10	-0.72%	Fertility rate (per woman)	1.3
Pop. under 15	13.8%	Urban population	73.0%
Pop. over 60	29.9%		*per 1,000 pop.*
No. of men per 100 women	94	Crude birth rate	8.9
Human Development Index	81.6	Crude death rate	14.8

The economy

GDP	BGL41.9bn	GDP per head	$3,460
GDP	$26.6bn	GDP per head in purchasing	
Av. ann. growth in real		power parity (USA=100)	21.6
GDP 1995–2005	2.0%	Economic freedom index	62.2

Origins of GDP		**Components of GDP**	
	% of total		*% of total*
Agriculture	9.3	Private consumption	78.8
Industry, of which:	30.4	Public consumption	9.8
manufacturing	...	Investment	23.8
Services	60.3	Exports	60.8
		Imports	-77.4

Structure of employment

	% of total		*% of labour force*
Agriculture	9	Unemployed 2005	12.1
Industry	34	Av. ann. rate 1995–2005	15.2
Services	57		

Energy

		m TOE	
Total output	10.3	Net energy imports as %	
Total consumption	18.9	of energy use	46
Consumption per head,			
kg oil equivalent	2,434		

Inflation and finance

Consumer price			*av. ann change 2000–05*
inflation 2006	7.3%	Narrow money (M1)	21.0%
Av. ann. inflation 2001–06	5.3%	Broad money	21.3%
Money market rate, 2006	2.79%		

Exchange rates

	end 2006		*December 2006*
BGL per $	1.49	Effective rates	*2000 = 100*
BGL per SDR	2.23	– nominal	113.20
BGL per €	1.97	– real	127.62

Trade

Principal exports		**Principal imports**	
	$bn fob		*$bn cif*
Clothing	2.0	Mineral fuels	2.9
Other metals	1.2	Machinery & equipment	1.8
Iron & steel	1.0	Textiles	1.7
Chemicals	0.7	Chemicals	1.2
Total incl. others	**11.7**	Total incl. others	**18.2**

Main export destinations		**Main origins of imports**	
	% of total		*% of total*
Italy	12.0	Italy	15.6
Turkey	10.5	Germany	13.6
Germany	9.8	Russia	9.0
Greece	9.4	Turkey	5.0

Balance of payments, reserves and debt, $bn

Visible exports fob	11.8	Change in reserves	-0.6
Visible imports fob	-17.1	Level of reserves	
Trade balance	-5.4	end Dec.	8.7
Invisibles inflows	5.8	No. months of import cover	4.8
Invisibles outflows	-4.6	Official gold holdings, m oz	1.3
Net transfers	1.2	Foreign debt	16.8
Current account balance	-3.0	– as % of GDP	68
– as % of GDP	-11.3	– as % of total exports	105
Capital balance	4.9	Debt service ratio	32
Overall balance	2.2		

Health and education

Health spending, % of GDP	8.0	Education spending, % of GDP	4.2
Doctors per 1,000 pop.	3.6	Enrolment, %: primary	104
Hospital beds per 1,000 pop.	6.4	secondary	102
Improved-water source access,		tertiary	43
% of pop.	99		

Society

No. of households	2.9m	Colour TVs per 100 households	67.8
Av. no. per household	2.6	Telephone lines per 100 pop.	32.2
Marriages per 1,000 pop.	4.0	Mobile telephone subscribers	
Divorces per 1,000 pop.	2.0	per 100 pop.	80.8
Cost of living, Dec. 2006		Computers per 100 pop.	5.9
New York = 100	60	Internet hosts per 1,000 pop.	28.6

CAMEROON

Area	475,442 sq km	Capital	Yaoundé
Arable as % of total land	13	Currency	CFA franc (CFAfr)

People

Population	16.3m	Life expectancy: men	50.0 yrs
Pop. per sq km	34.3	women	50.8 yrs
Av. ann. growth		Adult literacy	67.9%
in pop. 2005–10	2.00%	Fertility rate (per woman)	4.3
Pop. under 15	41.8%	Urban population	54.6%
Pop. over 60	5.4%		per 1,000 pop.
No. of men per 100 women	100	Crude birth rate	34.5
Human Development Index	50.6	Crude death rate	14.4

The economy

GDP	CFAfr8,901bn	GDP per head	$1,040
GDP	$16.9bn	GDP per head in purchasing	
Av. ann. growth in real		power parity (USA=100)	5.5
GDP 1995–2005	4.3%	Economic freedom index	54.4

Origins of GDP		Components of GDP	
	% of total		% of total
Agriculture	41	Private consumption	71
Industry, of which:	14	Public consumption	10
manufacturing	7	Investment	21
Services	45	Exports	23
		Imports	-25

Structure of employment

	% of total		% of labour force
Agriculture	70	Unemployed 2005	...
Industry	13	Av. ann. rate 1995–2005	...
Services	17		

Energy

	m TOE		
Total output	12.5	Net energy imports as %	
Total consumption	6.9	of energy use	-80
Consumption per head,			
kg oil equivalent	433		

Inflation and finance

			av. ann. change 2000–05
Consumer price			
inflation 2005	2.0%	Narrow money (M1)	5.7%
Av. ann. inflation 2001–05	2.3%	Broad money	8.6%
Deposit rate, 2006	4.33%		

Exchange rates

	end 2006		December 2006
CFAfr per $	498.07	Effective rates	2000 = 100
CFAfr per SDR	749.30	– nominal	112.1
CFAfr per €	657.45	– real	114.3

Trade

Principal exports[a]		Principal imports[a]	
	$bn fob		*$bn cif*
Crude oil	1.3	Capital goods	0.4
Cocoa	0.2	Intermediate goods	0.4
Cotton	0.2	Minerals & raw materials	0.3
Total incl. others	**2.5**	**Total incl. others**	**2.5**

Main export destinations		Main origins of imports	
	% of total		*% of total*
Spain	16.7	France	24.5
Italy	13.2	Nigeria	11.3
France	9.2	China	5.8
United Kingdom	8.8	United States	5.2

Balance of payments[b], reserves and debt, $bn

Visible exports fob	2.4	Change in reserves	0.1
Visible imports fob	-2.1	Level of reserves	
Trade balance	0.3	end Dec.	1.0
Invisibles inflows	0.5	No. months of import cover	2.9
Invisibles outflows	-1.6	Official gold holdings, m oz	0.0
Net transfers	0.1	Foreign debt	7.2
Current account balance	-0.7	– as % of GDP	14
– as % of GDP	-3.3	– as % of total exports	61
Capital balance	1.0	Debt service ratio	1
Overall balance	0.5		

Health and education

Health spending, % of GDP	5.2	Education spending, % of GDP	1.8
Doctors per 1,000 pop.	0.2	Enrolment, %: primary	91
Hospital beds per 1,000 pop.	...	secondary	44
Improved-water source access,		tertiary	5
% of pop.	66		

Society

No. of households	4.3m	Colour TVs per 100 households	...
Av. no. per household	3.7	Telephone lines per 100 pop.	0.6
Marriages per 1,000 pop.	...	Mobile telephone subscribers	
Divorces per 1,000 pop.	...	per 100 pop.	13.8
Cost of living, Dec. 2006		Computers per 100 pop.	1.2
New York = 100	...	Internet hosts per 1,000 pop.	...

a 2004
b 2003

CANADA

Area[a]	9,970,610 sq km	Capital	Ottawa
Arable as % of total land	5	Currency	Canadian dollar (C$)

People

Population	32.3m	Life expectancy:	men	78.3 yrs
Pop. per sq km	3.2		women	82.9 yrs
Av. ann. growth		Adult literacy		...
in pop. 2005–10	0.90%	Fertility rate (per woman)		1.5
Pop. under 15	17.6%	Urban population		80.1%
Pop. over 60	17.8%			*per 1,000 pop.*
No. of men per 100 women	98	Crude birth rate		10.3
Human Development Index	95.0	Crude death rate		7.4

The economy

GDP	C$1,350bn	GDP per head	$34,480
GDP	$1,114bn	GDP per head in purchasing	
Av. ann. growth in real		power parity (USA=100)	79.7
GDP 1995–2005	3.4%	Economic freedom index	78.7

Origins of GDP		**Components of GDP**	
	% of total		*% of total*
Agriculture	2.2	Private consumption	55.4
Industry, of which:	29.5	Public consumption	19.3
manufacturing & mining	20.9	Investment	20.7
Services	68.3	Exports	37.9
		Imports	-34.1

Structure of employment

	% of total		*% of labour force*
Agriculture	3	Unemployed 2004	7.2
Industry	22	Av. ann. rate 1995–2004	8.1
Services	75		

Energy

	m TOE		
Total output	397.5	Net energy imports as %	
Total consumption	269.0	of energy use	-48
Consumption per head,			
kg oil equivalent	8,411		

Inflation and finance

		av. ann. increase 2000–05	
Consumer price			
inflation 2006	2.0%	Narrow money (M1)	13.5%
Av. ann. inflation 2001–06	2.2%	Broad money	21.6%
Money market rate, 2006	4.02%	Household saving rate, 2006	1.5%

Exchange rates

	end 2006		*December 2006*
C$ per $	1.17	Effective rates	*2000 = 100*
C$ per SDR	1.75	– nominal	122.3
C$ per €	1.54	– real	129.9

Trade

Principal exports		Principal imports	
	$bn fob		*$bn fob*
Machinery & equipment	78.2	Machinery & equipment	91.0
Motor vehicles and parts	72.9	Industrial goods	64.8
Energy products	72.1	Motor vehicles & parts	64.6
Other industrial goods	69.8	Consumer goods	40.8
Forest products	30.0	Energy products	27.9
Total incl. others	**358.9**	Total incl. others	**323.2**

Main export destinations		Main origins of imports	
	% of total		*% of total*
United States	83.2	United States	63.4
Japan	2.1	China	8.2
United Kingdom	1.8	Mexico	4.2
China	1.6	Japan	3.7
EU25	5.5	EU25	11.6

Balance of payments, reserves and aid, $bn

Visible exports fob	374.3	Overall balance	1.3
Visible imports fob	-320.5	Change in reserves	-1.5
Trade balance	53.8	Level of reserves	
Invisibles inflows	93.5	end Dec.	33.0
Invisibles outflows	-120.3	No. months of import cover	0.9
Net transfers	-0.4	Official gold holdings, m oz	0.1
Current account balance	26.6	Aid given	3.76
– as % of GDP	2.4	– as % of GDP	0.34
Capital balance	-22.6		

Health and education

Health spending, % of GDP	9.8	Education spending, % of GDP	5.2
Doctors per 1,000 pop.	2.1	Enrolment, %: primary	99
Hospital beds per 1,000 pop.	3.6	secondary	109
Improved-water source access,		tertiary	60
% of pop.	100		

Society

No. of households	12.2m	Colour TVs per 100 households	98.8
Av. no. per household	2.7	Telephone lines per 100 pop.	64.1
Marriages per 1,000 pop.	4.5	Mobile telephone subscribers	
Divorces per 1,000 pop.	2.2	per 100 pop.	52.5
Cost of living, Dec. 2006		Computers per 100 pop.	69.8
New York = 100	96	Internet hosts per 1,000 pop.	131.8

a Including freshwater.

CHILE

Area	756,945 sq km	Capital	Santiago
Arable as % of total land	3	Currency	Chilean peso (Ps)

People

Population	16.3m	Life expectancy: men	75.5 yrs
Pop. per sq km	21.5	women	81.5 yrs
Av. ann. growth		Adult literacy	95.7%
in pop. 2005–10	1.00%	Fertility rate (per woman)	1.9
Pop. under 15	24.9%	Urban population	87.6%
Pop. over 60	11.6%		per 1,000 pop.
No. of men per 100 women	98	Crude birth rate	15.0
Human Development Index	85.9	Crude death rate	5.4

The economy

GDP	64.549bn pesos	GDP per head	$7,070
GDP	$115bn	GDP per head in purchasing	
Av. ann. growth in real		power parity (USA=100)	28.7
GDP 1995–2005	4.3%	Economic freedom index	78.3

Origins of GDP

	% of total
Agriculture	6.0
Industry, of which:	49.3
manufacturing	35.6
Services	44.7

Components of GDP

	% of total
Private consumption	57.1
Public consumption	11.6
Investment	22.1
Exports	41.8
Imports	-33.6

Structure of employment

	% of total		% of labour force
Agriculture	13	Unemployed 2004	7.8
Industry	23	Av. ann. rate 1995–2004	7.1
Services	64		

Energy

	m TOE		
Total output	8.4	Net energy imports as %	
Total consumption	27.9	of energy use	70
Consumption per head,			
kg oil equivalent	1,732		

Inflation and finance

Consumer price			av. ann. increase 2000–05
inflation 2005	3.1%	Narrow money (M1)	12.4%
Av. ann. inflation 2001–06	2.4%	Broad money	12.4%
Money market rate, 2006	5.02%		

Exchange rates

	end 2006		December 2006
Ps per $	534.43	Effective rates	2000 = 100
Ps per SDR	804.00	– nominal	97.0
Ps per €	705.45	– real	95.0

Trade

Principal exports		Principal imports	
	$bn fob		*$bn cif*
Copper	18.3	Intermediate goods	18.5
Fruit	2.1	Capital goods	7.2
Paper products	1.7	Consumer goods	4.7
Total incl. others	**40.6**	Total incl. others	**32.6**

Main export destinations		Main origins of imports	
	% of total		*% of total*
United States	15.4	Argentina	14.7
China	10.8	United States	13.6
Japan	10.8	Brazil	10.8
Netherlands	5.6	China	7.1
South Korea	5.3	South Korea	4.8

Balance of payments, reserves and debt, $bn

Visible exports fob	40.6	Change in reserves	0.9
Visible imports fob	-30.4	Level of reserves	
Trade balance	10.2	end Dec.	16.9
Invisibles inflows	9.3	No. months of import cover	4.0
Invisibles outflows	-20.5	Official gold holdings, m oz	0.0
Net transfers	1.7	Foreign debt	45.2
Current account balance	0.7	– as % of GDP	52
– as % of GDP	0.6	– as % of total exports	114
Capital balance	2.1	Debt service ratio	15
Overall balance	1.7		

Health and education

Health spending, % of GDP	6.1	Education spending, % of GDP	3.7
Doctors per 1,000 pop.	1.1	Enrolment, %: primary	107
Hospital beds per 1,000 pop.	2.4	secondary	89
Improved-water source access,		tertiary	38
% of pop.	95		

Society

No. of households	4.4m	Colour TVs per 100 households	63.4
Av. no. per household	3.7	Telephone lines per 100 pop.	22.0
Marriages per 1,000 pop.	3.4	Mobile telephone subscribers	
Divorces per 1,000 pop.	0.5	per 100 pop.	67.8
Cost of living, Dec. 2006		Computers per 100 pop.	14.8
New York = 100	68	Internet hosts per 1,000 pop.	38.1

CHINA

Area	9,560,900 sq km	Capital	Beijing
Arable as % of total land	11	Currency	Yuan

People

Population	1,315.8m	Life expectancy: men	71.3 yrs
Pop. per sq km	137.6	women	74.8 yrs
Av. ann. growth		Adult literacy	90.9%
in pop. 2005–10	0.58%	Fertility rate (per woman)	1.7
Pop. under 15	21.6%	Urban population	40.4%
Pop. over 60	11.0%		*per 1,000 pop.*
No. of men per 100 women	107	Crude birth rate	13.1
Human Development Index	76.8	Crude death rate	7.1

The economy

GDP	Yuan18,309bn	GDP per head	$1,700
GDP	$2,234bn	GDP per head in purchasing	
Av. ann. growth in real		power parity (USA=100)	16.1
GDP 1995–2005	9.0%	Economic freedom index	54.0

Origins of GDP		**Components of GDP**	
	% of total		*% of total*
Agriculture	13	Private consumption	38.0
Industry, of which:	48	Public consumption	13.9
manufacturing	34	Investment	41.5
Services	40	Exports	36.7
		Imports	-31.3

Structure of employment

	% of total		*% of labour force*
Agriculture	49	Unemployed 2005	4.2
Industry	22	Av. ann. rate 1995–2005	3.5
Services	29		

Energy

	m TOE		
Total output	1,536.8	Net energy imports as %	
Total consumption	1,609.3	of energy use	5
Consumption per head,			
kg oil equivalent	1,242		

Inflation and finance

		av. ann. increase 2000–05	
Consumer price			
inflation 2006	1.5%	Narrow money (M1)	14.4%
Av. ann. inflation 2001–06	1.5%	Broad money	17.0%
Deposit rate, 2006	2.52%		

Exchange rates

	end 2006		*December 2006*
Yuan per $	7.81	Effective rates	2000 = 100
Yuan per SDR	11.75	– nominal	97.18
Yuan per €	10.31	– real	95.83

Trade

Principal exports		Principal imports	
	$bn fob		*$bn cif*
Office equipment	110.7	Electrical machinery	137.7
Telecoms equipment	94.9	Petroleum products	59.5
Electrical machinery	75.5	Professional &	
Apparel & clothing	74.2	scientific instruments	41.4
Misc. manufactures	47.2	Office equipment	35.8
		Other machinery	24.3
Total incl. others	**762.0**	Total incl. others	**660.0**

Main export destinations		Main origins of imports	
	% of total		*% of total*
United States	21.4	Japan	15.2
Hong Kong	16.3	South Korea	11.6
Japan	11.0	Taiwan	11.3
South Korea	4.6	United States	7.4
Germany	4.3	Germany	4.7

Balance of payments, reserves and debt, $bn

Visible exports fob	762.5	Change in reserves	208.5
Visible imports fob	-628.3	Level of reserves	
Trade balance	134.2	end Dec.	831.4
Invisibles inflows	113.4	No. months of import cover	13.5
Invisibles outflows	-112.1	Official gold holdings, m oz	19.3
Net transfers	25.4	Foreign debt	281.6
Current account balance	160.8	– as % of GDP	14
– as % of GDP	7.2	– as % of total exports	40
Capital balance	63.0	Debt service ratio	3
Overall balance	207.3		

Health and education

Health spending, % of GDP	4.7	Education spending, % of GDP	...
Doctors per 1,000 pop.	1.1	Enrolment, %: primary	106
Hospital beds per 1,000 pop.	2.5	secondary	73
Improved-water source access,		tertiary	7
% of pop.	77		

Society

No. of households	372.1m	Colour TVs per 100 households	46.8
Av. no. per household	3.5	Telephone lines per 100 pop.	26.6
Marriages per 1,000 pop.	5.9	Mobile telephone subscribers	
Divorces per 1,000 pop.	1.3	per 100 pop.	29.9
Cost of living, Dec. 2006		Computers per 100 pop.	4.1
New York = 100	80	Internet hosts per 1,000 pop.	1.5

Note: Data excludes Special Administrative Regions ie, Hong Kong and Macau.

COLOMBIA

Area	1,141,748 sq km	Capital	Bogota
Arable as % of total land	2	Currency	Colombian peso (peso)

People

Population	45.6m	Life expectancy: men	69.2 yrs
Pop. per sq km	40.0	women	76.6 yrs
Av. ann. growth		Adult literacy	92.8%
in pop. 2005–10	1.27%	Fertility rate (per woman)	2.2
Pop. under 15	30.3%	Urban population	72.7%
Pop. over 60	7.5%		per 1,000 pop.
No. of men per 100 women	97	Crude birth rate	18.7
Human Development Index	79.0	Crude death rate	5.4

The economy

GDP	283,848bn pesos	GDP per head	$2,680
GDP	$122bn	GDP per head in purchasing	
Av. ann. growth in real		power parity (USA=100)	17.4
GDP 1995–2005	2.2%	Economic freedom index	60.5

Origins of GDP

Components of GDP

	% of total		% of total
Agriculture	12.3	Private consumption	60.3
Industry, of which:	34.3	Public consumption	20.1
manufacturing	15.4	Investment	19.0
Services	53.4	Exports	21.6
		Imports	-21.3

Structure of employment

	% of total		% of labour force
Agriculture	22	Unemployed 2004	13.7
Industry	19	Av. ann. rate 1995–2004	14.7
Services	59		

Energy

	m TOE		
Total output	76.2	Net energy imports as %	
Total consumption	27.7	of energy use	-175
Consumption per head,			
kg oil equivalent	616		

Inflation and finance

Consumer price		av. ann. increase 2000–05	
inflation 2006	4.3%	Narrow money (M1)	15.2%
Av. ann. inflation 2001–06	5.7%	Broad money	15.3%
Money market rate, 2006	6.49%		

Exchange rates

	end 2006		December 2006
Peso per $	2,225	Effective rates	2000 = 100
Peso per SDR	3,348	– nominal	98.5
Peso per €	2,938	– real	106.9

Trade

Principal exports		**Principal imports**	
	$bn fob		*$bn cif*
Oil	5.6	Intermediate goods &	
Coal	2.6	raw materials	9.5
Coffee	1.5	Capital goods	7.7
		Consumer goods	4.0
Total incl. others	**21.1**	Total	**21.2**

Main export destinations		**Main origins of imports**	
	% of total		*% of total*
United States	40.4	United States	28.1
Venezuela	9.2	Venezuela	6.4
Ecuador	5.7	Mexico	5.9
Peru	3.5	Brazil	5.5

Balance of payments, reserves and debt, $bn

Visible exports fob	21.7	Change in reserves	1.4
Visible imports fob	-20.1	Level of reserves	
Trade balance	1.6	end Dec.	15.0
Invisibles inflows	3.7	No. months of import cover	5.7
Invisibles outflows	-11.3	Official gold holdings, m oz	0.3
Net transfers	4.0	Foreign debt	37.7
Current account balance	-1.9	– as % of GDP	43
– as % of GDP	-1.5	– as % of total exports	171
Capital balance	3.2	Debt service ratio	35
Overall balance	1.7		

Health and education

Health spending, % of GDP	7.8	Education spending, % of GDP	4.8
Doctors per 1,000 pop.	1.4	Enrolment, %: primary	113
Hospital beds per 1,000 pop.	1.2	secondary	75
Improved-water source access,		tertiary	22
% of pop.	93		

Society

No. of households	12.0m	Colour TVs per 100 households	87.2
Av. no. per household	3.8	Telephone lines per 100 pop.	16.8
Marriages per 1,000 pop.	1.7	Mobile telephone subscribers	
Divorces per 1,000 pop.	0.2	per 100 pop.	47.9
Cost of living, Dec. 2006		Computers per 100 pop.	4.2
New York = 100	69	Internet hosts per 1,000 pop.	15.8

CÔTE D'IVOIRE

| Area | 322,463 sq km | Capital | Abidjan/Yamoussoukro |
| Arable as % of total land | 10 | Currency | CFA franc (CFAfr) |

People

Population	18.2m	Life expectancy: men	47.5 yrs
Pop. per sq km	56.4	women	49.3 yrs
Av. ann. growth		Adult literacy	48.7%
in pop. 2005–10	1.84%	Fertility rate (per woman)	4.5
Pop. under 15	41.7%	Urban population	45.0%
Pop. over 60	5.1%		per 1,000 pop.
No. of men per 100 women	103	Crude birth rate	35.3
Human Development Index	42.1	Crude death rate	15.4

The economy

GDP	CFAfr8,621bn	GDP per head	$900
GDP	$16.3bn	GDP per head in purchasing	
Av. ann. growth in real		power parity (USA=100)	3.9
GDP 1995–2005	1.4%	Economic freedom index	55.5

Origins of GDP		Components of GDP	
	% of total		% of total
Agriculture	23	Private consumption	74
Industry, of which:	26	Public consumption	8
manufacturing	19	Investment	11
Services	51	Exports	50
		Imports	-42

Structure of employment

	% of total		% of labour force
Agriculture	...	Unemployed 2005	...
Industry	...	Av. ann. rate 1995–2005	...
Services	...		

Energy

	m TOE		
Total output	7.2	Net energy imports as %	
Total consumption	6.9	of energy use	-4
Consumption per head,			
kg oil equivalent	388		

Inflation and finance

		av. ann. change 2000–05	
Consumer price			
inflation 2005	3.9%	Narrow money (M1)	3.9%
Av. ann. inflation 2001–05	2.9%	Broad money	4.8%
Money market rate, 2006	4.95%		

Exchange rates

	end 2006		December 2006
CFAfr per $	498.1	Effective rates	2000 = 100
CFAfr per SDR	749.3	– nominal	115.0
CFAfr per €	657.5	– real	119.6

Trade

Principal exports[a]		**Principal imports**[a]	
	$bn fob		*$bn cif*
Cocoa beans & products	2.2	Capital equipment	1.2
Petroleum products	1.0	Foodstuffs	0.9
Timber	0.3	Fuel & lubricants	0.9
Coffee & products	0.2		
Total incl. others	**6.9**	Total incl. others	**5.7**

Main export destinations		**Main origins of imports**	
	% of total		*% of total*
France	18.3	France	27.7
United States	14.1	Nigeria	24.5
Netherlands	11.0	Singapore	6.6
Nigeria	8.0	China	3.1
Panama	4.4	United Kingdom	3.0

Balance of payments, reserves and debt, $bn

Visible exports fob	7.5	Change in reserves	-0.4
Visible imports fob	-5.1	Level of reserves	
Trade balance	2.4	end Dec.	1.3
Invisibles inflows	1.0	No. months of import cover	2.0
Invisibles outflows	-2.9	Official gold holdings, m oz	0.0
Net transfers	-0.5	Foreign debt	10.7
Current account balance	-0.0	– as % of GDP	69
– as % of GDP	-0.1	– as % of total exports	131
Capital balance	-0.9	Debt service ratio	6
Overall balance	-0.9		

Health and education

Health spending, % of GDP	3.8	Education spending, % of GDP	4.6
Doctors per 1,000 pop.	0.1	Enrolment, %: primary	77
Hospital beds per 1,000 pop.	...	secondary	25
Improved-water source access,		tertiary	7
% of pop.	84		

Society

No. of households	3.6m	Colour TVs per 100 households	28.0
Av. no. per household	4.7	Telephone lines per 100 pop.	1.4
Marriages per 1,000 pop.	...	Mobile telephone subscribers	
Divorces per 1,000 pop.	...	per 100 pop.	12.9
Cost of living, Dec. 2006		Computers per 100 pop.	1.6
New York = 100	89	Internet hosts per 1,000 pop.	0.1

a 2004

CZECH REPUBLIC

Area	78,864 sq km	Capital	Prague
Arable as % of total land	39	Currency	Koruna (Kc)

People

Population	10.2m	Life expectancy: men	73.4 yrs
Pop. per sq km	129.3	women	79.5 yrs
Av. ann. growth		Adult literacy	...
in pop. 2005–10	-0.03%	Fertility rate (per woman)	1.2
Pop. under 15	14.8%	Urban population	73.5%
Pop. over 60	19.9%		per 1,000 pop.
No. of men per 100 women	95	Crude birth rate	9.2
Human Development Index	88.5	Crude death rate	10.9

The economy

GDP	Kc2,978bn	GDP per head	$12,190
GDP	$124bn	GDP per head in purchasing	
Av. ann. growth in real		power parity (USA=100)	49.0
GDP 1995–2005	2.5%	Economic freedom index	69.7

Origins of GDP		**Components of GDP**	
	% of total		% of total
Agriculture	2.9	Private consumption	48.7
Industry, of which:	38.6	Public consumption	22.3
manufacturing	...	Investment	25.5
Services	58.5	Exports	71.7
		Imports	-69.8

Structure of employment

	% of total		% of labour force
Agriculture	4	Unemployed 2004	8.3
Industry	40	Av. ann. rate 1995–2004	6.8
Services	56		

Energy

	m TOE		
Total output	34.2	Net energy imports as %	
Total consumption	45.5	of energy use	25
Consumption per head,			
kg oil equivalent	4,460		

Inflation and finance

Consumer price		av. ann. increase 2000–05	
inflation 2006	2.5%	Narrow money (M1)	18.4%
Av. ann. inflation 2001–06	1.8%	Broad money	7.6%
Money market rate, 2005	2.17%	Household saving rate, 2005	1.2%

Exchange rates

	end 2006		December 2006
Kc per $	20.88	Effective rates	2000 = 100
Kc per SDR	31.41	– nominal	134.75
Kc per €	27.56	– real	134.67

Trade

Principal exports		**Principal imports**	
	$bn fob		*$bn cif*
Machinery & transport		Machinery & transport	
equipment	39.9	equipment	30.9
Semi-manufactures	16.9	Semi-manufactures	15.5
Chemicals	4.9	Raw materials & fuels	9.2
Raw materials & fuels	4.4	Chemicals	8.5
Total incl. others	**78.0**	Total incl. others	**76.4**

Main export destinations		**Main origins of imports**	
	% of total		*% of total*
Germany	33.6	Germany	33.0
Slovakia	8.7	Russia	6.3
Austria	5.5	Slovakia	6.0
Poland	5.5	China	5.7
France	5.3	Poland	4.9
EU25	84.2	EU25	70.8

Balance of payments, reserves and debt, $bn

Visible exports fob	78.2	Change in reserves	1.1
Visible imports fob	-76.5	Level of reserves	
Trade balance	1.7	end Dec.	29.6
Invisibles inflows	15.4	No. months of import cover	3.7
Invisibles outflows	-20.5	Official gold holdings, m oz	0.4
Net transfers	0.9	Foreign debt	46.8
Current account balance	-2.5	– as % of GDP	38
– as % of GDP	-2.0	– as % of total exports	50
Capital balance	5.9	Debt service ratio	12
Overall balance	3.9		

Health and education

Health spending, % of GDP	7.3	Education spending, % of GDP	4.5
Doctors per 1,000 pop.	3.5	Enrolment, %: primary	104
Hospital beds per 1,000 pop.	8.4	secondary	96
Improved-water source access,		tertiary	29
% of pop.	100		

Society

No. of households	3.8m	Colour TVs per 100 households	91.2
Av. no. per household	2.7	Telephone lines per 100 pop.	31.5
Marriages per 1,000 pop.	5.1	Mobile telephone subscribers	
Divorces per 1,000 pop.	3.3	per 100 pop.	115.2
Cost of living, Dec. 2006		Computers per 100 pop.	24.0
New York = 100	84	Internet hosts per 1,000 pop.	147.3

DENMARK

Area	43,075 sq km	Capital	Copenhagen
Arable as % of total land	53	Currency	Danish krone (DKr)

People

Population	5.4m	Life expectancy: men	76.0 yrs
Pop. per sq km	125.4	women	80.6 yrs
Av. ann. growth		Adult literacy	...
in pop. 2005–10	0.21	Fertility rate (per woman)	1.8
Pop. under 15	18.8%	Urban population	85.6%
Pop. over 60	21.2%		per 1,000 pop.
No. of men per 100 women	98	Crude birth rate	11.2
Human Development Index	94.3	Crude death rate	10.3

The economy

GDP	DKr1,552bn	GDP per head	$47,910
GDP	$259bn	GDP per head in purchasing	
Av. ann. growth in real		power parity (USA=100)	81.1
GDP 1995–2005	2.1%	Economic freedom index	77.6

Origins of GDP		**Components of GDP**	
	% of total		% of total
Agriculture	2.6	Private consumption	48.5
Industry, of which:	31.8	Public consumption	25.9
manufacturing	...	Investment	20.8
Services	65.6	Exports	18.6
		Imports	-43.9

Structure of employment

	% of total		% of labour force
Agriculture	3	Unemployed 2004	5.6
Industry	24	Av. ann. rate 1995–2004	5.6
Services	73		

Energy

	m TOE		
Total output	31.0	Net energy imports as %	
Total consumption	20.1	of energy use	-55
Consumption per head,			
kg oil equivalent	3,716		

Inflation and finance

Consumer price		av. ann. increase 1999–2004	
inflation 2006	1.9%	Narrow money (M1)	10.8%
Av. ann. inflation 2001–06	1.9%	Broad money	8.1%
Money market rate, 2006	3.18%	Household saving rate, 2006	-2.2%

Exchange rates

	end 2006		December 2006
DKr per $	5.66	Effective rates	2000 = 100
DKr per SDR	8.52	– nominal	108.3
DKr per €	7.47	– real	115.1

Trade

Principal exports		Principal imports	
	$bn fob		*$bn cif*
Manufactured goods	61.7	Intermediate goods	30.6
Energy & products	8.7	Consumer goods	21.1
Agric. products	8.3	Capital goods excl. ships	10.5
Total incl. others	**83.6**	Total incl. others	**74.3**

Main export destinations		Main origins of imports	
	% of total		*% of total*
Germany	17.6	Germany	20.8
Sweden	13.2	Sweden	13.7
United Kingdom	8.7	Netherlands	6.7
United States	6.4	Norway	6.6
France	5.5	United Kingdom	5.9
Netherlands	5.3	United States	5.9
Norway	5.1	France	4.2
EU25	70.6	EU25	71.2

Balance of payments, reserves and aid, $bn

Visible exports fob	82.7	Overall balance	-1.5
Visible imports fob	-74.6	Change in reserves	-5.9
Trade balance	8.0	Level of reserves	
Invisibles inflows	66.0	end Dec.	34.0
Invisibles outflows	-61.2	No. months of import cover	3.0
Net transfers	-4.2	Official gold holdings, m oz	2.1
Current account balance	8.6	Aid given	2.11
– as % of GDP	3.4	– as % of GDP	0.81
Capital balance	-9.6		

Health and education

Health spending, % of GDP	8.6	Education spending, % of GDP	8.4
Doctors per 1,000 pop.	2.9	Enrolment, %: primary	102
Hospital beds per 1,000 pop.	3.8	secondary	124
Improved-water source access,		tertiary	56
% of pop.	100		

Society

No. of households	2.5m	Colour TVs per 100 households	92.6
Av. no. per household	2.2	Telephone lines per 100 pop.	61.7
Marriages per 1,000 pop.	7.1	Mobile telephone subscribers	
Divorces per 1,000 pop.	3.0	per 100 pop.	100.3
Cost of living, Dec. 2006		Computers per 100 pop.	65.5
New York = 100	126	Internet hosts per 1,000 pop.	519.9

EGYPT

Area	1,000,250 sq km	Capital	Cairo
Arable as % of total land	3	Currency	Egyptian pound (£E)

People

Population	74.0m	Life expectancy: men	69.1 yrs
Pop. per sq km	74.0	women	73.6 yrs
Av. ann. growth		Adult literacy	71.4%
in pop. 2005–10	1.76%	Fertility rate (per woman)	2.9
Pop. under 15	33.3%	Urban population	42.8%
Pop. over 60	7.2%		per 1,000 pop.
No. of men per 100 women	100	Crude birth rate	24.2
Human Development Index	70.2	Crude death rate	5.6

The economy

GDP	£E537bn	GDP per head	$1,210
GDP	$89.4bn	GDP per head in purchasing	
Av. ann. growth in real		power parity (USA=100)	10.4
GDP 1995–2005	4.7%	Economic freedom index	53.2

Origins of GDP

	% of total
Agriculture	15
Industry, of which:	36
manufacturing	17
Services	49

Components of GDP[a]

	% of total
Private consumption	71.4
Public consumption	12.3
Investment	18.7
Exports	31.3
Imports	-33.7

Structure of employment

	% of total		% of labour force
Agriculture	27	Unemployed 2004	11.0
Industry	21	Av. ann. rate 1995–2004	9.6
Services	52		

Energy

	m TOE		
Total output	64.7	Net energy imports as %	
Total consumption	56.9	of energy use	-14
Consumption per head,			
kg oil equivalent	783		

Inflation and finance

Consumer price			av. ann. increase 2000–05
inflation 2006	4.2%	Narrow money (M1)	10.2%
Av. ann. inflation 2001–06	5.3%	Broad money	14.9%
Treasury bill rate, 2006	9.50%		

Exchange rates

	end 2006		December 2006
£E per $	5.70	Effective rates	2000 = 100
£E per SDR	8.58	– nominal	...
£E per €	7.52	– real	...

Trade

Principal exports[b]		**Principal imports**[b]	
	$bn fob		*$bn fob*
Petroleum & products	5.3	Intermediate goods	6.8
Cotton yarn & textiles	0.9	Investment goods	4.9
Metals	0.9	Fuels	4.0
Agricultural products	0.2	Consumer goods	3.2
Pharmaceuticals	0.2		
Total incl. others	**13.1**	Total incl. others	**20.0**

Main export destinations		**Main origins of imports**	
	% of total		*% of total*
United States	30.6	United States	18.9
Italy	11.3	United Kingdom	9.7
Spain	7.3	Germany	6.5
India	5.3	Switzerland	5.3

Balance of payments, reserves and debt, $bn

Visible exports fob	16.1	Change in reserves	6.5
Visible imports fob	-23.8	Level of reserves	
Trade balance	-7.7	end Dec.	21.9
Invisibles inflows	16.1	No. months of import cover	7.3
Invisibles outflows	-12.0	Official gold holdings, m oz	2.4
Net transfers	5.7	Foreign debt	34.1
Current account balance	2.1	– as % of GDP	36
– as % of GDP	2.4	– as % of total exports	99
Capital balance	5.5	Debt service ratio	7
Overall balance	5.2		

Health and education

Health spending, % of GDP	5.9	Education spending, % of GDP	...
Doctors per 1,000 pop.	0.5	Enrolment, %: primary	100
Hospital beds per 1,000 pop.	2.2	secondary	87
Improved-water source access,		tertiary	39
% of pop.	98		

Society

No. of households	16.0m	Colour TVs per 100 households	52.4
Av. no. per household	4.3	Telephone lines per 100 pop.	14.0
Marriages per 1,000 pop.	6.7	Mobile telephone subscribers	
Divorces per 1,000 pop.	0.8	per 100 pop.	18.4
Cost of living, Dec. 2006		Computers per 100 pop.	3.7
New York = 100	58	Internet hosts per 1,000 pop.	1.2

a Year ending June 30, 2006.
b Year ending June 30, 2005.

ESTONIA

Area	45,200 sq km	Capital	Tallinn
Arable as % of total land	14	Currency	Kroon (EEK)

People

Population	1.3m	Life expectancy: men	65.9 yrs
Pop. per sq km	28.8	women	76.8 yrs
Av. ann. growth		Adult literacy	99.8%
in pop. 2005–10	-0.35%	Fertility rate (per woman)	1.5
Pop. under 15	15.2%	Urban population	69.1%
Pop. over 60	21.6%		per 1,000 pop.
No. of men per 100 women	85	Crude birth rate	10.8
Human Development Index	85.8	Crude death rate	14.3

The economy

GDP	EEK165bn	GDP per head	$10,080
GDP	$13.1bn	GDP per head in purchasing	
Av. ann. growth in real		power parity (USA=100)	36.9
GDP 1995–2005	6.6%	Economic freedom index	78.1

Origins of GDP		**Components of GDP**	
	% of total		% of total
Agriculture	3.7	Private consumption	51.8
Industry, of which:	28.5	Public consumption	17.4
manufacturing	...	Investment	31.1
Services	67.8	Exports	80.0
		Imports	-86.1

Structure of employment

	% of total		% of labour force
Agriculture	5	Unemployed 2004	9.6
Industry	34	Av. ann. rate 1995–2004	10.7
Services	61		

Energy

	m TOE		
Total output	3.6	Net energy imports as %	
Total consumption	5.2	of energy use	31
Consumption per head,			
kg oil equivalent	3,835		

Inflation and finance

		av. ann. increase 2000–05	
Consumer price			
inflation 2006	4.4%	Narrow money (M1)	18.4%
Av. ann. inflation 2001–06	3.3%	Broad money	20.0%
Money market rate, 2006	3.16%		

Exchange rates

	end 2006		December 2006
EEK per $	11.88	Effective rates	2000 = 100
EEK per SDR	17.80	– nominal	...
EEK per €	15.68	– real	...

Trade

Principal exports		**Principal imports**	
	$bn fob		*$bn cif*
Machinery & equipment	1.6	Machinery & equipment	2.4
Wood & paper	0.9	Transport equipment	1.0
Clothing & footwear	0.6	Metals	0.9
Food	0.5	Chemicals	0.8
Furniture	0.5	Food	0.8
Total incl. others	**7.7**	Total incl. others	**10.2**

Main export destinations		**Main origins of imports**	
	% of total		*% of total*
Finland	26.8	Finland	19.6
Sweden	13.2	Germany	14.0
Latvia	8.8	Russia	9.2
Russia	6.5	Sweden	8.7
Germany	6.3	Lithuania	6.0

Balance of payments, reserves and debt, $bn

Visible exports fob	7.8	Change in reserves	0.2
Visible imports fob	-9.6	Level of reserves	
Trade balance	-1.8	end Dec.	1.9
Invisibles inflows	3.8	No. months of import cover	1.8
Invisibles outflows	-3.5	Official gold holdings, m oz	0.0
Net transfers	0.1	Foreign debt	11.3
Current account balance	-1.4	– as % of GDP	102
– as % of GDP	-11.0	– as % of total exports	115
Capital balance	1.8	Debt service ratio	14
Overall balance	0.4		

Health and education

Health spending, % of GDP	5.3	Education spending, % of GDP	5.7
Doctors per 1,000 pop.	4.5	Enrolment, %: primary	103
Hospital beds per 1,000 pop.	5.8	secondary	98
Improved-water source access,		tertiary	53
% of pop.	100		

Society

No. of households	0.6m	Colour TVs per 100 households	89.0
Av. no. per household	2.4	Telephone lines per 100 pop.	33.3
Marriages per 1,000 pop.	4.5	Mobile telephone subscribers	
Divorces per 1,000 pop.	3.1	per 100 pop.	108.8
Cost of living, Dec. 2006		Computers per 100 pop.	48.9
New York = 100	...	Internet hosts per 1,000 pop.	345.4

FINLAND

Area	338,145 sq km	Capital	Helsinki
Arable as % of total land	7	Currency	Euro (€)

People

Population	5.2m	Life expectancy: men	76.1 yrs
Pop. per sq km	15.4	women	82.4 yrs
Av. ann. growth		Adult literacy	...
in pop. 2005–10	0.29%	Fertility rate (per woman)	1.8
Pop. under 15	17.4%	Urban population	61.1%
Pop. over 60	21.4%		per 1,000 pop.
No. of men per 100 women	96	Crude birth rate	11.1
Human Development Index	94.7	Crude death rate	9.7

The economy

GDP	€155bn	GDP per head	$37,150
GDP	$193bn	GDP per head in purchasing	
Av. ann. growth in real		power parity (USA=100)	76.8
GDP 1995–2005	3.5%	Economic freedom index	76.5

Origins of GDP		Components of GDP	
	% of total		% of total
Agriculture	3.0	Private consumption	51.6
Industry, of which:	35.6	Public consumption	19.6
manuf., mining & utilities	30.5	Investment	19.5
Services	61.4	Exports	45.8
		Imports	-37.9

Structure of employment

	% of total		% of labour force
Agriculture	5	Unemployed 2004	8.9
Industry	26	Av. ann. rate 1995–2004	10.9
Services	69		

Energy

	m TOE		
Total output	15.9	Net energy imports as %	
Total consumption	38.1	of energy use	58
Consumption per head,			
kg oil equivalent	7,286		

Inflation and finance

Consumer price		av. ann. increase 2001–05	
inflation 2006	1.3%	Euro area:	
Av. ann. inflation 2001–06	1.1%	Narrow money (M1)	10.8%
Money market rate, 2006	3.08%	Broad money	7.7%
		Household saving rate, 2006	-1.5%

Exchange rates

	end 2006		December 2006
			2000 = 100
€ per $	0.76	Effective rates	
€ per SDR	1.14	– nominal	109.9
		– real	111.1

Trade

Principal exports		Principal imports	
	$bn fob		*$bn cif*
Metals, machinery &		Raw materials	22.9
transport equipment	28.7	Energy	8.0
Basic manufactures	19.6	Basic manufactures	6.9
Chemicals	5.0	Chemicals & plastics	6.6
Crude materials	3.8		
Total incl. others	**65.2**	Total incl. others	**58.5**

Main export destinations		Main origins of imports	
	% of total		*% of total*
Russia	11.0	Germany	14.9
Sweden	10.8	Russia	13.9
Germany	10.6	Sweden	10.6
United Kingdom	6.7	China	6.0
United States	5.8	United Kingdom	4.5
Netherlands	4.8	United States	4.2

Balance of payments, reserves and aid, $bn

Visible exports fob	65.5	Overall balance	-0.2
Visible imports fob	-55.9	Change in reserves	-1.7
Trade balance	9.6	Level of reserves	
Invisibles inflows	31.0	end Dec.	11.3
Invisibles outflows	-29.5	No. months of import cover	1.6
Net transfers	-1.6	Official gold holdings, m oz	1.6
Current account balance	9.5	Aid given	0.90
– as % of GDP	4.9	– as % of GDP	0.46
Capital balance	-3.5		

Health and education

Health spending, % of GDP	7.4	Education spending, % of GDP	6.5
Doctors per 1,000 pop.	3.2	Enrolment, %: primary	101
Hospital beds per 1,000 pop.	7.0	secondary	109
Improved-water source access,		tertiary	84
% of pop.	100		

Society

No. of households	2.4m	Colour TVs per 100 households	98.7
Av. no. per household	2.1	Telephone lines per 100 pop.	40.4
Marriages per 1,000 pop.	5.7	Mobile telephone subscribers	
Divorces per 1,000 pop.	2.5	per 100 pop.	100.4
Cost of living, Dec. 2006		Computers per 100 pop.	48.2
New York = 100	116	Internet hosts per 1,000 pop.	613.0

FRANCE

Area	543,965 sq km	Capital	Paris
Arable as % of total land	34	Currency	Euro (€)

People

Population	60.5m	Life expectancy: men	77.1 yrs
Pop. per sq km	111.2	women	84.1 yrs
Av. ann. growth		Adult literacy	...
in pop. 2005–10	0.49%	Fertility rate (per woman)	1.9
Pop. under 15	18.4%	Urban population	76.7%
Pop. over 60	20.8%		per 1,000 pop.
No. of men per 100 women	95	Crude birth rate	12.2
Human Development Index	94.2	Crude death rate	8.9

The economy

GDP	€1,710bn	GDP per head	$35,150
GDP	$2,127bn	GDP per head in purchasing	
Av. ann. growth in real		power parity (USA=100)	72.5
GDP 1995–2005	2.2%	Economic freedom index	66.1

Origins of GDP		**Components of GDP**	
	% of total		% of total
Agriculture	2.2	Private consumption	56.5
Industry, of which:	21.4	Public consumption	24.1
manufacturing	...	Investment	19.6
Services	76.4	Exports	26.3
		Imports	-27.4

Structure of employment

	% of total		% of labour force
Agriculture	2	Unemployed 2004	9.9
Industry	24	Av. ann. rate 1995–2004	10.7
Services	74		

Energy

	m TOE		
Total output	137.4	Net energy imports as %	
Total consumption	275.2	of energy use	50
Consumption per head,			
kg oil equivalent	4,547		

Inflation and finance

Consumer price		av. ann. increase 2000–05	
inflation 2006	1.9%	Euro area:	
Av. ann. inflation 2001–06	2.0%	Narrow money (M1)	10.8%
Deposit rate, households, 2006	2.85%	Broad money	7.7%
		Household saving rate, 2006	11.5%

Exchange rates

	end 2006		December 2006
€ per $	0.76	Effective rates	2000 = 100
€ per SDR	1.14	– nominal	109.2
		– real	102.3

Trade

Principal exports

	$bn fob
Intermediate goods	132.8
Capital goods	100.6
Consumer goods	67.4
Motor vehicles & other transport equipment	64.5
Food & drink	37.5
Total incl. others	**437.6**

Principal imports

	$bn cif
Intermediate goods	141.2
Capital goods	98.4
Consumer goods	78.3
Motor vehicles & other transport equipment	78.3
Energy	65.7
Total incl. others	**473.8**

Main export destinations

	% of total
Germany	14.5
Spain	10.2
Italy	9.2
United Kingdom	8.8
Belgium-Luxembourg	8.0
EU25	65.0

Main origins of imports

	% of total
Germany	17.2
Italy	8.6
Belgium-Luxembourg	8.5
Spain	7.1
United Kingdom	5.9
EU25	61.3

Balance of payments, reserves and aid, $bn

Visible exports fob	439.2	Overall balance	-9.1
Visible imports fob	-471.4	Change in reserves	-3.0
Trade balance	-32.1	Level of reserves	
Invisibles inflows	251.5	end Dec.	74.4
Invisibles outflows	-235.2	No. months of import cover	1.3
Net transfers	-27.4	Official gold holdings, m oz	91.0
Current account balance	-33.3	Aid given	10.03
– as % of GDP	-1.6	– as % of GDP	0.47
Capital balance	-37.8		

Health and education

Health spending, % of GDP	10.5	Education spending, % of GDP	5.9
Doctors per 1,000 pop.	3.4	Enrolment, %: primary	105
Hospital beds per 1,000 pop.	7.5	secondary	111
Improved-water source access,		tertiary	53
% of pop.	100		

Society

No. of households	25.3m	Colour TVs per 100 households	95.9
Av. no. per household	2.4	Telephone lines per 100 pop.	55.7
Marriages per 1,000 pop.	4.2	Mobile telephone subscribers	
Divorces per 1,000 pop.	2.2	per 100 pop.	79.5
Cost of living, Dec. 2006		Computers per 100 pop.	57.9
New York = 100	130	Internet hosts per 1,000 pop.	170.8

GERMANY

Area	357,868 sq km	Capital	Berlin
Arable as % of total land	34	Currency	Euro (€)

People

Population	82.7m	Life expectancy: men	76.5 yrs
Pop. per sq km	231.0	women	82.1 yrs
Av. ann. growth		Adult literacy	...
in pop. 2005–10	-0.07%	Fertility rate (per woman)	1.4
Pop. under 15	14.4%	Urban population	75.2%
Pop. over 60	25.1%		per 1,000 pop.
No. of men per 100 women	96	Crude birth rate	8.2
Human Development Index	93.2	Crude death rate	10.7

The economy

GDP	€2,247bn	GDP per head	$33,800
GDP	$2,795bn	GDP per head in purchasing	
Av. ann. growth in real		power parity (USA=100)	70.3
GDP 1995–2005	1.4%	Economic freedom index	73.5

Origins of GDP

	% of total
Agriculture	0.9
Industry, of which:	29.6
manufacturing	...
Services	69.5

Components of GDP

	% of total
Private consumption	58.9
Public consumption	18.7
Investment	17.3
Exports	40.7
Imports	-35.5

Structure of employment

	% of total		% of labour force
Agriculture	2	Unemployed 2004	9.8
Industry	30	Av. ann. rate 1995–2004	9.1
Services	68		

Energy

	m TOE		
Total output	136.0	Net energy imports as %	
Total consumption	348.0	of energy use	61
Consumption per head,			
kg oil equivalent	4,218		

Inflation and finance

Consumer price		av. ann. increase 1999–2004
inflation 2006	1.8%	Euro area:
Av. ann. inflation 2001–06	1.6%	Narrow money (M1) 10.8%
Deposit rate, households, 2006	2.56%	Broad money 7.7%
		Household saving rate, 2006 10.5%

Exchange rates

	end 2006		December 2006
€ per $	0.76	Effective rates	2000 = 100
€ per SDR	1.14	– nominal	111.2
		– real	95.9

Trade

Principal exports		Principal imports	
	$bn fob		*$bn cif*
Road vehicles	187.1	Chemicals	87.4
Machinery	137.6	Road vehicles	79.2
Chemicals	127.5	Fuels	64.2
Metals	50.9	Machinery	52.2
Electricity devices	48.3	Computer technology	49.3
Total incl. others	**977.9**	Total incl. others	**780.4**

Main export destinations		Main origins of imports	
	% of total		*% of total*
France	10.2	France	9.0
United States	8.8	Netherlands	7.8
United Kingdom	7.8	United States	7.3
Italy	6.9	China	6.1
Netherlands	6.1	United Kingdom	6.1
Belgium	5.6	Italy	4.9
Austria	5.4	Belgium	3.8
		Austria	2.8

Balance of payments, reserves and aid, $bn

Visible exports fob	972.1	Overall balance	-2.6
Visible imports fob	-782.8	Change in reserves	4.5
Trade balance	189.3	Level of reserves	
Invisibles inflows	327.6	end Dec.	101.7
Invisibles outflows	-364.9	No. months of import cover	1.1
Net transfers	-36.0	Official gold holdings, m oz	110.2
Current account balance	116.0	Aid given	10.08
– as % of GDP	4.2	– as % of GDP	0.36
Capital balance	-132.7		

Health and education

Health spending, % of GDP	10.6	Education spending, % of GDP	4.7
Doctors per 1,000 pop.	3.4	Enrolment, %: primary	105
Hospital beds per 1,000 pop.	8.4	secondary	100
Improved-water source access,		tertiary	46
% of pop.	100		

Society

No. of households	39.3m	Colour TVs per 100 households	97.4
Av. no. per household	2.1	Telephone lines per 100 pop.	66.6
Marriages per 1,000 pop.	4.8	Mobile telephone subscribers	
Divorces per 1,000 pop.	2.7	per 100 pop.	95.8
Cost of living, Dec. 2006		Computers per 100 pop.	54.5
New York = 100	106	Internet hosts per 1,000 pop.	158.3

GREECE

Area	131,957 sq km	Capital	Athens
Arable as % of total land	20	Currency	Euro (€)

People

Population	11.1m	Life expectancy: men	77.1 yrs
Pop. per sq km	84.1	women	81.9 yrs
Av. ann. growth		Adult literacy	96.0%
in pop. 2005–10	0.21%	Fertility rate (per woman)	1.3
Pop. under 15	14.3%	Urban population	59.0%
Pop. over 60	23.3%		per 1,000 pop.
No. of men per 100 women	98	Crude birth rate	9.3
Human Development Index	92.1	Crude death rate	9.9

The economy

GDP	€181bn	GDP per head	$20,290
GDP	$225bn	GDP per head in purchasing	
Av. ann. growth in real		power parity (USA=100)	55.8
GDP 1995–2005	3.8%	Economic freedom index	57.6

Origins of GDP		Components of GDP	
	% of total		% of total
Agriculture	4.1	Private consumption	68.7
Industry, of which:	17.2	Public consumption	14.2
mining & manufacturing	9.7	Investment	23.4
Services	78.7	Exports	18.4
		Imports	-25.6

Structure of employment

	% of total		% of labour force
Agriculture	13	Unemployed 2004	10.2
Industry	22	Av. ann. rate 1995–2004	10.4
Services	65		

Energy

	m TOE		
Total output	10.3	Net energy imports as %	
Total consumption	30.5	of energy use	66
Consumption per head,			
kg oil equivalent	2,755		

Inflation and finance

Consumer price		av. ann. increase 2000–05	
inflation 2006	3.3%	Euro area:	
Av. ann. inflation 2001–06	3.4%	Narrow money (M1)	10.8%
Treasury bill rate, 2006	3.44%	Broad money	7.7%

Exchange rates

	end 2006		December 2006
€ per $	0.76	Effective rates	2000 = 100
€ per SDR	1.14	– nominal	105.5
		– real	123.9

Trade

Principal exports[a]		Principal imports[a]	
	$bn fob		*$bn cif*
Machinery	3.0	Machinery	10.3
Food	2.7	Chemicals & plastics	7.1
Transport equipment	2.1	Food	6.8
Total incl. others	**15.5**	Total incl. others	**49.8**

Main export destinations		Main origins of imports	
	% of total		*% of total*
Germany	12.4	Germany	12.7
Italy	10.4	Italy	12.4
United Kingdom	6.7	Russia	7.8
United States	5.3	France	5.2
EU25	53.0	EU25	55.7

Balance of payments, reserves and debt, $bn

Visible exports fob	17.6	Overall balance	-0.1
Visible imports fob	-51.9	Change in reserves	-0.4
Trade balance	-34.3	Level of reserves	
Invisibles inflows	38.2	end Dec.	2.3
Invisibles outflows	-25.8	No. months of import cover	0.4
Net transfers	4.0	Official gold holdings, m oz	3.5
Current account balance	-17.9	Aid given	0.38
– as % of GDP	-8.4	– as % of GDP	0.17
Capital balance	18.2		

Health and education

Health spending, % of GDP	7.9	Education spending, % of GDP	4.0
Doctors per 1,000 pop.	4.4	Enrolment, %: primary	99
Hospital beds per 1,000 pop.	4.7	secondary	96
Improved-water source access,		tertiary	55
% of pop.	...		

Society

No. of households	3.8m	Colour TVs per 100 households	91.8
Av. no. per household	2.8	Telephone lines per 100 pop.	56.8
Marriages per 1,000 pop.	5.6	Mobile telephone subscribers	
Divorces per 1,000 pop.	1.2	per 100 pop.	92.3
Cost of living, Dec. 2006		Computers per 100 pop.	8.9
New York = 100	84	Internet hosts per 1,000 pop.	71.9

a 2004

HONG KONG

Area	1,075 sq km	Capital	Victoria
Arable as % of total land	5	Currency	Hong Kong dollar (HK$)

People

Population	7.0m	Life expectancy: men	79.4 yrs
Pop. per sq km	6,511.6	women	85.1 yrs
Av. ann. growth		Adult literacy	93.5%
in pop. 2005–10	1.00%	Fertility rate (per woman)	1.0
Pop. under 15	15.1%	Urban population	100.0%
Pop. over 60	15.4%		per 1,000 pop.
No. of men per 100 women	92	Crude birth rate	7.6
Human Development Index	92.7	Crude death rate	5.9

The economy

GDP	HK$1,382bn	GDP per head	$25,390
GDP	$178bn	GDP per head in purchasing	
Av. ann. growth in real		power parity (USA=100)	83.2
GDP 1995–2005	3.9%	Economic freedom index	89.3

Origins of GDP		**Components of GDP**	
	% of total		% of total
Agriculture	0	Private consumption	53.2
Industry, of which:	10	Public consumption	8.0
manufacturing	4	Investment	22.7
Services	90	Exports	180.8
		Imports	-164.4

Structure of employment

	% of total		% of labour force
Agriculture	0	Unemployed 2004	6.8
Industry	15	Av. ann. rate 1995–2004	5.1
Services	85		

Energy

	m TOE		
Total output	0.0	Net energy imports as %	
Total consumption	17.1	of energy use	100
Consumption per head,			
kg oil equivalent	2,488		

Inflation and finance

Consumer price			av. ann. increase 2000–05
inflation 2006	2.2%	Narrow money (M1)	11.3%
Av. ann. inflation 2001–06	-0.6%	Broad money	3.4%
Money market rate, 2006	3.94%		

Exchange rates

	end 2006		December 2006
HK$ per $	7.78	Effective rates	2000 = 100
HK$ per SDR	11.67	– nominal	...
HK$ per €	10.27	– real	...

Trade

Principal exports[a]		**Principal imports**	
	$bn fob		*$bn cif*
Clothing	7.2	Raw materials &	
Electrical machinery		semi-manufactures	27.9
& apparatus	2.4	Capital goods	16.7
Jewellery	0.9	Consumer goods	16.2
Textiles	0.6	Fuel	7.3
Printed matter	0.4	Food	6.5
Total incl. others	**17.5**	**Total incl. others**	**299.9**

Main export destinations		**Main origins of imports**	
	% of total		*% of total*
China	45.8	China	45.0
United States	15.3	Japan	11.0
Japan	5.4	Taiwan	7.2
Germany	3.2	Singapore	5.8

Balance of payments, reserves and debt, $bn

Visible exports fob	289.6	Change in reserves	0.7
Visible imports fob	-297.2	Level of reserves	
Trade balance	-7.6	end Dec.	124.3
Invisibles inflows	127.0	No. months of import cover	3.8
Invisibles outflows	-97.0	Official gold holdings, m oz	0.1
Net transfers	-2.1	Foreign debt	72.3
Current account balance	20.2	– as % of GDP	41
– as % of GDP	11.4	– as % of total exports	17
Capital balance	-22.1	Debt service ratio	2
Overall balance	1.4		

Health and education

Health spending, % of GDP	...	Education spending, % of GDP	4.2
Doctors per 1,000 pop.	...	Enrolment, %: primary	94
Hospital beds per 1,000 pop.	...	secondary	85
Improved-water source access,		tertiary	27
% of pop.	...		

Society

No. of households	2.2m	Colour TVs per 100 households	99.1
Av. no. per household	3.2	Telephone lines per 100 pop.	53.9
Marriages per 1,000 pop.	6.0	Mobile telephone subscribers	
Divorces per 1,000 pop.	2.3	per 100 pop.	123.5
Cost of living, Dec. 2006		Computers per 100 pop.	59.3
New York = 100	107	Internet hosts per 1,000 pop.	114.5

a Domestic, excluding re-exports.
Note: Hong Kong became a Special Administrative Region of China on July 1 1997.

HUNGARY

Area	93,030 sq km	Capital	Budapest
Arable as % of total land	51	Currency	Forint (Ft)

People

Population	10.1m	Life expectancy: men		69.2 yrs
Pop. per sq km	108.6	women		77.4 yrs
Av. ann. growth		Adult literacy		...
in pop. 2005–10	-0.29%	Fertility rate (per woman)		1.3
Pop. under 15	15.8%	Urban population		66.3%
Pop. over 60	20.8%		per 1,000 pop.	
No. of men per 100 women	91	Crude birth rate		9.3
Human Development Index	86.9	Crude death rate		13.2

The economy

GDP	Ft21,802bn	GDP per head	$10,820
GDP	$109bn	GDP per head in purchasing	
Av. ann. growth in real		power parity (USA=100)	42.7
GDP 1995–2005	4.1%	Economic freedom index	66.2

Origins of GDP[a]		Components of GDP	
	% of total		% of total
Agriculture	3.9	Private consumption	68.2
Industry, of which:	27.4	Public consumption	10.3
manufacturing	...	Investment	23.2
Services	68.7	Exports	66.4
		Imports	-68.5

Structure of employment

	% of total		% of labour force
Agriculture	5	Unemployed 2004	6.1
Industry	32	Av. ann. rate 1995–2004	7.3
Services	63		

Energy

	m TOE		
Total output	10.2	Net energy imports as %	
Total consumption	26.4	of energy use	61
Consumption per head,			
kg oil equivalent	2,608		

Inflation and finance

Consumer price		av. ann. increase 2000–05	
inflation 2006	3.9%	Narrow money (M1)	14.3%
Av. ann. inflation 2001–06	4.8%	Broad money	13.0%
Treasury bill rate, 2006	6.87%	Household saving rate, 2006	13.2%

Exchange rates

	end 2006		December 2006
Ft per $	191.62	Effective rates	2000 = 100
Ft per SDR	288.27	– nominal	109.9
Ft per €	252.94	– real	137.1

Trade

Principal exports		Principal imports	
	$bn fob		$bn cif
Machinery & equipment	37.7	Machinery & equipment	33.1
Other manufactures	17.4	Other manufactures	21.9
Food, drink & tobacco	3.8	Fuels	6.7
Fuels & electricity	1.7	Food, drink & tobacco	2.6
Raw materials	1.3	Raw materials	1.2
Total incl. others	**62.2**	Total incl. others	**65.8**

Main export destinations		Main origins of imports	
	% of total		% of total
Germany	29.3	Germany	27.6
Austria	6.4	Russia	7.2
Italy	5.6	China	7.0
France	4.9	Austria	6.7

Balance of payments, reserves and debt, $bn

Visible exports fob	62.2	Change in reserves	2.6
Visible imports fob	-64.0	Level of reserves	
Trade balance	-1.8	end Dec.	18.6
Invisibles inflows	15.0	No. months of import cover	2.6
Invisibles outflows	-20.9	Official gold holdings, m oz	0.1
Net transfers	0.2	Foreign debt	66.1
Current account balance	-7.5	– as % of GDP	69
– as % of GDP	-7.4	– as % of total exports	96
Capital balance	14.7	Debt service ratio	31
Overall balance	4.9		

Health and education

Health spending, % of GDP	7.9	Education spending, % of GDP	5.9
Doctors per 1,000 pop.	3.3	Enrolment, %: primary	103
Hospital beds per 1,000 pop.	7.9	secondary	97
Improved-water source access,		tertiary	37
% of pop.	99		

Society

No. of households	3.7m	Colour TVs per 100 households	92.2
Av. no. per household	2.7	Telephone lines per 100 pop.	33.2
Marriages per 1,000 pop.	4.3	Mobile telephone subscribers	
Divorces per 1,000 pop.	2.4	per 100 pop.	92.3
Cost of living, Dec. 2006		Computers per 100 pop.	15.0
New York = 100	67	Internet hosts per 1,000 pop.	116.5

a 2003

INDIA

Area	3,287,263 sq km	Capital	New Delhi
Arable as % of total land	54	Currency	Indian rupee (Rs)

People

Population	1,103.4m	Life expectancy: men		63.2 yrs
Pop. per sq km	335.7	women		66.4 yrs
Av. ann. growth		Adult literacy		61.0%
in pop. 2005–10	1.46%	Fertility rate (per woman)		2.8
Pop. under 15	33.0%	Urban population		28.7%
Pop. over 60	7.1%			*per 1,000 pop.*
No. of men per 100 women	107	Crude birth rate		23.0
Human Development Index	61.1	Crude death rate		8.2

The economy

GDP	Rs35,672bn	GDP per head	$730
GDP	$806bn	GDP per head in purchasing	
Av. ann. growth in real		power parity (USA=100)	8.2
GDP 1995–2005	6.3%	Economic freedom index	55.6

Origins of GDP[a]   **Components of GDP**[b]

	% of total		*% of total*
Agriculture	19.0	Private consumption	61.7
Industry, of which:	27.4	Public consumption	10.6
manufacturing	15.9	Investment	24.8
Services	53.6	Exports	19.1
		Imports	-16.3

Structure of employment

	% of total		*% of labour force*
Agriculture	...	Unemployed 2004	5.0
Industry	...	Av. ann. rate 1995–2004	3.3
Services	...		

Energy

	m TOE		
Total output	466.9	Net energy imports as %	
Total consumption	572.9	of energy use	19
Consumption per head,			
kg oil equivalent	531		

Inflation and finance

Consumer price		*av. ann. increase 2000–05*	
inflation 2006	6.1%	Narrow money (M1)	15.6%
Av. ann. inflation 2001–06	4.4%	Broad money	15.3%
Lending rate, 2006	11.19%		

Exchange rates

	end 2006		*December 2006*
Rs per $	44.25	Effective rates	*2000 = 100*
Rs per SDR	66.56	– nominal	...
Rs per €	58.41	– real	...

Trade

Principal exports[a]		**Principal imports**[a]	
	$bn fob		*$bn cif*
Engineering goods	20.9	Petroleum & products	26.2
Textiles	15.6	Capital goods	13.8
Gems & jewellery	15.1	Electronic goods	9.9
Petroleum & products	11.2	Gold & silver	8.4
Agricultural goods	9.9	Gems	6.9
Total incl. others	**102.9**	Total incl. others	**145.7**

Main export destinations		**Main origins of imports**	
	% of total		*% of total*
United States	19.1	China	7.3
China	9.4	United States	6.5
United Arab Emirates	8.4	Belgium	5.2
United Kingdom	4.9	Singapore	4.8

Balance of payments[a], reserves and debt, $bn

Visible exports fob	105.2	Change in reserves	6.2
Visible imports fob	-157.0	Level of reserves	
Trade balance	-51.8	end Dec.	137.8
Invisibles inflows	67.1	No. months of import cover	8.0
Invisibles outflows	-48.7	Official gold holdings, m oz	11.5
Net transfers	24.3	Foreign debt	123.1
Current account balance	-9.2	– as % of GDP	16
– as % of GDP	-1.5	– as % of total exports	73
Capital balance	17.2	Debt service ratio	12
Overall balance	15.1		

Health and education

Health spending, % of GDP	5.8	Education spending, % of GDP	3.7
Doctors per 1,000 pop.	0.6	Enrolment, %: primary	101
Hospital beds per 1,000 pop.	0.7	secondary	54
Improved-water source access,		tertiary	7
% of pop.	86		

Society

No. of households	206.3m	Colour TVs per 100 households	36.5
Av. no. per household	5.3	Telephone lines per 100 pop.	4.5
Marriages per 1,000 pop.	...	Mobile telephone subscribers	
Divorces per 1,000 pop.	...	per 100 pop.	8.2
Cost of living, Dec. 2006		Computers per 100 pop.	1.5
New York = 100	45	Internet hosts per 1,000 pop.	1.5

a Year ending March 31, 2006.
b Year ending March 31, 2005.

INDONESIA

Area	1,904,443 sq km	Capital	Jakarta
Arable as % of total land	13	Currency	Rupiah (Rp)

People

Population	222.8m	Life expectancy: men	68.7 yrs
Pop. per sq km	116.9	women	72.7 yrs
Av. ann. growth		Adult literacy	90.4%
in pop. 2005–10	1.16%	Fertility rate (per woman)	2.2
Pop. under 15	28.4%	Urban population	48.1%
Pop. over 60	8.3%		*per 1,000 pop.*
No. of men per 100 women	100	Crude birth rate	18.7
Human Development Index	71.1	Crude death rate	6.3

The economy

GDP	Rp2,730trn	GDP per head	$1,290
GDP	$287bn	GDP per head in purchasing	
Av. ann. growth in real		power parity (USA=100)	9.2
GDP 1995–2005	2.7%	Economic freedom index	55.1

Origins of GDP   **Components of GDP**

	% of total		*% of total*
Agriculture	14.5	Private consumption	65.4
Industry, of which:	44.0	Public consumption	8.2
manufacturing	28.1	Investment	22.0
Services	41.5	Exports	33.5
		Imports	-29.2

Structure of employment

	% of total		*% of labour force*
Agriculture	44	Unemployed 2004	9.9
Industry	18	Av. ann. rate 1995–2004	6.7
Services	38		

Energy

	m TOE		
Total output	258.0	Net energy imports as %	
Total consumption	174.0	of energy use	-48
Consumption per head,			
kg oil equivalent	800		

Inflation and finance

Consumer price		*av. ann. increase 2000–05*	
inflation 2006	13.1%	Narrow money (M1)	11.0%
Av. ann. inflation 2001–06	9.6%	Broad money	9.9%
Money market rate, 2006	9.18%		

Exchange rates

	end 2006		*December 2006*
Rp per $	9,020	Effective rates	*2000 = 100*
Rp per SDR	13,570	– nominal	...
Rp per €	11,906	– real	...

Trade

Principal exports		Principal imports	
	$bn fob		*$bn cif*
Petroleum & products	10.1	Raw materials	44.1
Natural gas	9.2	Capital goods	8.3
Garments & textiles	8.6	Consumer goods	4.6
Total incl. others	**84.6**	**Total incl. others**	**69.5**

Main export destinations		Main origins of imports	
	% of total		*% of total*
Japan	22.3	Japan	18.0
United States	13.9	China	16.1
China	9.1	Singapore	12.8
Singapore	8.9	Thailand	7.7

Balance of payments, reserves and debt, $bn

Visible exports fob	86.2	Change in reserves	-1.7
Visible imports fob	-63.9	Level of reserves	
Trade balance	22.3	end Dec.	34.6
Invisibles inflows	15.3	No. months of import cover	4.1
Invisibles outflows	-37.9	Official gold holdings, m oz	3.1
Net transfers	1.2	Foreign debt	138.3
Current account balance	0.9	– as % of GDP	55
– as % of GDP	0.3	– as % of total exports	159
Capital balance	-4.5	Debt service ratio	17
Overall balance	-5.6		

Health and education

Health spending, % of GDP	2.8	Education spending, % of GDP	0.9
Doctors per 1,000 pop.	0.1	Enrolment, %: primary	108
Hospital beds per 1,000 pop.	0.6	secondary	64
Improved-water source access,		tertiary	11
% of pop.	77		

Society

No. of households	58.6m	Colour TVs per 100 households	53.4
Av. no. per household	3.8	Telephone lines per 100 pop.	5.7
Marriages per 1,000 pop.	7.3	Mobile telephone subscribers	
Divorces per 1,000 pop.	0.8	per 100 pop.	21.1
Cost of living, Dec. 2006		Computers per 100 pop.	1.4
New York = 100	76	Internet hosts per 1,000 pop.	1.2

IRAN

Area	1,648,000 sq km	Capital	Tehran
Arable as % of total land	10	Currency	Rial (IR)

People

Population	69.5m	Life expectancy: men	69.4 yrs
Pop. per sq km	42.2	women	72.6 yrs
Av. ann. growth		Adult literacy	77.0%
in pop. 2005–10	1.35%	Fertility rate (per woman)	2.0
Pop. under 15	28.8%	Urban population	66.9%
Pop. over 60	6.4%		per 1,000 pop.
No. of men per 100 women	103	Crude birth rate	20.3
Human Development Index	74.6	Crude death rate	5.4

The economy

GDP	IR1,701trn	GDP per head	$2,730
GDP	$190bn	GDP per head in purchasing	
Av. ann. growth in real		power parity (USA=100)	19.0
GDP 1995–2005	4.6%	Economic freedom index	43.1

Origins of GDP

	% of total
Agriculture	10
Industry, of which:	45
manufacturing	12
Services	45

Components of GDP

	% of total
Private consumption	46
Public consumption	12
Investment	33
Exports	39
Imports	-30

Structure of employment

	% of total		% of labour force
Agriculture	25	Unemployed 2003	11.6
Industry	30	Av. ann. rate 2000–2003	13.2
Services	45		

Energy

	m TOE		
Total output	278.0	Net energy imports as %	
Total consumption	145.8	of energy use	-91
Consumption per head,			
kg oil equivalent	2,167		

Inflation and finance

		av. ann. increase 2000–05	
Consumer price			
inflation 2005	12.1%	Narrow money (M1)	20.6%
Av. ann. inflation 2001–05	14.7%	Broad money	24.5%
Deposit rate, 2006	11.78%		

Exchange rates

	end 2006		December 2006
IR per $	9,223	Effective rates	2000 = 100
IR per SDR	13,875	– nominal	73.87
IR per €	12,174	– real	140.71

Trade

Principal exports[a]		Principal imports[a]	
	$bn fob		*$bn cif*
Oil & gas	36.8	Capital goods	12.1
Chemicals & petrochemicals	1.4	Industrial goods	12.0
Fruits	0.8	Consumer goods	6.4
Total incl. others	**44.4**	Total incl. others	**35.2**

Main export destinations		Main origins of imports	
	% of total		*% of total*
Japan	16.0	Germany	14.6
China	10.6	United Arab Emirates	8.8
Italy	5.7	China	8.7
South Korea	5.5	Italy	7.4
Turkey	5.4	France	6.6

Balance of payments[b], reserves and debt, $bn

Visible exports fob	60.0	Change in reserves	...
Visible imports fob	-41.0	Level of reserves	
Trade balance	19.0	end Dec.	...
Invisibles net	-5.9	No. months of import cover	...
Net transfers	0.9	Official gold holdings, m oz	...
Current account balance	14.0	Foreign debt	21.3
– as % of GDP	7.1	– as % of GDP	13
Capital balance	-0.4	– as % of total exports	39
		Debt service ratio	4

Health and education

Health spending, % of GDP	6.6	Education spending, % of GDP	4.7
Doctors per 1,000 pop.	0.9	Enrolment, %: primary	88
Hospital beds per 1,000 pop.	1.7	secondary	82
Improved-water source access,		tertiary	10
% of pop.	94		

Society

No. of households	13.0m	Colour TVs per 100 households	9.5
Av. no. per household	5.4	Telephone lines per 100 pop.	27.3
Marriages per 1,000 pop.	8.9	Mobile telephone subscribers	
Divorces per 1,000 pop.	0.9	per 100 pop.	10.4
Cost of living, Dec. 2006		Computers per 100 pop.	10.5
New York = 100	34	Internet hosts per 1,000 pop.	...

a 2004
b Iranian year ending March 20, 2006.

IRELAND

Area	70,282 sq km	Capital	Dublin
Arable as % of total land	18	Currency	Euro (€)

People

Population	4.1m	Life expectancy: men	76.5 yrs
Pop. per sq km	58.3	women	81.4 yrs
Av. ann. growth		Adult literacy	...
in pop. 2005–10	1.77%	Fertility rate (per woman)	2.0
Pop. under 15	20.7%	Urban population	60.5%
Pop. over 60	15.3%		per 1,000 pop.
No. of men per 100 women	100	Crude birth rate	15.5
Human Development Index	95.6	Crude death rate	7.0

The economy

GDP	€162bn	GDP per head	$49,220
GDP	$202bn	GDP per head in purchasing	
Av. ann. growth in real		power parity (USA=100)	91.9
GDP 1995–2005	7.4%	Economic freedom index	81.3

Origins of GDP		**Components of GDP**	
	% of total		% of total
Agriculture	3.3	Private consumption	46.1
Industry, of which:	38.8	Public consumption	14.2
manufacturing	...	Investment	27.0
Services	57.9	Exports	79.4
		Imports	-66.2

Structure of employment

	% of total		% of labour force
Agriculture	6	Unemployed 2004	4.4
Industry	28	Av. ann. rate 1995–2004	6.9
Services	66		

Energy

	m TOE		
Total output	1.9	Net energy imports as %	
Total consumption	15.2	of energy use	87
Consumption per head,			
kg oil equivalent	3,738		

Inflation and finance

Consumer price			av. ann. increase 2000–05
inflation 2006	2.7%	Euro area:	
Av. ann. inflation 2001–06	3.2%	Narrow money (M1)	10.8%
Money market rate, 2004	2.21%	Broad money	7.7%
Deposit rate, households, 2006	2.64%		

Exchange rates

	end 2006		December 2006
€ per $	0.76	Effective rates	2000 = 100
€ per SDR	1.14	– nominal	...
		– real	...

Trade

Principal exports		Principal imports	
	$bn fob		*$bn cif*
Chemicals	50.1	Machinery & transport	
Machinery & transport		equipment	30.8
equipment	29.2	Chemicals	9.1
Manufactured materials	12.9	Miscellaneous manufactures	8.6
Food & live animals	7.9	Fuels	4.8
Total incl. others	**109.6**	Total incl. others	**69.2**

Main export destinations		Main origins of imports	
	% of total		*% of total*
United States	18.7	United Kingdom	31.2
United Kingdom	17.4	Germany	14.1
Belgium	15.1	United States	14.1
Germany	7.5	China	6.6
France	6.4	Netherlands	4.0
EU25	63.3	EU25	57.4

Balance of payments, reserves and aid, $bn

Visible exports fob	104.1	Overall balance	-1.8
Visible imports fob	-67.3	Change in reserves	-2.0
Trade balance	36.8	Level of reserves	
Invisibles inflows	111.2	end Dec.	0.9
Invisibles outflows	-156.0	No. months of import cover	0.0
Net transfers	0.7	Official gold holdings, m oz	0.2
Current account balance	-5.3	Aid given	0.72
– as % of GDP	-2.7	– as % of GDP	0.42
Capital balance	-2.7		

Health and education

Health spending, % of GDP	7.2	Education spending, % of GDP	4.5
Doctors per 1,000 pop.	2.8	Enrolment, %: primary	119
Hospital beds per 1,000 pop.	5.7	secondary	112
Improved-water source access,		tertiary	46
% of pop.	...		

Society

No. of households	1.4m	Colour TVs per 100 households	99.4
Av. no. per household	2.9	Telephone lines per 100 pop.	49.5
Marriages per 1,000 pop.	5.1	Mobile telephone subscribers	
Divorces per 1,000 pop.	0.7	per 100 pop.	102.9
Cost of living, Dec. 2006		Computers per 100 pop.	49.7
New York = 100	104	Internet hosts per 1,000 pop.	294.7

ISRAEL

Area	20,770 sq km	Capital	Jerusalem
Arable as % of total land	15	Currency	New Shekel (NIS)

People

Population	6.7m	Life expectancy: men	78.6 yrs
Pop. per sq km	322.6	women	82.8 yrs
Av. ann. growth		Adult literacy	97.1%
in pop. 2005–10	1.66%	Fertility rate (per woman)	2.8
Pop. under 15	27.9%	Urban population	91.6%
Pop. over 60	13.2%		per 1,000 pop.
No. of men per 100 women	98	Crude birth rate	19.7
Human Development Index	92.7	Crude death rate	5.5

The economy

GDP	NIS554bn	GDP per head	$18,420
GDP	$123bn	GDP per head in purchasing	
Av. ann. growth in real		power parity (USA=100)	61.7
GDP 1995–2005	3.2%	Economic freedom index	68.4

Origins of GDP		Components of GDP	
	% of total		% of total
Agriculture	2.6	Private consumption	55.1
Industry, of which:	31.7	Public consumption	26.9
manufacturing	21.2	Investment	16.8
Services	65.7	Exports	44.6
		Imports	-44.3

Structure of employment

	% of total		% of labour force
Agriculture	2	Unemployed 2003	10.7
Industry	22	Av. ann. rate 1995–2003	8.7
Services	76		

Energy

	m TOE		
Total output	1.7	Net energy imports as %	
Total consumption	20.7	of energy use	92
Consumption per head,			
kg oil equivalent	3,049		

Inflation and finance

Consumer price		av. ann. increase 2000–05	
inflation 2006	2.1%	Narrow money (M1)	14.5%
Av. ann. inflation 2001–06	1.9%	Broad money	6.1%
Treasury bill rate, 2005	4.3%		

Exchange rates

	end 2006		December 2006
NIS per $	4.23	Effective rates	2000 = 100
NIS per SDR	6.36	– nominal	84.68
NIS per €	5.58	– real	79.45

Trade

Principal exports		**Principal imports**	
	$bn fob		*$bn fob*
Diamonds	12.1	Diamonds	9.6
Chemicals	6.8	Fuel	6.8
Communications, medical &		Machinery & equipment	4.9
scientific equipment	6.0	Chemicals	2.9
Electronics	2.4		
Total incl. others	**42.8**	Total incl. others	**47.1**

Main export destinations		**Main origins of imports**	
	% of total		*% of total*
United States	42.4	United States	19.7
Belgium	8.6	Belgium	9.9
Hong Kong	4.9	Germany	7.2
United Kingdom	4.6	Switzerland	6.6
Germany	3.9	United Kingdom	6.0

Balance of payments, reserves and debt, $bn

Visible exports fob	40.1	Change in reserves	1.0
Visible imports fob	-43.9	Level of reserves	
Trade balance	-3.8	end Dec.	28.1
Invisibles inflows	22.4	No. months of import cover	5.2
Invisibles outflows	-21.0	Official gold holdings, m oz	0.0
Net transfers	6.0	Foreign debt	76.4
Current account balance	3.8	– as % of GDP	60
– as % of GDP	3.0	– as % of total exports	117
Capital balance	-5.1	Debt service ratio	11
Overall balance	1.3		

Health and education

Health spending, % of GDP	8.7	Education spending, % of GDP	7.3
Doctors per 1,000 pop.	3.8	Enrolment, %: primary	114
Hospital beds per 1,000 pop.	6.3	secondary	93
Improved-water source access,		tertiary	50
% of pop.	100		

Society

No. of households	2.0m	Colour TVs per 100 households	96.9
Av. no. per household	3.5	Telephone lines per 100 pop.	42.6
Marriages per 1,000 pop.	5.3	Mobile telephone subscribers	
Divorces per 1,000 pop.	1.6	per 100 pop.	112.4
Cost of living, Dec. 2006		Computers per 100 pop.	73.4
New York = 100	88	Internet hosts per 1,000 pop.	195.8

ITALY

Area	301,245 sq km	Capital	Rome
Arable as % of total land	26	Currency	Euro (€)

People

Population	58.1m	Life expectancy: men	77.5 yrs
Pop. per sq km	192.9	women	83.5 yrs
Av. ann. growth		Adult literacy	98.4%
in pop. 2005–10	0.13%	Fertility rate (per woman)	1.4
Pop. under 15	14.0%	Urban population	67.6%
Pop. over 60	25.3%		*per 1,000 pop.*
No. of men per 100 women	94	Crude birth rate	9.2
Human Development Index	94.0	Crude death rate	10.5

The economy

GDP	€1,417bn	GDP per head	$30,340
GDP	$1,763bn	GDP per head in purchasing	
Av. ann. growth in real		power parity (USA=100)	68.1
GDP 1995–2005	1.3%	Economic freedom index	63.4

Origins of GDP		**Components of GDP**	
	% of total		*% of total*
Agriculture	2.1	Private consumption	58.5
Industry, of which:	29.1	Public consumption	20.7
manufacturing	...	Investment	20.6
Services	68.8	Exports	26.3
		Imports	-26.4

Structure of employment

	% of total		*% of labour force*
Agriculture	4	Unemployed 2004	8.0
Industry	31	Av. ann. rate 1995–2004	10.3
Services	65		

Energy

	m TOE		
Total output	30.1	Net energy imports as %	
Total consumption	184.5	of energy use	84
Consumption per head,			
kg oil equivalent	3,171		

Inflation and finance

Consumer price		*av. ann. increase 2000–05*	
inflation 2006	2.2%	Euro area:	
Av. ann. inflation 2001–06	2.4%	Narrow money (M1)	10.8%
Money market rate, 2006	3.09%	Broad money	7.7%
		Household saving rate, 2004	10.2%

Exchange rates

	end 2006		*December 2006*
€ per $	0.76	Effective rates	*2000 = 100*
€ per SDR	1.14	– nominal	108.9
		– real	132.4

Trade

Principal exports		Principal imports	
	$bn fob		*$bn cif*
Engineering products	107.5	Engineering products	73.9
Textiles & clothing	47.9	Energy products	51.1
Transport equipment	40.2	Transport equipment	51.1
Chemicals	37.5	Chemicals	50.8
Food, drink & tobacco	20.0	Food, drink & tobacco	24.9
Total incl. others	**372.9**	Total incl. others	**384.8**

Main export destinations		Main origins of imports	
	% of total		*% of total*
Germany	13.6	Germany	18.0
France	12.4	France	11.0
United States	7.9	Netherlands	5.9
Spain	7.3	United Kingdom	4.3
United Kingdom	7.1	United States	3.5
EU25	58.6	EU25	57.2

Balance of payments, reserves and aid, $bn

Visible exports fob	372.8	Overall balance	-1.0
Visible imports fob	-372.7	Change in reserves	3.6
Trade balance	0.1	Level of reserves	
Invisibles inflows	151.4	end Dec.	66.0
Invisibles outflows	-169.0	No. months of import cover	1.5
Net transfers	-10.0	Official gold holdings, m oz	78.8
Current account balance	-27.7	Aid given	5.09
– as % of GDP	-1.6	– as % of GDP	0.29
Capital balance	25.2		

Health and education

Health spending, % of GDP	8.7	Education spending, % of GDP	4.9
Doctors per 1,000 pop.	4.2	Enrolment, %: primary	101
Hospital beds per 1,000 pop.	4.0	secondary	99
Improved-water source access, % of pop.	...	tertiary	47

Society

No. of households	22.4m	Colour TVs per 100 households	96.0
Av. no. per household	2.6	Telephone lines per 100 pop.	43.1
Marriages per 1,000 pop.	4.5	Mobile telephone subscribers	
Divorces per 1,000 pop.	0.8	per 100 pop.	124.3
Cost of living, Dec. 2006		Computers per 100 pop.	37.0
New York = 100	98	Internet hosts per 1,000 pop.	238.5

JAPAN

Area	377,727 sq km	Capital	Tokyo
Arable as % of total land	12	Currency	Yen (¥)

People

Population	128.1m	Life expectancy:	men	79.0 yrs
Pop. per sq km	339.1		women	86.1 yrs
Av. ann. growth		Adult literacy		...
in pop. 2005–10	-0.02%	Fertility rate (per woman)		1.3
Pop. under 15	13.9%	Urban population		65.8%
Pop. over 60	26.4%			*per 1,000 pop.*
No. of men per 100 women	95	Crude birth rate		8.3
Human Development Index	94.9	Crude death rate		9.0

The economy

GDP	¥500trn	GDP per head	$35,390
GDP	$4,534bn	GDP per head in purchasing	
Av. ann. growth in real		power parity (USA=100)	74.6
GDP 1995–2005	1.3%	Economic freedom index	73.6

Origins of GDP[a]		**Components of GDP**	
	% of total		*% of total*
Agriculture	1.7	Private consumption	57.4
Industry, of which:	30.0	Public consumption	18.0
manufacturing	21.0	Investment	23.2
Services	68.3	Exports	14.3
		Imports	-12.9

Structure of employment

	% of total		*% of labour force*
Agriculture	4	Unemployed 2004	4.7
Industry	28	Av. ann. rate 1995–2004	4.4
Services	68		

Energy

	m TOE		
Total output	96.8	Net energy imports as %	
Total consumption	533.2	of energy use	82
Consumption per head,			
kg oil equivalent	4,173		

Inflation and finance

Consumer price		*av. ann. increase 2000–05*	
inflation 2006	0.2%	Narrow money (M1)	7.8%
Av. ann. inflation 2001–06	-0.3%	Broad money	-3.2%
Money market rate, 2006	0.12%	Household saving rate, 2006	2.9%

Exchange rates

	end 2006		*December 2006*
¥ per $	118.0	Effective rates	*2000 = 100*
¥ per SDR	179.0	– nominal	77.7
¥ per €	157.0	– real	65.7

Trade

Principal exports		Principal imports	
	$bn fob		*$bn cif*
Transport machinery	137.9	Mineral fuels	132.1
Electrical equipment	132.1	Machinery & equipment	118.4
Non-electrical machinery	120.9	Food	50.4
Chemicals	53.1	Chemicals	39.2
Metals	27.6	Raw materials	31.5
Total incl. others	**594.9**	Total incl. others	**514.9**

Main export destinations		Main origins of imports	
	% of total		*% of total*
United States	22.6	China	21.0
China	13.5	United States	12.4
South Korea	7.8	Australia	4.7
Taiwan	7.3	South Korea	4.7
Hong Kong	6.0	Taiwan	3.5

Balance of payments, reserves and aid, $bn

Visible exports fob	567.6	Overall balance	22.3
Visible imports fob	-473.6	Change in reserves	2.2
Trade balance	94.0	Level of reserves	
Invisibles inflows	251.3	end Dec.	846.9
Invisibles outflows	-171.9	No. months of import cover	15.7
Net transfers	-7.6	Official gold holdings, m oz	24.6
Current account balance	165.8	Aid given	13.15
– as % of GDP	3.7	– as % of GDP	0.28
Capital balance	-127.6		

Health and education

Health spending, % of GDP	7.8	Education spending, % of GDP	3.7
Doctors per 1,000 pop.	2.0	Enrolment, %: primary	101
Hospital beds per 1,000 pop.	14.3	secondary	102
Improved-water source access,		tertiary	46
% of pop.	100		

Society

No. of households	48.5m	Colour TVs per 100 households	99.0
Av. no. per household	2.6	Telephone lines per 100 pop.	45.3
Marriages per 1,000 pop.	5.6	Mobile telephone subscribers	
Divorces per 1,000 pop.	2.0	per 100 pop.	75.3
Cost of living, Dec. 2006		Computers per 100 pop.	54.2
New York = 100	124	Internet hosts per 1,000 pop.	240.8

a 2003

KENYA

Area	582,646 sq km	Capital	Nairobi
Arable as % of total land	8	Currency	Kenyan shilling (KSh)

People

Population	34.3m	Life expectancy:	men	53.0 yrs
Pop. per sq km	58.9		women	55.2 yrs
Av. ann. growth		Adult literacy		73.6%
in pop. 2005–10	2.65%	Fertility rate (per woman)		5.0
Pop. under 15	42.6%	Urban population		20.7%
Pop. over 60	3.9%			*per 1,000 pop.*
No. of men per 100 women	99	Crude birth rate		39.2
Human Development Index	49.1	Crude death rate		11.8

The economy

GDP	KSh1,415bn	GDP per head	$550
GDP	$18.7bn	GDP per head in purchasing	
Av. ann. growth in real		power parity (USA=100)	3.0
GDP 1995–2005	2.5%	Economic freedom index	59.4

Origins of GDP		**Components of GDP**	
	% of total		*% of total*
Agriculture	26.0	Private consumption	75.3
Industry, of which:	...	Public consumption	17.6
manufacturing	9.9	Investment	16.1
Other	64.1	Exports	26.2
		Imports	-33.9

Structure of employment

	% of total		*% of labour force*
Agriculture	...	Unemployed 2004	...
Industry	...	Av. ann. rate 1995–2004	...
Services	...		

Energy

	m TOE		
Total output	13.7	Net energy imports as %	
Total consumption	16.9	of energy use	19
Consumption per head,			
kg oil equivalent	506		

Inflation and finance

		av. ann. increase 2000–05	
Consumer price			
inflation 2006	14.1%	Narrow money (M1)	14.2%
Av. ann. inflation 2001–06	9.5%	Broad money	10.0%
Treasury bill rate, 2006	6.43%		

Exchange rates

	end 2006		*December 2006*
KSh per $	69.4	Effective rates	*2000 = 100*
KSh per SDR	104.4	– nominal	...
KSh per €	91.6	– real	...

Trade

Principal exports	$m fob	Principal imports	$m cif
Horticultural products	590	Industrial supplies	1,781
Tea	560	Machinery & transport equip.	735
Coffee	128	Consumer goods	399
Fish products	61	Food & drink	342
Total incl. others	**3,293**	Total incl. others	**6,149**

Main export destinations	% of total	Main origins of imports	% of total
Uganda	14.0	United Arab Emirates	13.0
United Kingdom	10.4	United States	10.2
United States	9.2	Saudi Arabia	9.4
Netherlands	7.8	South Africa	8.6

Balance of payments, reserves and debt, $bn

Visible exports fob	3.2	Change in reserves	0.3
Visible imports fob	-5.4	Level of reserves	
Trade balance	-2.2	end Dec.	1.8
Invisibles inflows	2.0	No. months of import cover	3.2
Invisibles outflows	-1.3	Official gold holdings, m oz	0.0
Net transfers	1.0	Foreign debt	6.2
Current account balance	-0.5	– as % of GDP	28
– as % of GDP	-2.8	– as % of total exports	103
Capital balance	0.6	Debt service ratio	4
Overall balance	0.1		

Health and education

Health spending, % of GDP	4.1	Education spending, % of GDP	6.7
Doctors per 1,000 pop.	0.1	Enrolment, %: primary	91
Hospital beds per 1,000 pop.	1.9	secondary	33
Improved-water source access,		tertiary	1
% of pop.	61		

Society

No. of households	7.7m	Colour TVs per 100 households	11.9
Av. no. per household	4.2	Telephone lines per 100 pop.	0.8
Marriages per 1,000 pop.	...	Mobile telephone subscribers	
Divorces per 1,000 pop.	...	per 100 pop.	13.5
Cost of living, Dec. 2006		Computers per 100 pop.	1.0
New York = 100	68	Internet hosts per 1,000 pop.	0.4

LATVIA

Area	63,700 sq km	Capital	Riga
Arable as % of total land	18	Currency	Lats (LVL)

People

Population	2.3m	Life expectancy: men		67.3 yrs
Pop. per sq km	36.1	women		77.7 yrs
Av. ann. growth		Adult literacy		99.7%
in pop. 2005–10	-0.52%	Fertility rate (per woman)		1.3
Pop. under 15	14.4%	Urban population		67.8%
Pop. over 60	22.4%			per 1,000 pop.
No. of men per 100 women	85	Crude birth rate		9.3
Human Development Index	84.5	Crude death rate		13.6

The economy

GDP	LVL8.9bn	GDP per head	$6,880
GDP	$15.8bn	GDP per head in purchasing	
Av. ann. growth in real		power parity (USA=100)	32.6
GDP 1995–2005	6.9%	Economic freedom index	68.2

Origins of GDP		**Components of GDP**	
	% of total		% of total
Agriculture	4.1	Private consumption	62.4
Industry, of which:	21.7	Public consumption	17.7
manufacturing	12.8	Investment	29.8
Services	74.2	Exports	48.1
		Imports	-62.4

Structure of employment

	% of total		% of labour force
Agriculture	12	Unemployed 2005	8.7
Industry	26	Av. ann. rate 1996–2005	13.3
Services	62		

Energy

			m TOE
Total output	2.1	Net energy imports as %	
Total consumption	4.6	of energy use	53
Consumption per head,			
kg oil equivalent	1,988		

Inflation and finance

Consumer price		av. ann. increase 2000–05	
inflation 2006	6.5%	Narrow money (M1)	21.8%
Av. ann. inflation 2001–06	4.8%	Broad money	25.2%
Money market rate, 2006	3.24%		

Exchange rates

	end 2006		December 2006
LVL per $	0.54	Effective rates	2000 = 100
LVL per SDR	0.81	– nominal	...
LVL per €	0.71	– real	...

Trade

Principal exports		Principal imports	
	$bn fob		*$bn cif*
Wood & wood products	1.3	Machinery & equipment	1.7
Metals	0.7	Mineral products	1.3
Machinery & equipment	0.5	Transport equipment	0.9
Textiles	0.4	Base metals	0.8
Total incl. others	**5.1**	Total incl. others	**8.6**

Main export destinations		Main origins of imports	
	% of total		*% of total*
Estonia	10.8	Germany	13.8
Lithuania	10.8	Lithuania	13.7
Germany	10.3	Russia	8.6
United Kingdom	10.1	Estonia	7.9
Russia	8.0	Poland	6.3
EU25	76.2	EU25	75.0

Balance of payments, reserves and debt, $bn

Visible exports fob	5.4	Change in reserves	0.3
Visible imports fob	-8.4	Level of reserves	
Trade balance	-3.0	end Dec.	2.4
Invisibles inflows	2.9	No. months of import cover	2.6
Invisibles outflows	-2.5	Official gold holdings, m oz	0.2
Net transfers	0.6	Foreign debt	14.3
Current account balance	-2.0	– as % of GDP	104
– as % of GDP	-12.7	– as % of total exports	211
Capital balance	2.8	Debt service ratio	37
Overall balance	0.5		

Health and education

Health spending, % of GDP	7.1	Education spending, % of GDP	5.3
Doctors per 1,000 pop.	3.0	Enrolment, %: primary	101
Hospital beds per 1,000 pop.	7.7	secondary	97
Improved-water source access,		tertiary	50
% of pop.	99		

Society

No. of households	0.8m	Colour TVs per 100 households	72.2
Av. no. per household	2.9	Telephone lines per 100 pop.	31.7
Marriages per 1,000 pop.	4.6	Mobile telephone subscribers	
Divorces per 1,000 pop.	2.3	per 100 pop.	81.1
Cost of living, Dec. 2006		Computers per 100 pop.	21.9
New York = 100	...	Internet hosts per 1,000 pop.	57.5

LITHUANIA

Area	65,200 sq km	Capital	Vilnius
Arable as % of total land	30	Currency	Litas (LTL)

People

Population	3.4m	Life expectancy: men	67.5 yrs
Pop. per sq km	52.1	women	78.3 yrs
Av. ann. growth		Adult literacy	99.6%
in pop. 2005–10	-0.53%	Fertility rate (per woman)	1.3
Pop. under 15	16.8%	Urban population	66.6%
Pop. over 60	20.3%		per 1,000 pop.
No. of men per 100 women	87	Crude birth rate	9.1
Human Development Index	85.7	Crude death rate	12.3

The economy

GDP	LTL71.1bn	GDP per head	$7,540
GDP	$25.6bn	GDP per head in purchasing	
Av. ann. growth in real		power parity (USA=100)	34.6
GDP 1995–2005	5.9%	Economic freedom index	72.0

Origins of GDP		**Components of GDP**	
	% of total		% of total
Agriculture	5.7	Private consumption	65.3
Industry, of which:	34.3	Public consumption	16.7
manufacturing	...	Investment	22.4
Services	60.0	Exports	58.3
		Imports	-65.3

Structure of employment

	% of total		% of labour force
Agriculture	14	Unemployed 2005	8.3
Industry	29	Av. ann. rate 1995–2005	14.1
Services	57		

Energy

		m TOE	
Total output	5.2	Net energy imports as %	
Total consumption	9.2	of energy use	43
Consumption per head,			
kg oil equivalent	2,666		

Inflation and finance

Consumer price		av. ann. increase 2000–05	
inflation 2006	3.8%	Narrow money (M1)	24.1%
Av. ann. inflation 2001–06	1.3%	Broad money	22.6%
Money market rate, 2006	2.72%		

Exchange rates

	end 2006		December 2006
LTL per $	2.63	Effective rates	2000 = 100
LTL per SDR	3.96	– nominal	...
LTL per €	3.47	– real	...

Trade

Principal exports		**Principal imports**	
	$bn fob		*$bn cif*
Mineral products	3.2	Mineral products	4.0
Machinery & equipment	1.5	Machinery & equipment	2.8
Textiles	1.1	Transport equipment	1.8
Transport equipment	1.0	Chemicals	1.2
Total incl. others	**11.8**	Total incl. others	**15.5**

Main export destinations		**Main origins of imports**	
	% of total		*% of total*
Russia	10.4	Russia	27.8
Latvia	10.3	Germany	15.2
Germany	9.4	Poland	8.3
France	7.0	Latvia	4.0
Estonia	5.9	Netherlands	3.7
EU25	65.4	EU25	59.3

Balance of payments, reserves and debt, $bn

Visible exports fob	11.8	Change in reserves	0.2
Visible imports fob	-14.7	Level of reserves	
Trade balance	-2.9	end Dec.	3.8
Invisibles inflows	3.6	No. months of import cover	2.6
Invisibles outflows	-3.1	Official gold holdings, m oz	0.2
Net transfers	0.7	Foreign debt	11.2
Current account balance	-1.8	– as % of GDP	52
– as % of GDP	-7.2	– as % of total exports	90
Capital balance	2.6	Debt service ratio	17
Overall balance	0.7		

Health and education

Health spending, % of GDP	6.5	Education spending, % of GDP	5.2
Doctors per 1,000 pop.	4.0	Enrolment, %: primary	101
Hospital beds per 1,000 pop.	8.1	secondary	102
Improved-water source access,		tertiary	40
% of pop.	...		

Society

No. of households	1.4m	Colour TVs per 100 households	76.0
Av. no. per household	2.5	Telephone lines per 100 pop.	22.1
Marriages per 1,000 pop.	5.8	Mobile telephone subscribers	
Divorces per 1,000 pop.	3.3	per 100 pop.	127.1
Cost of living, Dec. 2006		Computers per 100 pop.	15.5
New York = 100	...	Internet hosts per 1,000 pop.	70.8

MALAYSIA

Area	332,665 sq km	Capital	Kuala Lumpur
Arable as % of total land	6	Currency	Malaysian dollar/ringgit (M$)

People

Population	25.3m	Life expectancy: men		72.0 yrs
Pop. per sq km	76.0	women		76.7 yrs
Av. ann. growth		Adult literacy		88.7%
in pop. 2005–10	1.69%	Fertility rate (per woman)		2.6
Pop. under 15	31.4%	Urban population		67.3%
Pop. over 60	6.7%		*per 1,000 pop.*	
No. of men per 100 women	103	Crude birth rate		20.6
Human Development Index	80.5	Crude death rate		4.5

The economy

GDP	M$495bn	GDP per head	$5,150
GDP	$130bn	GDP per head in purchasing	
Av. ann. growth in real		power parity (USA=100)	26.0
GDP 1995–2005	4.6%	Economic freedom index	65.8

Origins of GDP		**Components of GDP**	
	% of total		*% of total*
Agriculture	8.7	Private consumption	43.7
Industry, of which:	48.7	Public consumption	13.1
manufacturing	30.5	Investment	20.0
Services	42.6	Exports	123.1
		Imports	-99.7

Structure of employment

	% of total		*% of labour force*
Agriculture	15	Unemployed 2004	3.5
Industry	30	Av. ann. rate 1995–2004	3.2
Services	55		

Energy

	m TOE		
Total output	88.5	Net energy imports as %	
Total consumption	56.7	of energy use	-56
Consumption per head,			
kg oil equivalent	2,279		

Inflation and finance

Consumer price		*av. ann. increase 2000–05*	
inflation 2006	3.6%	Narrow money (M1)	9.1%
Av. ann. inflation 2001–06	2.2%	Broad money	7.8%
Money market rate, 2006	3.38%		

Exchange rates

	end 2006		*December 2006*
M$ per $	3.53	Effective rates	*2000 = 100*
M$ per SDR	5.31	– nominal	99.5
M$ per €	4.66	– real	101.6

Trade

Principal exports	$bn fob	Principal imports	$bn cif
Electronics & electrical mach.	48.5	Intermediate goods	71.0
Chemicals & products	4.9	Capital goods & transport	14.0
Palm oil	4.4	equipment	
Wood products	2.7	Consumption goods	5.7
		Re-exports	5.0
Total incl. others	**140.9**	Total incl. others	**114.4**

Main export destinations	% of total	Main origins of imports	% of total
United States	22.4	Singapore	29.2
Singapore	17.6	Japan	12.1
China	13.0	China	10.2
Japan	9.5	United States	10.0
Thailand	5.2	Thailand	5.5

Balance of payments, reserves and debt, $bn

Visible exports fob	141.8	Change in reserves	3.6
Visible imports fob	-108.7	Level of reserves	
Trade balance	33.2	end Dec.	70.5
Invisibles inflows	24.9	No. months of import cover	5.9
Invisibles outflows	-33.7	Official gold holdings, m oz	1.2
Net transfers	-4.5	Foreign debt	51.0
Current account balance	20.0	– as % of GDP	46
– as % of GDP	15.4	– as % of total exports	35
Capital balance	-9.8	Debt service ratio	6
Overall balance	3.6		

Health and education

Health spending, % of GDP	3.8	Education spending, % of GDP	8.0
Doctors per 1,000 pop.	0.7	Enrolment, %: primary	101
Hospital beds per 1,000 pop.	1.8	secondary	76
Improved-water source access,		tertiary	23
% of pop.	99		

Society

No. of households	5.6m	Colour TVs per 100 households	90.2
Av. no. per household	4.7	Telephone lines per 100 pop.	16.8
Marriages per 1,000 pop.	5.9	Mobile telephone subscribers	
Divorces per 1,000 pop.	...	per 100 pop.	75.2
Cost of living, Dec. 2006		Computers per 100 pop.	19.2
New York = 100	68	Internet hosts per 1,000 pop.	6.6

MEXICO

Area	1,972,545 sq km	Capital	Mexico city
Arable as % of total land	13	Currency	Mexican peso (PS)

People

Population	107.0m	Life expectancy:	men	73.7 yrs
Pop. per sq km	54.2		women	78.6 yrs
Av. ann. growth		Adult literacy		91.0%
in pop. 2005–10	1.12%	Fertility rate (per woman)		2.2
Pop. under 15	30.8%	Urban population		76.0%
Pop. over 60	8.4%			*per 1,000 pop.*
No. of men per 100 women	95	Crude birth rate		19.3
Human Development Index	82.1	Crude death rate		4.8

The economy

GDP	8,374bn pesos	GDP per head	$7,180
GDP	$768bn	GDP per head in purchasing	
Av. ann. growth in real		power parity (USA=100)	25.7
GDP 1995–2005	3.6%	Economic freedom index	65.8

Origins of GDP		**Components of GDP**	
	% of total		*% of total*
Agriculture	3.8	Private consumption	68.3
Industry, of which:	25.9	Public consumption	11.5
manufacturing & mining	19.2	Investment	19.3
Services	70.3	Exports	29.9
		Imports	-31.5

Structure of employment

	% of total		*% of labour force*
Agriculture	15	Unemployed 2004	3.0
Industry	26	Av. ann. rate 1995–2004	2.7
Services	59		

Energy

	m TOE		
Total output	253.9	Net energy imports as %	
Total consumption	165.5	of energy use	-53
Consumption per head,			
kg oil equivalent	1,622		

Inflation and finance

		av. ann. increase 2000–05	
Consumer price			
inflation 2006	3.6%	Narrow money (M1)	13.2%
Av. ann. inflation 2001–06	4.4%	Broad money	9.3%
Money market rate, 2006	7.51%		

Exchange rates

	end 2006		*December 2006*
PS per $	10.88	Effective rates	*2000 = 100*
PS per SDR	16.37	– nominal	...
PS per €	14.36	– real	...

Trade

Principal exports		**Principal imports**	
	$bn fob		*$bn fob*
Manufactured products	175.2	Intermediate goods	164.1
(Maquiladora[a]	*97.4)*	*(Maquiladora[a]*	*75.7)*
Crude oil & products	31.9	Consumer goods	31.5
Agricultural products	6.0	Capital goods	26.2
Total incl. others	**213.9**	Total	**221.4**

Main export destinations		**Main origins of imports**	
	% of total		*% of total*
United States	85.7	United States	59.5
Canada	2.0	Germany	3.8
Spain	1.3	Japan	3.4
Japan	1.1	South Korea	3.1

Balance of payments, reserves and debt, $bn

Visible exports fob	214.2	Change in reserves	9.9
Visible imports fob	-221.8	Level of reserves	
Trade balance	-7.6	end Dec.	74.1
Invisibles inflows	21.9	No. months of import cover	3.4
Invisibles outflows	-39.8	Official gold holdings, m oz	0.1
Net transfers	20.5	Foreign debt	167.2
Current account balance	-5.1	– as % of GDP	26
– as % of GDP	-0.7	– as % of total exports	79
Capital balance	12.0	Debt service ratio	17
Overall balance	7.0		

Health and education

Health spending, % of GDP	6.5	Education spending, % of GDP	5.8
Doctors per 1,000 pop.	2.0	Enrolment, %: primary	113
Hospital beds per 1,000 pop.	1.0	secondary	80
Improved-water source access,		tertiary	20
% of pop.	97		

Society

No. of households	24.6m	Colour TVs per 100 households	90.9
Av. no. per household	4.3	Telephone lines per 100 pop.	18.2
Marriages per 1,000 pop.	5.3	Mobile telephone subscribers	
Divorces per 1,000 pop.	0.6	per 100 pop.	44.0
Cost of living, Dec. 2006		Computers per 100 pop.	13.1
New York = 100	79	Internet hosts per 1,000 pop.	62.6

a Manufacturing assembly plants near the Mexican-US border where goods for processing may be imported duty-free and all output is exported.

MOROCCO

Area	446,550 sq km	Capital	Rabat
Arable as % of total land	19	Currency	Dirham (Dh)

People

Population	31.5m	Life expectancy:	men	69.0 yrs
Pop. per sq km	70.5		women	73.4 yrs
Av. ann. growth		Adult literacy		52.3%
in pop. 2005–10	1.20%	Fertility rate (per woman)		2.4
Pop. under 15	30.3%	Urban population		58.7%
Pop. over 60	7.5%			per 1,000 pop.
No. of men per 100 women	97	Crude birth rate		20.5
Human Development Index	64.0	Crude death rate		5.8

The economy

GDP	Dh458bn	GDP per head	$1,640
GDP	$51.6bn	GDP per head in purchasing	
Av. ann. growth in real		power parity (USA=100)	10.9
GDP 1995–2005	3.9%	Economic freedom index	57.4

Origins of GDP		Components of GDP	
	% of total		% of total
Agriculture	12.4	Private consumption	62.4
Industry, of which:	30.7	Public consumption	20.5
manufacturing	17.6	Investment	23.5
Services	56.9	Exports	29.6
		Imports	-36.6

Structure of employment

	% of total		% of labour force
Agriculture	47	Unemployed 2004	11.2
Industry	21	Av. ann. rate 1995–2004	15.1
Services	32		

Energy

	m TOE		
Total output	0.7	Net energy imports as %	
Total consumption	11.5	of energy use	94
Consumption per head,			
kg oil equivalent	384		

Inflation and finance

Consumer price		av. ann. increase 2000–05	
inflation 2006	3.3%	Narrow money (M1)	11.7%
Av. ann. inflation 2001–06	2.0%	Broad money	10.2%
Money market rate, 2006	2.58%		

Exchange rates

	end 2006		December 2006
Dh per $	8.46	Effective rates	2000 = 100
Dh per SDR	12.72	– nominal	95.4
Dh per €	11.17	– real	93.1

Trade

Principal exports		Principal imports	
	$bn fob		*$bn cif*
Textiles	2.0	Semi-finished goods	4.5
Phosphoric acid	0.9	Energy & lubricants	4.4
Electrical components	0.7	Consumer goods	4.1
Phosphate rock	0.5	Capital goods	4.0
Citrus fruits	0.3	Food, drink & tobacco	1.7
Total incl. others	**10.5**	Total incl. others	**20.3**

Main export destinations		Main origins of imports	
	% of total		*% of total*
France	37.5	France	30.0
Spain	16.4	Spain	11.6
United Kingdom	5.1	Italy	5.4
Italy	4.0	China	5.3

Balance of payments, reserves and debt, $bn

Visible exports fob	10.7	Change in reserves	-0.1
Visible imports fob	-18.9	Level of reserves	
Trade balance	-8.2	end Dec.	16.6
Invisibles inflows	8.8	No. months of import cover	8.4
Invisibles outflows	-4.9	Official gold holdings, m oz	0.7
Net transfers	5.3	Foreign debt	16.8
Current account balance	1.0	– as % of GDP	34
– as % of GDP	2.0	– as % of total exports	77
Capital balance	-0.2	Debt service ratio	11
Overall balance	0.4		

Health and education

Health spending, % of GDP	5.1	Education spending, % of GDP	6.7
Doctors per 1,000 pop.	0.5	Enrolment, %: primary	90
Hospital beds per 1,000 pop.	0.9	secondary	48
Improved-water source access,		tertiary	9
% of pop.	81		

Society

No. of households	6.0m	Colour TVs per 100 households	49.6
Av. no. per household	5.2	Telephone lines per 100 pop.	4.4
Marriages per 1,000 pop.	...	Mobile telephone subscribers	
Divorces per 1,000 pop.	...	per 100 pop.	40.9
Cost of living, Dec. 2006		Computers per 100 pop.	2.5
New York = 100	72	Internet hosts per 1,000 pop.	8.5

NETHERLANDS

Area[a]	41,526 sq km	Capital	Amsterdam
Arable as % of total land	27	Currency	Euro (€)

People

Population	16.3m	Life expectancy: men		77.5 yrs
Pop. per sq km	392.5	women		81.9 yrs
Av. ann. growth		Adult literacy		...
in pop. 2005–10	0.21%	Fertility rate (per woman)		1.7
Pop. under 15	18.4%	Urban population		80.2%
Pop. over 60	19.3%			*per 1,000 pop.*
No. of men per 100 women	98	Crude birth rate		11.1
Human Development Index	94.7	Crude death rate		8.6

The economy

GDP	€502bn	GDP per head	$38,290
GDP	$624bn	GDP per head in purchasing	
Av. ann. growth in real		power parity (USA=100)	78.0
GDP 1995–2005	2.2%	Economic freedom index	77.1

Origins of GDP		**Components of GDP**	
	% of total		*% of total*
Agriculture	2.7	Private consumption	48.9
Industry, of which:	23.1	Public consumption	24.1
manufacturing	...	Investment	19.3
Services	74.2	Exports	69.9
		Imports	-62.2

Structure of employment

	% of total		*% of labour force*
Agriculture	3	Unemployed 2003	4.3
Industry	20	Av. ann. rate 1995–2003	4.5
Services	77		

Energy

	m TOE		
Total output	67.9	Net energy imports as %	
Total consumption	82.1	of energy use	17
Consumption per head,			
kg oil equivalent	5,045		

Inflation and finance

Consumer price		*av. ann. increase 1999–2004*	
inflation 2006	1.7%	Euro area:	
Av. ann. inflation 2001–06	2.1%	Narrow money (M1)	10.8%
Lending rate, 2004	2.75%	Broad money	7.7%
Deposit rate, households, 2006	3.23%	Household saving rate, 2006	7.0%

Exchange rates

	end 2006		*December 2006*
€ per $	0.76	Effective rates	*2000 = 100*
€ per SDR	1.14	– nominal	109.2
		– real	114.4

Trade

Principal exports[b]		**Principal imports**[b]	
	$bn fob		*$bn cif*
Machinery & transport equipment	103	Machinery & transport equipment	108
Chemicals	54	Chemicals	36
Food, drink & tobacco	46	Food, drink & tobacco	33
Fuels	29	Fuels	26
Total incl. others	**318**	Total incl. others	**284**

Main export destinations		**Main origins of imports**	
	% of total		*% of total*
Germany	28.7	Germany	19.6
Belgium	14.0	Belgium	10.8
France	10.7	China	10.2
United Kingdom	10.7	United States	9.1
EU25	75.8	EU25	56.9

Balance of payments, reserves and aid, $bn

Visible exports fob	347.9	Overall balance	-1.8
Visible imports fob	-301.4	Change in reserves	-0.6
Trade balance	46.5	Level of reserves	
Invisibles inflows	177.1	end Dec.	20.4
Invisibles outflows	-164.1	No. months of import cover	0.5
Net transfers	-10.5	Official gold holdings, m oz	22.3
Current account balance	48.9	Aid given	5.12
– as % of GDP	8.2	– as % of GDP	0.82
Capital balance	-46.3		

Health and education

Health spending, % of GDP	9.2	Education spending, % of GDP	5.3
Doctors per 1,000 pop.	3.2	Enrolment, %: primary	108
Hospital beds per 1,000 pop.	5.0	secondary	119
Improved-water source access,		tertiary	52
% of pop.	100		

Society

No. of households	7.1m	Colour TVs per 100 households	98.7
Av. no. per household	2.3	Telephone lines per 100 pop.	46.6
Marriages per 1,000 pop.	4.3	Mobile telephone subscribers	
Divorces per 1,000 pop.	1.8	per 100 pop.	102.9
Cost of living, Dec. 2006		Computers per 100 pop.	68.5
New York = 100	101	Internet hosts per 1,000 pop.	553.0

a   Includes water.
b   2004

NEW ZEALAND

Area	270,534 sq km	Capital	Wellington
Arable as % of total land	6	Currency	New Zealand dollar (NZ$)

People

Population	4.0m	Life expectancy:	men	78.2 yrs
Pop. per sq km	14.8		women	82.2 yrs
Av. ann. growth		Adult literacy		...
in pop. 2005–10	0.90%	Fertility rate (per woman)		2.0
Pop. under 15	21.5%	Urban population		86.2%
Pop. over 60	16.6%		*per 1,000 pop.*	
No. of men per 100 women	97	Crude birth rate		13.7
Human Development Index	93.6	Crude death rate		7.1

The economy

GDP	NZ$155bn	GDP per head	$27,320
GDP	$109bn	GDP per head in purchasing	
Av. ann. growth in real		power parity (USA=100)	59.7
GDP 1995–2005	3.1%	Economic freedom index	81.6

Origins of GDP		**Components of GDP**	
	% of total		*% of total*
Agriculture & mining	6.7	Private consumption	61.4
Manufacturing	14.7	Public consumption	17.3
Other	78.6	Investment	27.4
		Exports	31.8
		Imports	-37.9

Structure of employment

	% of total		*% of labour force*
Agriculture	7	Unemployed 2004	3.9
Industry	22	Av. ann. rate 1995–2004	5.8
Services	71		

Energy

	m TOE		
Total output	13.0	Net energy imports as %	
Total consumption	17.6	of energy use	26
Consumption per head,			
kg oil equivalent	4,344		

Inflation and finance

Consumer price		*av. ann. increase 2000–05*	
inflation 2006	3.4%	Narrow money (M1)	7.4%
Av. ann. inflation 2001–06	2.6%	Broad money	8.5%
Money market rate, 2006	7.26%		

Exchange rates

	end 2006		*December 2006*
NZ$ per $	1.42	Effective rates	*2000 = 100*
NZ$ per SDR	2.13	– nominal	128.3
NZ$ per €	1.87	– real	132.5

Trade

Principal exports		Principal imports	
	$bn fob		*$bn cif*
Dairy produce	3.6	Machinery & electrical	
Meat	3.3	equipment	5.9
Forestry products	1.3	Transport equipment	4.7
Fish	0.8	Mineral fuels	3.1
Total incl. others	**21.7**	Total incl. others	**26.2**

Main export destinations		Main origins of imports	
	% of total		*% of total*
Australia	21.4	Australia	20.6
United States	14.2	United States	11.0
Japan	10.6	Japan	10.9
China	5.1	China	10.8

Balance of payments, reserves and aid, $bn

Visible exports fob	22.0	Overall balance	2.4
Visible imports fob	-24.7	Change in reserves	3.6
Trade balance	-2.7	Level of reserves	
Invisibles inflows	10.0	end Dec.	8.9
Invisibles outflows	-17.3	No. months of import cover	2.5
Net transfers	0.4	Official gold holdings, m oz	0.0
Current account balance	-9.6	Aid given	0.27
– as % of GDP	-8.8	– as % of GDP	0.27
Capital balance	11.0		

Health and education

Health spending, % of GDP	8.4	Education spending, % of GDP	6.8
Doctors per 1,000 pop.	2.4	Enrolment, %: primary	101
Hospital beds per 1,000 pop.	6.0	secondary	118
Improved-water source access,		tertiary	66
% of pop.	...		

Society

No. of households	1.5m	Colour TVs per 100 households	98.2
Av. no. per household	2.7	Telephone lines per 100 pop.	42.9
Marriages per 1,000 pop.	5.2	Mobile telephone subscribers	
Divorces per 1,000 pop.	2.7	per 100 pop.	87.6
Cost of living, Dec. 2006		Computers per 100 pop.	48.2
New York = 100	86	Internet hosts per 1,000 pop.	338.9

NIGERIA

Area	923,768 sq km	Capital	Abuja
Arable as % of total land	34	Currency	Naira (N)

People

Population	131.5m	Life expectancy: men		46.4 yrs
Pop. per sq km	142.4	women		47.3 yrs
Av. ann. growth		Adult literacy		...
in pop. 2005–10	2.27%	Fertility rate (per woman)		5.3
Pop. under 15	44.3%	Urban population		48.2%
Pop. over 60	4.6%		*per 1,000 pop.*	
No. of men per 100 women	100	Crude birth rate		39.9
Human Development Index	44.8	Crude death rate		16.8

The economy

GDP	N12,990bn	GDP per head	$750
GDP	$99.0bn	GDP per head in purchasing	
Av. ann. growth in real		power parity (USA=100)	2.7
GDP 1995–2005	4.2%	Economic freedom index	52.6

Origins of GDP		**Components of GDP**	
	% of total		*% of total*
Agriculture	41.2	Private consumption	61.9
Manufacturing	3.8	Public consumption	15.1
Other	55.0	Investment	16.0
		Exports	33.3
		Imports	-26.3

Structure of employment

	% of total		*% of labour force*
Agriculture	...	Unemployed 2001	3.9
Industry	...	Av. ann. rate 1995–2001	3.7
Services	...		

Energy

	m TOE		
Total output	229.4	Net energy imports as %	
Total consumption	99.0	of energy use	-132
Consumption per head,			
kg oil equivalent	769		

Inflation and finance

Consumer price		*av. ann. increase 2000–05*	
inflation 2006	8.3%	Narrow money (M1)	18.9%
Av. ann. inflation 2001–06	13.7%	Broad money	20.5%
Treasury bill rate 2005	7.63%		

Exchange rates

	end 2006		*December 2006*
N per $	134.0	Effective rates	*2000 = 100*
N per SDR	201.0	– nominal	67.3
N per €	176.9	– real	130.4

Trade

Principal exports		Principal imports	
	$bn fob		*$bn cif*
Oil	46.8	Manufactured goods	6.1
Gas	0.5	Chemicals	4.6
		Machinery & transport equipment	4.2
		Agric products & foodstuffs	1.3
Total incl. others	**48.1**	Total incl. others	**17.7**

Main export destinations[a]		Main origins of imports[a]	
	% of total		*% of total*
United States	54.0	China	10.5
Brazil	10.4	United States	7.4
Spain	8.3	United Kingdom	6.9
France	3.2	Netherlands	6.2

Balance of payments, reserves and debt, $bn

Visible exports fob	48.1	Change in reserves	11.4
Visible imports fob	-17.3	Level of reserves	
Trade balance	30.8	end Dec.	28.6
Invisibles inflows	4.9	No. months of import cover	10.7
Invisibles outflows	-14.8	Official gold holdings, m oz	0.7
Net transfers	3.3	Foreign debt	22.2
Current account balance	24.2	– as % of GDP	34
– as % of GDP	24.5	– as % of total exports	53
Capital balance	-23.6	Debt service ratio	16
Overall balance	10.4		

Health and education

Health spending, % of GDP	4.6	Education spending, % of GDP	...
Doctors per 1,000 pop.	0.3	Enrolment, %: primary	98
Hospital beds per 1,000 pop.	1.2	secondary	35
Improved-water source access, % of pop.	48	tertiary	4

Society

No. of households	26.8m	Colour TVs per 100 households	54.8
Av. no. per household	4.8	Telephone lines per 100 pop.	0.9
Marriages per 1,000 pop.	...	Mobile telephone subscribers	
Divorces per 1,000 pop.	...	per 100 pop.	14.1
Cost of living, Dec. 2006		Computers per 100 pop.	0.9
New York = 100	83	Internet hosts per 1,000 pop.	...

a Estimate.

NORWAY

Area	323,878 sq km	Capital	Oslo
Arable as % of total land	3	Currency	Norwegian krone (Nkr)

People

Population	4.6m	Life expectancy: men	77.8 yrs
Pop. per sq km	14.2	women	82.5 yrs
Av. ann. growth		Adult literacy	...
in pop. 2005–10	0.62%	Fertility rate (per woman)	1.9
Pop. under 15	19.6%	Urban population	77.4%
Pop. over 60	19.7%		*per 1,000 pop.*
No. of men per 100 women	99	Crude birth rate	11.9
Human Development Index	96.5	Crude death rate	9.1

The economy

GDP	Nkr1,904bn	GDP per head	$64,240
GDP	$296bn	GDP per head in purchasing	
Av. ann. growth in real		power parity (USA=100)	98.9
GDP 1995–2005	2.7%	Economic freedom index	70.1

Origins of GDP		**Components of GDP**	
	% of total		*% of total*
Agriculture	1.9	Private consumption	41.9
Industry, of which:	41.4	Public consumption	20.4
manufacturing	...	Investment	18.7
Services	56.7	Exports	45.2
		Imports	-27.8

Structure of employment

	% of total		*% of labour force*
Agriculture	3	Unemployed 2004	4.4
Industry	21	Av. ann. rate 1995–2004	4.0
Services	76		

Energy

	m TOE		
Total output	238.6	Net energy imports as %	
Total consumption	27.7	of energy use	-763
Consumption per head,			
kg oil equivalent	6,024		

Inflation and finance

Consumer price		*av. ann. increase 2000–03*	
inflation 2006	2.3%	Narrow money (M1)	9.8%
Av. ann. inflation 2001–06	1.6%	Broad money	6.6%
Interbank rate, 2006	3.10%	Household saving rate, 2006	5.2%

Exchange rates

	end 2006		*December 2006*
Nkr per $	6.26	Effective rates	*2000 = 100*
Nkr per SDR	9.42	– nominal	109.4
Nkr per €	8.26	– real	130.8

Trade

Principal exports		Principal imports	
	$bn fob		*$bn cif*
Oil, gas & products	70.5	Machinery & transport equip.	21.5
Machinery & transport equip.	9.6	Metals	6.2
Metals	7.8	Chemicals	5.7
Food, drink & tobacco	3.6	Textiles	3.2
Total incl. others	**101.9**	Total incl. others	**54.8**

Main export destinations		Main origins of imports	
	% of total		*% of total*
United Kingdom	24.3	Sweden	14.7
Germany	14.7	Germany	14.0
France	9.2	Denmark	7.7
Netherlands	8.4	United Kingdom	7.2
United States	6.9	Netherlands	4.7
Sweden	6.7	United States	4.7
EU25	80.2	EU25	71.9

Balance of payments, reserves and aid, $bn

Visible exports fob	104.2	Overall balance	4.5
Visible imports fob	-54.5	Change in reserves	2.7
Trade balance	49.7	Level of reserves	
Invisibles inflows	48.1	end Dec.	47.0
Invisibles outflows	-48.4	No. months of import cover	5.5
Net transfers	-2.8	Official gold holdings, m oz	0.0
Current account balance	46.6	Aid given	2.79
– as % of GDP	16.4	– as % of GDP	0.94
Capital balance	-34.0		

Health and education

Health spending, % of GDP	9.7	Education spending, % of GDP	7.7
Doctors per 1,000 pop.	3.1	Enrolment, %: primary	101
Hospital beds per 1,000 pop.	4.2	secondary	116
Improved-water source access,		tertiary	68
% of pop.	100		

Society

No. of households	2.0m	Colour TVs per 100 households	94.0
Av. no. per household	2.2	Telephone lines per 100 pop.	45.7
Marriages per 1,000 pop.	4.8	Mobile telephone subscribers	
Divorces per 1,000 pop.	2.4	per 100 pop.	102.9
Cost of living, Dec. 2006		Computers per 100 pop.	57.2
New York = 100	132	Internet hosts per 1,000 pop.	515.2

PAKISTAN

Area	803,940 sq km	Capital	Islamabad
Arable as % of total land	28	Currency	Pakistan rupee (PRs)

People

Population	157.9m	Life expectancy:	men	65.2 yrs
Pop. per sq km	196.4		women	65.8 yrs
Av. ann. growth		Adult literacy		49.9%
in pop. 2005–10	1.84%	Fertility rate (per woman)		3.5
Pop. under 15	37.2%	Urban population		34.9%
Pop. over 60	5.9%			per 1,000 pop.
No. of men per 100 women	106	Crude birth rate		27.2
Human Development Index	53.9	Crude death rate		7.1

The economy

GDP	PRs6,548bn	GDP per head	$700
GDP	$111bn	GDP per head in purchasing	
Av. ann. growth in real		power parity (USA=100)	5.7
GDP 1995–2005	4.0%	Economic freedom index	58.2

Origins of GDP		Components of GDP[a]	
	% of total		% of total
Agriculture	21.6	Private consumption	80.0
Industry, of which:	25.0	Public consumption	7.8
manufacturing & mining	20.2	Investment	16.9
Other	53.4	Exports	15.3
		Imports	-19.9

Structure of employment

	% of total		% of labour force
Agriculture	42	Unemployed 2004	7.7
Industry	21	Av. ann. rate 1995–2004	6.4
Services	37		

Energy

	m TOE		
Total output	59.0	Net energy imports as %	
Total consumption	74.4	of energy use	21
Consumption per head,			
kg oil equivalent	489		

Inflation and finance

Consumer price		av. ann. increase 2000–05	
inflation 2006	7.9%	Narrow money (M1)	21.4%
Av. ann. inflation 2001–06	5.4%	Broad money	16.6%
Money market rate, 2006	8.89%		

Exchange rates

	end 2006		December 2006
PRs per $	60.92	Effective rates	2000 = 100
PRs per SDR	91.65	– nominal	76.80
PRs per €	80.41	– real	96.31

Trade

Principal exports[a]		Principal imports[a]	
	$bn fob		*$bn fob*
Cotton fabrics	1.9	Machinery & transport equip.	6.0
Knitwear	1.6	Fuels etc	4.3
Bedwear	1.5	Chemicals	3.6
Cotton yarn & thread	1.1	Manufactures	2.3
Rice	0.9		
Total incl. others	**13.4**	Total incl. others	**17.9**

Main export destinations[a]		Main origins of imports[a]	
	% of total		*% of total*
United States	24.0	Saudi Arabia	12.3
United Arab Emirates	7.6	China	8.9
United Kingdom	6.2	United Arab Emirates	8.3
Afghanistan	5.2	United States	7.6
Germany	4.8	Japan	7.0

Balance of payments, reserves and debt, $bn

Visible exports fob	15.4	Change in reserves	0.4
Visible imports fob	-21.8	Level of reserves	
Trade balance	-6.3	end Dec.	11.1
Invisibles inflows	4.3	No. months of import cover	4.1
Invisibles outflows	-10.7	Official gold holdings, m oz	2.1
Net transfers	9.1	Foreign debt	33.7
Current account balance	-3.6	– as % of GDP	30
– as % of GDP	-3.3	– as % of total exports	134
Capital balance	4.3	Debt service ratio	10
Overall balance	0.5		

Health and education

Health spending, % of GDP	2.2	Education spending, % of GDP	2.3
Doctors per 1,000 pop.	0.7	Enrolment, %: primary	96
Hospital beds per 1,000 pop.	0.7	secondary	27
Improved-water source access,		tertiary	4
% of pop.	91		

Society

No. of households	27.1m	Colour TVs per 100 households	39.4
Av. no. per household	7.2	Telephone lines per 100 pop.	3.4
Marriages per 1,000 pop.	...	Mobile telephone subscribers	
Divorces per 1,000 pop.	...	per 100 pop.	8.3
Cost of living, Dec. 2006		Computers per 100 pop.	...
New York = 100	44	Internet hosts per 1,000 pop.	0.6

a Fiscal year ending June 30, 2005.

PERU

Area	1,285,216 sq km	Capital	Lima
Arable as % of total land	3	Currency	Nuevo Sol (New Sol)

People

Population	28.0m	Life expectancy: men	68.9 yrs
Pop. per sq km	21.8	women	74.0 yrs
Av. ann. growth		Adult literacy	87.7%
in pop. 2005–10	1.15%	Fertility rate (per woman)	2.5
Pop. under 15	31.8%	Urban population	72.6%
Pop. over 60	8.1%		per 1,000 pop.
No. of men per 100 women	100	Crude birth rate	20.9
Human Development Index	76.7	Crude death rate	6.1

The economy

GDP	New Soles 262bn	GDP per head	$2,840
GDP	$79.4bn	GDP per head in purchasing	
Av. ann. growth in real		power parity (USA=100)	14.4
GDP 1995–2005	3.3%	Economic freedom index	62.1

Origins of GDP		Components of GDP	
	% of total		% of total
Agriculture	8.9	Private consumption	65.9
Industry, of which:	26.8	Public consumption	10.1
manufacturing	15.3	Investment	18.8
Services	64.3	Exports	24.2
		Imports	-18.8

Structure of employment

	% of total		% of labour force
Agriculture	1	Unemployed 2004	10.5
Industry	24	Av. ann. rate 1996–2004	8.5
Services	75		

Energy

	m TOE		
Total output	9.5	Net energy imports as %	
Total consumption	13.2	of energy use	28
Consumption per head,			
kg oil equivalent	479		

Inflation and finance

Consumer price		av. ann. increase 2000–05	
inflation 2006	2.0%	Narrow money (M1)	18.5%
Av. ann. inflation 2001–06	2.0%	Broad money	-3.6%
Deposit rate, 2006	3.21%		

Exchange rates

	end 2006		December 2006
New Soles per $	3.20	Effective rates	2000 = 100
New Soles per SDR	4.81	– nominal	...
New Soles per €	4.22	– real	...

Trade

Principal exports		Principal imports	
	$bn fob		*$bn fob*
Copper	3.4	Intermediate goods	6.6
Gold	3.1	Capital goods	3.1
Fishmeal	1.3	Consumer goods	2.3
Zinc	0.8	Other goods	0.1
Total incl. others	**16.6**	Total incl. others	**12.1**

Main export destinations		Main origins of imports	
	% of total		*% of total*
United States	31.0	United States	19.9
China	10.8	China	9.3
Chile	6.6	Brazil	8.7
Canada	5.9	Ecuador	8.1

Balance of payments, reserves and debt, $bn

Visible exports fob	17.2	Change in reserves	1.5
Visible imports fob	-12.1	Level of reserves	
Trade balance	5.2	end Dec.	14.2
Invisibles inflows	2.8	No. months of import cover	8.2
Invisibles outflows	-8.7	Official gold holdings, m oz	1.1
Net transfers	1.8	Foreign debt	28.7
Current account balance	1.0	– as % of GDP	49
– as % of GDP	1.3	– as % of total exports	198
Capital balance	-0.1	Debt service ratio	26
Overall balance	1.4		

Health and education

Health spending, % of GDP	4.1	Education spending, % of GDP	2.4
Doctors per 1,000 pop.	1.1	Enrolment, %: primary	128
Hospital beds per 1,000 pop.	1.1	secondary	90
Improved-water source access,		tertiary	29
% of pop.	83		

Society

No. of households	5.8m	Colour TVs per 100 households	50.5
Av. no. per household	4.7	Telephone lines per 100 pop.	8.1
Marriages per 1,000 pop.	2.9	Mobile telephone subscribers	
Divorces per 1,000 pop.	...	per 100 pop.	20.0
Cost of living, Dec. 2006		Computers per 100 pop.	10.0
New York = 100	60	Internet hosts per 1,000 pop.	10.1

PHILIPPINES

Area	300,000 sq km	Capital	Manila
Arable as % of total land	19	Currency	Philippine peso (P)

People

Population	83.1m	Life expectancy: men	69.5 yrs
Pop. per sq km	277.0	women	73.9 yrs
Av. ann. growth		Adult literacy	92.6%
in pop. 2005–10	1.90%	Fertility rate (per woman)	3.2
Pop. under 15	36.2%	Urban population	62.7%
Pop. over 60	6.0%		per 1,000 pop.
No. of men per 100 women	101	Crude birth rate	25.8
Human Development Index	76.3	Crude death rate	4.8

The economy

GDP	P5,419bn	GDP per head	$1,190
GDP	$99.0bn	GDP per head in purchasing	
Av. ann. growth in real		power parity (USA=100)	12.3
GDP 1995–2005	4.2%	Economic freedom index	57.4

Origins of GDP		Components of GDP	
	% of total		% of total
Agriculture	14.3	Private consumption	69.6
Industry, of which:	32.2	Public consumption	9.7
manufacturing	23.3	Investment	14.9
Services	53.5	Exports	47.3
		Imports	-52.0

Structure of employment

	% of total		% of labour force
Agriculture	37	Unemployed 2004	10.9
Industry	15	Av. ann. rate 1995–2004	9.4
Services	48		

Energy

	m TOE		
Total output	23.4	Net energy imports as %	
Total consumption	44.3	of energy use	47
Consumption per head,			
kg oil equivalent	542		

Inflation and finance

Consumer price			av. ann. increase 2000–05
inflation 2006	6.2%	Narrow money (M1)	9.7%
Av. ann. inflation 2001–06	5.2%	Broad money	6.7%
Money market rate, 2006	7.84%		

Exchange rates

	end 2006		December 2006
P per $	49.13	Effective rates	2000 = 100
P per SDR	73.91	– nominal	83.9
P per €	64.85	– real	105.4

Trade

Principal exports		Principal imports	
	$bn fob		*$bn fob*
Electrical & electronic equipment	27.3	Semi-processed raw materials	16.8
Semiconductors	20.2	Telecom & electrical machinery	8.9
Clothing	2.2	Crude petroleum	3.8
Coconut products	0.7	Manufactured goods	3.8
Petroleum products	0.6	Chemicals	3.3
Total incl. others	**39.9**	Total incl. others	**47.0**

Main export destinations		Main origins of imports	
	% of total		*% of total*
United States	18.0	United States	17.8
Japan	17.5	Japan	17.0
China	9.9	Singapore	8.0
Netherlands	9.8	Taiwan	7.5
Hong Kong	8.1	China	6.4
Singapore	6.6	South Korea	4.9

Balance of payments, reserves and debt, $bn

Visible exports fob	40.2	Change in reserves	2.2
Visible imports fob	-47.8	Level of reserves	
Trade balance	-7.5	end Dec.	18.5
Invisibles inflows	8.4	No. months of import cover	3.8
Invisibles outflows	-9.9	Official gold holdings, m oz	5.0
Net transfers	11.4	Foreign debt	61.5
Current account balance	2.3	– as % of GDP	67
– as % of GDP	2.4	– as % of total exports	120
Capital balance	0.1	Debt service ratio	17
Overall balance	1.6		

Health and education

Health spending, % of GDP	3.4	Education spending, % of GDP	3.2
Doctors per 1,000 pop.	0.6	Enrolment, %: primary	113
Hospital beds per 1,000 pop.	1.2	secondary	86
Improved-water source access, % of pop.	85	tertiary	29

Society

No. of households	17.1m	Colour TVs per 100 households	68.5
Av. no. per household	5.0	Telephone lines per 100 pop.	4.0
Marriages per 1,000 pop.	6.8	Mobile telephone subscribers	
Divorces per 1,000 pop.	...	per 100 pop.	41.3
Cost of living, Dec. 2006		Computers per 100 pop.	4.5
New York = 100	43	Internet hosts per 1,000 pop.	2.9

POLAND

Area	312,683 sq km	Capital	Warsaw
Arable as % of total land	40	Currency	Zloty (Zl)

People

Population	38.5m	Life expectancy: men	71.3 yrs
Pop. per sq km	123.1	women	79.8 yrs
Av. ann. growth		Adult literacy	...
in pop. 2005–10	-0.15%	Fertility rate (per woman)	1.2
Pop. under 15	16.3%	Urban population	62.1%
Pop. over 60	17.2%		*per 1,000 pop.*
No. of men per 100 women	93	Crude birth rate	9.5
Human Development Index	86.2	Crude death rate	10.0

The economy

GDP	Zl981bn	GDP per head	$7,880
GDP	$303bn	GDP per head in purchasing	
Av. ann. growth in real		power parity (USA=100)	33.1
GDP 1995–2005	4.2%	Economic freedom index	58.8

Origins of GDP[a]		**Components of GDP**	
	% of total		*% of total*
Agriculture	5	Private consumption	62.8
Industry, of which:	31	Public consumption	18.3
manufacturing	18	Investment	18.2
Services	64	Exports	37.2
		Imports	-37.5

Structure of employment

	% of total		*% of labour force*
Agriculture	17	Unemployed 2005	17.7
Industry	29	Av. ann. rate 1995–2005	15.6
Services	54		

Energy

	m TOE		
Total output	78.8	Net energy imports as %	
Total consumption	91.7	of energy use	14
Consumption per head,			
kg oil equivalent	2,403		

Inflation and finance

Consumer price		*av. ann. increase 2000–05*	
inflation 2006	1.0%	Narrow money (M1)	16.2%
Av. ann. inflation 2001–06	1.9%	Broad money	7.2%
Money market rate, 2006	4.1%	Household saving rate, 2006	7.4%

Exchange rates

	end 2006		*December 2006*
Zl per $	2.91	Effective rates	*2000 = 100*
Zl per SDR	4.38	– nominal	111.1
Zl per €	3.84	– real	112.0

Trade

Principal exports		Principal imports	
	$bn fob		*$bn cif*
Machinery &		Machinery &	
transport equipment	34.9	transport equipment	36.1
Manufactured goods	20.2	Manufactured goods	20.9
Other manufactured goods	13.0	Chemicals	14.4
Agric. products & foodstuffs	7.8	Mineral fuels	11.6
Total incl. others	**89.3**	Total incl. others	**100.9**

Main export destinations		Main origins of imports	
	% of total		*% of total*
Germany	28.1	Germany	29.3
France	6.2	Russia	8.6
Italy	6.1	Italy	6.5
United Kingdom	5.6	Netherlands	5.9

Balance of payments, reserves and debt, $bn

Visible exports fob	96.4	Change in reserves	5.8
Visible imports fob	-99.2	Level of reserves	
Trade balance	-2.8	end Dec.	42.6
Invisibles inflows	18.7	No. months of import cover	4.0
Invisibles outflows	-28.0	Official gold holdings, m oz	3.3
Net transfers	6.9	Foreign debt	98.8
Current account balance	-5.1	– as % of GDP	39
– as % of GDP	-1.7	– as % of total exports	98
Capital balance	15.5	Debt service ratio	29
Overall balance	8.1		

Health and education

Health spending, % of GDP	6.2	Education spending, % of GDP	5.6
Doctors per 1,000 pop.	2.5	Enrolment, %: primary	101
Hospital beds per 1,000 pop.	5.3	secondary	97
Improved-water source access,		tertiary	50
% of pop.	...		

Society

No. of households	13.6m	Colour TVs per 100 households	87.8
Av. no. per household	2.9	Telephone lines per 100 pop.	30.7
Marriages per 1,000 pop.	5.1	Mobile telephone subscribers	
Divorces per 1,000 pop.	1.5	per 100 pop.	75.7
Cost of living, Dec. 2006		Computers per 100 pop.	19.1
New York = 100	80	Internet hosts per 1,000 pop.	129.9

PORTUGAL

Area	88,940 sq km	Capital	Lisbon
Arable as % of total land	17	Currency	Euro (€)

People

Population	10.5m	Life expectancy: men	75.0 yrs
Pop. per sq km	118.0	women	81.2 yrs
Av. ann. growth		Adult literacy	...
in pop. 2005–10	0.37%	Fertility rate (per woman)	1.5
Pop. under 15	15.7%	Urban population	57.6%
Pop. over 60	22.1%		per 1,000 pop.
No. of men per 100 women	94	Crude birth rate	10.5
Human Development Index	90.4	Crude death rate	10.6

The economy

GDP	€147bn	GDP per head	$17,460
GDP	$183bn	GDP per head in purchasing	
Av. ann. growth in real		power parity (USA=100)	48.7
GDP 1995–2005	2.1%	Economic freedom index	66.7

Origins of GDP		Components of GDP	
	% of total		% of total
Agriculture	2.8	Private consumption	66.5
Industry, of which:	22.3	Public consumption	20.8
manufacturing	...	Investment	22.9
Services	74.9	Exports	32.6
		Imports	-42.7

Structure of employment

	% of total		% of labour force
Agriculture	13	Unemployed 2004	6.7
Industry	33	Av. ann. rate 1995–2004	5.7
Services	55		

Energy

	m TOE		
Total output	3.9	Net energy imports as %	
Total consumption	26.5	of energy use	85
Consumption per head,			
kg oil equivalent	2,528		

Inflation and finance

Consumer price		av. ann. increase 2000–05	
inflation 2006	3.1%	Euro area:	
Av. ann. inflation 2001–06	2.9%	Narrow money (M1)	10.8%
Deposit rate, h'holds, 2006	2.13%	Broad money	7.7%
		Household saving rate, 2006	9.4%

Exchange rates

	end 2006		December 2006
€ per $	0.76	Effective rates	2000 = 100
€ per SDR	1.14	– nominal	106.3
		– real	112.3

Trade

Principal exports		**Principal imports**	
	$bn fob		*$bn cif*
Machinery	6.0	Machinery	14.6
Clothing	4.7	Agricultural goods	8.9
Transport goods	4.1	Transport goods	8.4
Agricultural goods	2.8	Pharmaceuticals	2.4
Total incl. others	**32.2**	Total incl. others	**53.4**

Main export destinations		**Main origins of imports**	
	% of total		*% of total*
France	24.9	Spain	29.0
Germany	14.0	Germany	13.5
Spain	13.5	France	8.5
United Kingdom	9.6	Italy	5.2
United States	4.0	United Kingdom	4.6
EU25	79.4	EU25	73.5

Balance of payments, reserves and debt, $bn

Visible exports fob	38.2	Overall balance	-1.7
Visible imports fob	-59.0	Change in reserves	-1.3
Trade balance	-20.9	Level of reserves	
Invisibles inflows	22.8	end Dec.	10.4
Invisibles outflows	-21.7	No. months of import cover	1.5
Net transfers	2.7	Official gold holdings, m oz	13.4
Current account balance	-17.0	Aid given	0.38
– as % of GDP	-9.8	– as % of GDP	0.21
Capital balance	16.6		

Health and education

Health spending, % of GDP	9.8	Education spending, % of GDP	5.9
Doctors per 1,000 pop.	3.4	Enrolment, %: primary	123
Hospital beds per 1,000 pop.	3.7	secondary[a]	97
Improved-water source access,		tertiary	47
% of pop.	...		

Society

No. of households	3.9m	Colour TVs per 100 households	98.3
Av. no. per household	2.7	Telephone lines per 100 pop.	40.4
Marriages per 1,000 pop.	4.0	Mobile telephone subscribers	
Divorces per 1,000 pop.	2.3	per 100 pop.	109.1
Cost of living, Dec. 2006		Computers per 100 pop.	13.3
New York = 100	83	Internet hosts per 1,000 pop.	143.9

a Includes training for unemployed.

ROMANIA

Area	237,500 sq km	Capital	Bucharest
Arable as % of total land	40	Currency	Leu (RON)

People

Population	21.7m	Life expectancy: men	69.0 yrs
Pop. per sq km	91.4	women	76.1 yrs
Av. ann. growth		Adult literacy	97.3%
in pop. 2005–10	-0.45%	Fertility rate (per woman)	1.3
Pop. under 15	15.7%	Urban population	53.7%
Pop. over 60	19.3%		per 1,000 pop.
No. of men per 100 women	95	Crude birth rate	9.8
Human Development Index	80.5	Crude death rate	12.4

The economy

GDP	RON287bn	GDP per head	$4,540
GDP	$98.6bn	GDP per head in purchasing	
Av. ann. growth in real		power parity (USA=100)	21.6
GDP 1995–2005	2.1%	Economic freedom index	61.3

Origins of GDP		Components of GDP	
	% of total		% of total
Agriculture	10.1	Private consumption	75.2
Industry, of which:	35.0	Public consumption	12.3
manufacturing	...	Investment	23.4
Services	54.9	Exports	33.5
		Imports	-44.0

Structure of employment

	% of total		% of labour force
Agriculture	32	Unemployed 2004	8.0
Industry	30	Av. ann. rate 1995–2004	7.1
Services	38		

Energy

	m TOE		
Total output	28.1	Net energy imports as %	
Total consumption	38.6	of energy use	27
Consumption per head,			
kg oil equivalent	1,778		

Inflation and finance

Consumer price		av. ann. increase 2000–05	
inflation 2006	6.6%	Narrow money (M1)	39.6%
Av. ann. inflation 2001–06	12.9%	Broad money	29.2%
Bank rate, 2006	8.6%		

Exchange rates

	end 2006		December 2006
RON per $	2.57	Effective rates	2000 = 100
RON per SDR	3.86	– nominal	63.24
RON per €	3.39	– real	135.63

Trade

Principal exports		Principal imports	
	$bn fob		*$bn cif*
Textiles	5.2	Machinery & equipment	9.5
Basic metals & products	4.9	Fuels & minerals	6.3
Machinery & equipment	4.1	Textiles & footwear	4.1
Minerals & fuels	3.0	Chemicals	3.0
Total incl. others	**27.7**	Total incl. others	**40.5**

Main export destinations		Main origins of imports	
	% of total		*% of total*
Italy	19.2	Germany	15.5
Germany	14.0	Italy	14.0
France	7.9	Russia	8.3
EU25	67.6	EU25	62.2

Balance of payments, reserves and debt, $bn

Visible exports fob	27.7	Change in reserves	5.5
Visible imports fob	-37.3	Level of reserves	
Trade balance	-9.6	end Dec.	21.6
Invisibles inflows	6.6	No. months of import cover	5.5
Invisibles outflows	-10.0	Official gold holdings, m oz	3.4
Net transfers	4.3	Foreign debt	38.7
Current account balance	-8.6	– as % of GDP	351
– as % of GDP	-8.8	– as % of total exports	137
Capital balance	14.8	Debt service ratio	18
Overall balance	6.8		

Health and education

Health spending, % of GDP	5.1	Education spending, % of GDP	3.6
Doctors per 1,000 pop.	1.9	Enrolment, %: primary	102
Hospital beds per 1,000 pop.	6.6	secondary	85
Improved-water source access,		tertiary	24
% of pop.	57		

Society

No. of households	7.6m	Colour TVs per 100 households	55.4
Av. no. per household	2.9	Telephone lines per 100 pop.	20.3
Marriages per 1,000 pop.	6.1	Mobile telephone subscribers	
Divorces per 1,000 pop.	1.6	per 100 pop.	61.8
Cost of living, Dec. 2006		Computers per 100 pop.	11.3
New York = 100	66	Internet hosts per 1,000 pop.	53.9

RUSSIA

Area	17,075,400 sq km	Capital	Moscow
Arable as % of total land	7	Currency	Rouble (Rb)

People

Population	143.2m	Life expectancy: men	59.0 yrs
Pop. per sq km	8.4	women	72.6 yrs
Av. ann. growth		Adult literacy	99.4%
in pop. 2005–10	-0.51%	Fertility rate (per woman)	1.3
Pop. under 15	15.1%	Urban population	73.0%
Pop. over 60	17.1%		per 1,000 pop.
No. of men per 100 women	86	Crude birth rate	10.7
Human Development Index	79.7	Crude death rate	16.2

The economy

GDP	Rb21,598bn	GDP per head	$5,330
GDP	$764bn	GDP per head in purchasing	
Av. ann. growth in real		power parity (USA=100)	25.9
GDP 1995–2005	3.9%	Economic freedom index	54.0

Origins of GDP		**Components of GDP**a	
	% of total		% of total
Agriculture	5.6	Private consumption	49.8
Industry, of which:	38.0	Public consumption	16.6
manufacturing	...	Investment	20.1
Services	56.4	Exports	35.1
		Imports	-21.6

Structure of employment

	% of total		% of labour force
Agriculture	10	Unemployed 2004	7.9
Industry	30	Av. ann. rate 1995–2004	10.1
Services	60		

Energy

	m TOE		
Total output	1,158.5	Net energy imports as %	
Total consumption	641.5	of energy use	-81
Consumption per head,			
kg oil equivalent	4,460		

Inflation and finance

		av. ann. increase 2000–05	
Consumer price			
inflation 2006	9.7%	Narrow money (M1)	34.4%
Av. ann. inflation 2001–06	12.5%	Broad money	35.7%
Money market rate, 2006	3.43%		

Exchange rates

	end 2006		December 2006
			2000 = 100
Rb per $	26.33	Effective rates	
Rb per SDR	39.61	– nominal	99.71
Rb per 7	34.76	– real	166.16

Trade

Principal exports		Principal imports	
	$bn fob		*$bn fob*
Fuels	154.2	Machinery & equipment	60.6
Metals	34.3	Food & drink	24.3
Chemicals	14.4	Chemicals	22.7
Machinery & equipment	13.6	Metals	9.5
Total incl. others	**243.6**	Total incl. others	**137.8**

Main export destinations		Main origins of imports	
	% of total		*% of total*
Netherlands	10.1	Germany	13.4
Italy	9.6	Ukraine	7.9
Germany	8.1	China	7.3
China	5.4	United States	4.6

Balance of payments, reserves and debt, $bn

Visible exports fob	243.6	Change in reserves	56.0
Visible imports fob	-125.3	Level of reserves	
Trade balance	118.3	end Dec.	182.3
Invisibles inflows	42.0	No. months of import cover	10.9
Invisibles outflows	-75.8	Official gold holdings, m oz	12.4
Net transfers	-1.1	Foreign debt	229.0
Current account balance	83.3	– as % of GDP	40
– as % of GDP	10.9	– as % of total exports	104
Capital balance	-7.0	Debt service ratio	15
Overall balance	65.0		

Health and education

Health spending, % of GDP	6.0	Education spending, % of GDP	3.7
Doctors per 1,000 pop.	4.3	Enrolment, %: primary	85
Hospital beds per 1,000 pop.	9.7	secondary	93
Improved-water source access,		tertiary	65
% of pop.	97		

Society

No. of households	53.0m	Colour TVs per 100 households	75.7
Av. no. per household	2.8	Telephone lines per 100 pop.	27.9
Marriages per 1,000 pop.	6.8	Mobile telephone subscribers	
Divorces per 1,000 pop.	4.4	per 100 pop.	83.6
Cost of living, Dec. 2006		Computers per 100 pop.	12.1
New York = 100	101	Internet hosts per 1,000 pop.	16.4

a Production based.

SAUDI ARABIA

Area	2,200,000 sq km	Capital	Riyadh
Arable as % of total land	2	Currency	Riyal (SR)

People

Population	24.6m	Life expectancy: men	70.9 yrs
Pop. per sq km	11.2	women	75.3 yrs
Av. ann. growth		Adult literacy	79.4%
in pop. 2005–10	2.24%	Fertility rate (per woman)	3.4
Pop. under 15	34.5%	Urban population	81.0%
Pop. over 60	4.2%		per 1,000 pop.
No. of men per 100 women	122	Crude birth rate	24.9
Human Development Index	77.7	Crude death rate	3.7

The economy

GDP	SR1,161bn	GDP per head	$12,590
GDP	$310bn	GDP per head in purchasing	
Av. ann. growth in real		power parity (USA=100)	37.5
GDP 1995–2005	3.3%	Economic freedom index	59.1

Origins of GDP		**Components of GDP**	
	% of total		% of total
Agriculture	3.3	Private consumption	26.3
Industry, of which:	60.7	Public consumption	23.1
manufacturing	9.6	Investment	15.0
Services	36.0	Exports	60.7
		Imports	-26.4

Structure of employment

	% of total		% of labour force
Agriculture	5	Unemployed 2002	5.2
Industry	21	Av. ann. rate 1995–2002	4.4
Services	74		

Energy

	m TOE		
Total output	556.2	Net energy imports as %	
Total consumption	140.4	of energy use	-296
Consumption per head,			
kg oil equivalent	6,233		

Inflation and finance

Consumer price		*av. ann. increase 2000–05*	
inflation 2006	2.3%	Narrow money (M1)	11.4%
Av. ann. inflation 2001–06	0.8%	Broad money	11.8%
Deposit rate, 2006	5.02%		

Exchange rates

	end 2006		December 2006
SR per $	3.75	Effective rates	2000 = 100
SR per SDR	5.63	– nominal	88.1
SRE per €	4.95	– real	80.3

Trade

Principal exports	$bn fob	Principal imports	$bn cif
Crude oil & refined petroleum	120.6	Machinery & transport equipment	26.9
Oil products	24.0	Foodstuffs	8.8
Total incl. others	**180.6**	**Total incl. others**	**59.5**

Main export destinations	% of total	Main origins of imports	% of total
United States	17.0	United States	13.2
Japan	16.8	Japan	9.8
South Korea	8.7	Germany	8.1
China	7.2	United Kingdom	7.4

Balance of payments, reserves and aid, $bn

Visible exports fob	174.6	Overall balance	-0.5
Visible imports fob	-51.3	Change in reserves	-0.4
Trade balance	123.3	Level of reserves	
Invisibles inflows	10.9	end Dec.	28.9
Invisibles outflows	-32.6	No. months of import cover	4.1
Net transfers	-14.4	Official gold holdings, m oz	4.6
Current account balance	87.1	Aid given[a]	1.73
– as % of GDP	28.1	– as % of GDP[a]	0.69
Capital balance	-87.6		

Health and education

Health spending, % of GDP	3.3	Education spending, % of GDP	6.8
Doctors per 1,000 pop.	1.4	Enrolment, %: primary	68
Hospital beds per 1,000 pop.	2.3	secondary	68
Improved-water source access, % of pop.	...	tertiary	22

Society

No. of households	4.1m	Colour TVs per 100 households	99.1
Av. no. per household	5.9	Telephone lines per 100 pop.	15.5
Marriages per 1,000 pop.	4.2	Mobile telephone subscribers	
Divorces per 1,000 pop.	0.9	per 100 pop.	54.1
Cost of living, Dec. 2006		Computers per 100 pop.	35.4
New York = 100	65	Internet hosts per 1,000 pop.	2.8

a 2004

SINGAPORE

Area	639 sq km	Capital	Singapore
Arable as % of total land	1	Currency	Singapore dollar (S$)

People

Population	4.3m	Life expectancy: men	78.0 yrs
Pop. per sq km	6,729.3	women	81.9 yrs
Av. ann. growth		Adult literacy	92.5%
in pop. 2005–10	1.19%	Fertility rate (per woman)	1.3
Pop. under 15	19.5%	Urban population	100.0%
Pop. over 60	12.3%		per 1,000 pop.
No. of men per 100 women	101	Crude birth rate	8.2
Human Development Index	91.6	Crude death rate	5.3

The economy

GDP	S$194bn	GDP per head	$27,150
GDP	$117bn	GDP per head in purchasing	
Av. ann. growth in real		power parity (USA=100)	70.8
GDP 1995–2005	5.1%	Economic freedom index	85.7

Origins of GDP

	% of total
Agriculture	0
Industry, of which:	30.4
manufacturing	26.8
Services	69.6

Components of GDP

	% of total
Private consumption	41.9
Public consumption	10.6
Investment	21.8
Exports	243.0
Imports	-213.1

Structure of employment

	% of total		% of labour force
Agriculture	0	Unemployed 2003	5.4
Industry	30	Av. ann. rate 1995–2003	3.8
Services	70		

Energy

	m TOE		
Total output	0.1	Net energy imports as %	
Total consumption	25.6	of energy use	99
Consumption per head,			
kg oil equivalent	6,034		

Inflation and finance

		av. ann. increase 2000–05	
Consumer price			
inflation 2006	1.0%	Narrow money (M1)	6.7%
Av. ann. inflation 2001–06	0.6%	Broad money	5.2%
Money market rate, 2006	3.46%		

Exchange rates

	end 2006		December 2006
S$ per $	1.53	Effective rates	2000 = 100
S$ per SDR	2.31	– nominal	104.0
S$ per 7	2.02	– real	95.1

Trade

Principal exports		Principal imports	
	$bn fob		*$bn cif*
Machinery & equipment	135.2	Machinery & equipment	111.8
Mineral fuels	27.6	Petroleum	18.5
Chemicals	26.2	Manufactured products	15.0
Manufactured products	10.5	Chemicals	12.5
Food	2.3	Food	4.0
Total incl. others	229.6	Total incl. others	**200.0**

Main export destinations		Main origins of imports	
	% of total		*% of total*
Malaysia	14.3	Malaysia	14.2
United States	11.0	United States	12.1
Hong Kong	10.1	China	10.7
China	9.3	Japan	10.0
Japan	5.9	Saudi Arabia	4.7
Thailand	4.4	Thailand	3.9
South Korea	3.8	Hong Kong	2.2

Balance of payments, reserves and debt, $bn

Visible exports fob	232.3	Change in reserves	3.6
Visible imports fob	-194.4	Level of reserves	
Trade balance	37.9	end Dec.	115.8
Invisibles inflows	74.3	No. months of import cover	5.1
Invisibles outflows	-77.8	Official gold holdings, m oz	...
Net transfers	-1.2	Foreign debt	23.8
Current account balance	33.2	– as % of GDP	20
– as % of GDP	28.4	– as % of total exports	8
Capital balance	-20.2	Debt service ratio	1
Overall balance	12.1		

Health and education

Health spending, % of GDP	3.7	Education spending, % of GDP	3.7
Doctors per 1,000 pop.	1.4	Enrolment, %: primary	80
Hospital beds per 1,000 pop.	2.8	secondary	...
Improved-water source access,		tertiary	44
% of pop.	100		

Society

No. of households	1.0m	Colour TVs per 100 households	98.7
Av. no. per household	3.5	Telephone lines per 100 pop.	42.4
Marriages per 1,000 pop.	6.3	Mobile telephone subscribers	
Divorces per 1,000 pop.	2.1	per 100 pop.	100.8
Cost of living, Dec. 2006		Computers per 100 pop.	...
New York = 100	108	Internet hosts per 1,000 pop.	211.5

SLOVAKIA

Area	49,035 sq km	Capital	Bratislava
Arable as % of total land	29	Currency	Koruna (Sk)

People

Population	5.4m	Life expectancy: men	70.7 yrs
Pop. per sq km	110.1	women	78.5 yrs
Av. ann. growth		Adult literacy	99.6%
in pop. 2005–10	0.03%	Fertility rate (per woman)	1.3
Pop. under 15	16.8%	Urban population	56.2%
Pop. over 60	16.1%		per 1,000 pop.
No. of men per 100 women	94	Crude birth rate	10.0
Human Development Index	85.6	Crude death rate	10.0

The economy

GDP	Sk1,440bn	GDP per head	$8,590
GDP	$46.4bn	GDP per head in purchasing	
Av. ann. growth in real		power parity (USA=100)	37.9
GDP 1995–2005	4.3%	Economic freedom index	68.4

Origins of GDP

	% of total
Agriculture	3.9
Industry, of which:	31.2
Services	64.9

Components of GDP

	% of total
Private consumption	56.4
Public consumption	18.5
Investment	26.8
Exports	77.3
Imports	-82.4

Structure of employment

	% of total		% of labour force
Agriculture	5	Unemployed 2004	18.1
Industry	39	Av. ann. rate 1995–2004	15.7
Services	56		

Energy

	m TOE		
Total output	6.5	Net energy imports as %	
Total consumption	18.3	of energy use	65
Consumption per head,			
kg oil equivalent	3,407		

Inflation and finance

		av. ann. increase 2000–05	
Consumer price			
inflation 2006	4.4%	Narrow money	20.3%
Av. ann. inflation 2001–06	5.3%	Broad money	7.2%
Money market rate, 2006	4.83%	Household saving rate, 2006	7.3%

Exchange rates

	end 2006		December 2006
Sk per $	26.25	Effective rates	2000 = 100
Sk per SDR	39.48	– nominal	124.33
Sk per €	34.65	– real	152.89

Trade

Principal exports		Principal imports	
	$bn fob		*$bn fob*
Machinery & transport		Machinery & transport	
equipment	14.3	equipment	13.7
Semi-manufactures	8.0	Semi-manufactures	6.5
Other manufactured goods	3.3	Fuels	5.0
Chemicals	1.9	Chemicals	3.5
Total incl. others	**32.0**	Total incl. others	**36.2**

Main export destinations		Main origins of imports	
	% of total		*% of total*
Germany	26.1	Germany	21.0
Czech Republic	14.1	Czech Republic	12.7
Italy	7.1	Russia	10.7
Austria	6.6	Poland	4.1
EU25	85.4	EU25	71.1

Balance of payments, reserves and debt, $bn

Visible exports fob	32.0	Change in reserves	0.6
Visible imports fob	-34.5	Level of reserves	
Trade balance	-2.4	end Dec.	15.5
Invisibles inflows	6.1	No. months of import cover	4.4
Invisibles outflows	-7.7	Official gold holdings, m oz	1.1
Net transfers	0.0	Foreign debt	23.7
Current account balance	-4.1	– as % of GDP	61
– as % of GDP	-8.8	– as % of total exports	73
Capital balance	5.2	Debt service ratio	15
Overall balance	2.6		

Health and education

Health spending, % of GDP	7.2	Education spending, % of GDP	4.4
Doctors per 1,000 pop.	3.2	Enrolment, %: primary	103
Hospital beds per 1,000 pop.	6.9	secondary	94
Improved-water source access,		tertiary	29
% of pop.	100		

Society

No. of households	2.1m	Colour TVs per 100 households	84.1
Av. no. per household	2.5	Telephone lines per 100 pop.	22.2
Marriages per 1,000 pop.	4.9	Mobile telephone subscribers	
Divorces per 1,000 pop.	2.9	per 100 pop.	84.1
Cost of living, Dec. 2006		Computers per 100 pop.	35.7
New York = 100	...	Internet hosts per 1,000 pop.	90.0

SLOVENIA

Area	20,253 sq km	Capital	Ljubljana
Arable as % of total land	9	Currency	Tolars (SIT)

People

Population	2.0m	Life expectancy: men		74.1 yrs
Pop. per sq km	98.8		women	81.5 yrs
Av. ann. growth		Adult literacy		...
in pop. 2005–10	0.01%	Fertility rate (per woman)		1.3
Pop. under 15	14.1%	Urban population		51.0%
Pop. over 60	20.5%			per 1,000 pop.
No. of men per 100 women	95	Crude birth rate		9.0
Human Development Index	91.0	Crude death rate		9.9

The economy

GDP	SIT6,620bn	GDP per head	$17,180
GDP	$34.4bn	GDP per head in purchasing	
Av. ann. growth in real		power parity (USA=100)	53.2
GDP 1995–2005	3.9%	Economic freedom index	63.6

Origins of GDP		**Components of GDP**	
	% of total		% of total
Agriculture	2.5	Private consumption	55.0
Industry, of which:	34.1	Public consumption	19.5
manufacturing	24.6	Investment	24.5
Services	63.4	Exports	64.7
		Imports	-65.2

Structure of employment

	% of total		% of labour force
Agriculture	9	Unemployed 2004	6.1
Industry	37	Av. ann. rate 1995–2004	6.9
Services	54		

Energy

	m TOE		
Total output	3.4	Net energy imports as %	
Total consumption	7.2	of energy use	52
Consumption per head,			
kg oil equivalent	3,591		

Inflation and finance

Consumer price		av. ann. increase 2000–05	
inflation 2006	2.7%	Narrow money (M1)	23.5%
Av. ann. inflation 2001–06	4.4%	Broad money	12.5%
Money market rate, 2006	3.38%		

Exchange rates

	end 2006		December 2006
SIT per $	181.9	Effective rates	2000 = 100
SIT per SDR	273.7	– nominal	...
SIT per €	240.2	– real	...

Trade

Principal exports		**Principal imports**	
	$bn fob		*$bn fob*
Manufactures	7.2	Machinery & transport	
Machinery & transport		equipment	6.4
equipment	7.0	Manufactures	6.4
Chemicals	2.4	Chemicals	2.5
Food & live animals	0.4	Mineral fuels	2.0
Total incl. others	**17.9**	Total incl. others	**19.6**

Main export destinations		**Main origins of imports**	
	% of total		*% of total*
Germany	19.9	Germany	20.0
Italy	12.6	Italy	19.1
Croatia	9.1	Austria	12.3
France	8.2	France	7.4
Austria	8.0	Croatia	3.8
EU25	67.7	EU25	80.9

Balance of payments, reserves and debt, $bn

Visible exports fob	18.1	Change in reserves	-0.7
Visible imports fob	-19.4	Level of reserves	
Trade balance	-1.3	end Dec.	8.2
Invisibles inflows	4.8	No. months of import cover	4.2
Invisibles outflows	-4.1	Official gold holdings, m oz	0.2
Net transfers	-0.1	Foreign debt	18.4
Current account balance	-0.7	– as % of GDP	54
– as % of GDP	-2.0	– as % of total exports	80
Capital balance	0.7	Debt service ratio	18
Overall balance	0.2		

Health and education

Health spending, % of GDP	8.7	Education spending, % of GDP	6.0
Doctors per 1,000 pop.	2.3	Enrolment, %: primary	98
Hospital beds per 1,000 pop.	4.8	secondary	100
Improved-water source access,		tertiary	53
% of pop.	...		

Society

No. of households	0.7m	Colour TVs per 100 households	92.8
Av. no. per household	2.9	Telephone lines per 100 pop.	41.5
Marriages per 1,000 pop.	3.2	Mobile telephone subscribers	
Divorces per 1,000 pop.	1.2	per 100 pop.	89.5
Cost of living, Dec. 2006		Computers per 100 pop.	41.1
New York = 100	...	Internet hosts per 1,000 pop.	32.1

SOUTH AFRICA

Area	1,225,815 sq km	Capital	Pretoria
Arable as % of total land	12	Currency	Rand (R)

People

Population	47.4m	Life expectancy: men	48.8 yrs
Pop. per sq km	38.7	women	49.7 yrs
Av. ann. growth		Adult literacy	82.4%
in pop. 2005–10	0.55%	Fertility rate (per woman)	2.6
Pop. under 15	32.1%	Urban population	59.3%
Pop. over 60	6.7%		per 1,000 pop.
No. of men per 100 women	97	Crude birth rate	22.3
Human Development Index	65.3	Crude death rate	17.0

The economy

GDP	R1,523bn	GDP per head	$5,050
GDP	$240bn	GDP per head in purchasing	
Av. ann. growth in real		power parity (USA=100)	26.5
GDP 1995–2005	3.3%	Economic freedom index	64.1

Origins of GDP		**Components of GDP**	
	% of total		% of total
Agriculture	2.5	Private consumption	63.5
Industry, of which:	30.4	Public consumption	20.2
manufacturing	18.6	Investment	16.8
Services	67.1	Exports	27.1
		Imports	-28.6

Structure of employment

	% of total		% of labour force
Agriculture	10	Unemployed 2004	27.1
Industry	25	Av. ann. rate 1995–2004	24.1
Services	65		

Energy

	m TOE		
Total output	156.0	Net energy imports as %	
Total consumption	131.1	of energy use	-19
Consumption per head,			
kg oil equivalent	2,829		

Inflation and finance

Consumer price		av. ann. increase 2000–05	
inflation 2006	4.7%	Narrow money (M1)	1.8%
Av. ann. inflation 2001–06	4.9%	Broad money	13.4%
Money market rate, 2006	7.23%		

Exchange rates

	end 2006		December 2006
R per $	6.97	Effective rates	2000 = 100
R per SDR	10.49	– nominal	97.2
R per €	9.2	– real	97.2

Trade

Principal exports		Principal imports	
	$bn fob		*$bn cif*
Manufactures	33.4	Manufactures	46.4
Mining	16.2	Mining	8.0
Agriculture	2.4	Agriculture	0.7
Total incl. others	**52.1**	Total incl. others	**55.3**

Main export destinations		Main origins of imports	
	% of total		*% of total*
Japan	9.9	Germany	14.1
United Kingdom	9.7	China	9.0
United States	9.5	United States	7.8
Germany	6.5	Canada	6.2

Balance of payments, reserves and debt, $bn

Visible exports fob	55.3	Change in reserves	5.7
Visible imports fob	-56.5	Level of reserves	
Trade balance	-1.2	end Dec.	20.6
Invisibles inflows	15.8	No. months of import cover	3.2
Invisibles outflows	-21.7	Official gold holdings, m oz	4.0
Net transfers	-2.0	Foreign debt	30.6
Current account balance	-9.1	– as % of GDP	14
– as % of GDP	-3.8	– as % of total exports	47
Capital balance	11.4	Debt service ratio	7
Overall balance	5.8		

Health and education

Health spending, % of GDP	8.6	Education spending, % of GDP	5.4
Doctors per 1,000 pop.	0.8	Enrolment, %: primary	119
Hospital beds per 1,000 pop.	...	secondary	90
Improved-water source access,		tertiary	15
% of pop.	88		

Society

No. of households	12.5m	Colour TVs per 100 households	66.1
Av. no. per household	3.9	Telephone lines per 100 pop.	10.0
Marriages per 1,000 pop.	3.8	Mobile telephone subscribers	
Divorces per 1,000 pop.	0.9	per 100 pop.	71.1
Cost of living, Dec. 2006		Computers per 100 pop.	8.4
New York = 100	64	Internet hosts per 1,000 pop.	21.9

SOUTH KOREA

Area	99,274 sq km	Capital	Seoul
Arable as % of total land	17	Currency	Won (W)

People

Population	47.8m	Life expectancy: men		75.0 yrs
Pop. per sq km	481.5	women		82.2 yrs
Av. ann. growth		Adult literacy		...
in pop. 2005–10	0.33%	Fertility rate (per woman)		1.2
Pop. under 15	18.6%	Urban population		80.8%
Pop. over 60	13.7%		per 1,000 pop.	
No. of men per 100 women	100	Crude birth rate		9.3
Human Development Index	91.2	Crude death rate		5.9

The economy

GDP	W807trn	GDP per head	$16,480
GDP	$788bn	GDP per head in purchasing	
Av. ann. growth in real		power parity (USA=100)	52.6
GDP 1995–2005	4.4%	Economic freedom index	68.6

Origins of GDP		**Components of GDP**	
	% of total		% of total
Agriculture	3.3	Private consumption	52.6
Industry, of which:	37.6	Public consumption	14.1
manufacturing	28.4	Investment	29.3
Services	59.1	Exports	42.5
		Imports	-40.0

Structure of employment

	% of total		% of labour force
Agriculture	8	Unemployed 2004	3.5
Industry	27	Av. ann. rate 1995–2004	3.8
Services	65		

Energy

	m TOE		
Total output	38.0	Net energy imports as %	
Total consumption	213.0	of energy use	82
Consumption per head,			
kg oil equivalent	4,431		

Inflation and finance

		av. ann. increase 2000–05	
Consumer price			
inflation 2006	2.2%	Narrow money (M1)	10.5%
Av. ann. inflation 2001–06	3.0%	Broad money	6.5%
Money market rate, 2006	4.2%	Household saving rate, 2006	3.5%

Exchange rates

	end 2006		December 2006
W per $	930	Effective rates	2000 = 100
W per SDR	1,399	– nominal	...
W per €	1,227	– real	...

Trade

Principal exports		Principal imports	
	$bn fob		*$bn cif*
Electronic products	88.3	Electrical machinery	54.4
Machinery	32.1	Crude petroleum	42.7
Motor vehicles	27.2	Machinery & equipment	31.8
Chemicals	24.8	Consumer durables	26.8
Metal goods	22.5	Semiconductors	25.1
Total incl. others	**284.4**	Total incl. others	**261.2**

Main export destinations		Main origins of imports	
	% of total		*% of total*
China	21.8	Japan	18.5
United States	14.5	China	14.8
Japan	8.5	United States	11.7
Hong Kong	5.5	Saudi Arabia	6.2
Taiwan	3.8	Australia	3.8

Balance of payments, reserves and debt, $bn

Visible exports fob	289.0	Change in reserves	11.4
Visible imports fob	-255.5	Level of reserves	
Trade balance	33.5	end Dec.	210.6
Invisibles inflows	55.6	No. months of import cover	7.8
Invisibles outflows	-70.0	Official gold holdings, m oz	0.5
Net transfers	-2.5	Foreign debt	152.8
Current account balance	16.6	– as % of GDP	19
– as % of GDP	2.1	– as % of total exports	44
Capital balance	0.5	Debt service ratio	6
Overall balance	19.9		

Health and education

Health spending, % of GDP	5.6	Education spending, % of GDP	4.6
Doctors per 1,000 pop.	1.6	Enrolment, %: primary	99
Hospital beds per 1,000 pop.	6.6	secondary	93
Improved-water source access,		tertiary	72
% of pop.	92		

Society

No. of households	17.3m	Colour TVs per 100 households	93.8
Av. no. per household	2.7	Telephone lines per 100 pop.	49.2
Marriages per 1,000 pop.	6.5	Mobile telephone subscribers	
Divorces per 1,000 pop.	3.9	per 100 pop.	79.4
Cost of living, Dec. 2006		Computers per 100 pop.	53.2
New York = 100	115	Internet hosts per 1,000 pop.	6.4

SPAIN

Area	504,782 sq km	Capital	Madrid
Arable as % of total land	27	Currency	Euro (€)

People

Population	43.1m	Life expectancy: men	77.7 yrs
Pop. per sq km	85.4	women	84.2 yrs
Av. ann. growth		Adult literacy	
in pop. 2005–10	0.77%	Fertility rate (per woman)	1.4
Pop. under 15	14.4%	Urban population	76.7%
Pop. over 60	21.7%		per 1,000 pop.
No. of men per 100 women	97	Crude birth rate	10.8
Human Development Index	93.8	Crude death rate	8.8

The economy

GDP	€904bn	GDP per head	$26,090
GDP	$1,125bn	GDP per head in purchasing	
Av. ann. growth in real		power parity (USA=100)	64.9
GDP 1995–2005	3.5%	Economic freedom index	70.9

Origins of GDP

Components of GDP

	% of total		% of total
Agriculture	4.1	Private consumption	57.6
Industry, of which:	29.2	Public consumption	17.4
manufacturing	...	Investment	27.2
Services	66.8	Exports	26.3
		Imports	-28.7

Structure of employment

	% of total		% of labour force
Agriculture	5	Unemployed 2004	11.0
Industry	30	Av. ann. rate 1995–2004	16.2
Services	65		

Energy

	m TOE		
Total output	32.5	Net energy imports as %	
Total consumption	142.2	of energy use	77
Consumption per head,			
kg oil equivalent	3,331		

Inflation and finance

Consumer price		av. ann. increase 2000–05	
inflation 2006	3.6%	Euro area:	
Av. ann. inflation 2001–06	3.4%	Narrow money (M1)	10.8%
Money market rate, 2006	2.83%	Broad money	7.7%
		Household saving rate, 2006	10.0%

Exchange rates

	end 2006		December 2006
€ per $	0.76	Effective rates	2000 = 100
€ per SDR	1.14	– nominal	106.4
		– real	123.7

Trade

Principal exports		Principal imports	
	$bn fob		*$bn cif*
Raw materials &		Raw materials & intermediate	
intermediate products	91.9	products (excl. fuels)	130.6
Consumer goods	73.0	Consumer goods	83.1
Capital goods	18.5	Energy	39.7
Energy	7.8	Capital goods	33.9
Total incl. others	**191.0**	Total incl. others	**287.7**

Main export destinations		Main origins of imports	
	% of total		*% of total*
France	19.2	Germany	14.6
Germany	11.4	France	14.2
Italy	8.5	Italy	8.9
United Kingdom	8.4	United Kingdom	5.7
EU25	72.1	EU25	60.8

Balance of payments, reserves and aid, $bn

Visible exports fob	194.5	Overall balance	-1.9
Visible imports fob	-280.1	Change in reserves	-2.5
Trade balance	-85.6	Level of reserves	
Invisibles inflows	132.4	end Dec.	17.2
Invisibles outflows	-125.8	No. months of import cover	0.5
Net transfers	-4.1	Official gold holdings, m oz	14.7
Current account balance	-83.1	Aid given	3.02
– as % of GDP	-7.4	– as % of GDP	0.27
Capital balance	82.4		

Health and education

Health spending, % of GDP	8.1	Education spending, % of GDP	4.3
Doctors per 1,000 pop.	3.3	Enrolment, %: primary	105
Hospital beds per 1,000 pop.	3.8	secondary	119
Improved-water source access,		tertiary	58
% of pop.	100		

Society

No. of households	15.2m	Colour TVs per 100 households	98.7
Av. no. per household	2.7	Telephone lines per 100 pop.	42.9
Marriages per 1,000 pop.	5.3	Mobile telephone subscribers	
Divorces per 1,000 pop.	1.1	per 100 pop.	96.8
Cost of living, Dec. 2006		Computers per 100 pop.	28.1
New York = 100	97	Internet hosts per 1,000 pop.	68.0

SWEDEN

Area	449,964 sq km	Capital	Stockholm
Arable as % of total land	7	Currency	Swedish krona (Skr)

People

Population	9.0m	Life expectancy:	men	78.7 yrs
Pop. per sq km	20.0		women	83.0 yrs
Av. ann. growth		Adult literacy		...
in pop. 2005–10	0.45%	Fertility rate (per woman)		1.8
Pop. under 15	17.4%	Urban population		84.2%
Pop. over 60	23.4%			*per 1,000 pop.*
No. of men per 100 women	98	Crude birth rate		11.3
Human Development Index	95.1	Crude death rate		10.1

The economy

GDP	Skr2,673bn	GDP per head	$39,740
GDP	$358bn	GDP per head in purchasing	
Av. ann. growth in real		power parity (USA=100)	77.6
GDP 1995–2005	2.7%	Economic freedom index	72.6

Origins of GDP		**Components of GDP**	
	% of total		*% of total*
Agriculture	1.9	Private consumption	48.0
Industry, of which:	27.9	Public consumption	27.2
manufacturing	24.1	Investment	17.0
Services	70.2	Exports	48.6
		Imports	-40.9

Structure of employment

	% of total		*% of labour force*
Agriculture	2	Unemployed 2004	6.5
Industry	22	Av. ann. rate 1995–2004	6.4
Services	76		

Energy

	m TOE		
Total output	35.1	Net energy imports as %	
Total consumption	53.9	of energy use	35
Consumption per head,			
kg oil equivalent	5,998		

Inflation and finance

		av. ann. increase 2001–05	
Consumer price			
inflation 2006	1.5%	Narrow money	10.6%
Av. ann. inflation 2001–06	1.5%	Broad money	5.5%
Repurchase rate, 2005	1.50%	Household saving rate, 2006	7.8%

Exchange rates

	end 2006		*December 2006*
Skr per $	6.86	Effective rates	*2000 = 100*
Skr per SDR	10.33	– nominal	102.2
Skr per €	9.06	– real	95.9

Trade

Principal exports		Principal imports	
	$bn fob		*$bn cif*
Machinery & transport equipment	58.4	Machinery & transport equipment	43.8
Manufactured goods	26.6	Manufacturing goods	16.9
Chemicals	14.6	Miscellaneous manufactures	13.6
Miscellaneous manufactures	11.3	Mineral fuels	13.1
Total incl. others	**130.2**	Total incl. others	**111.2**

Main export destinations		Main origins of imports	
	% of total		*% of total*
United States	10.6	Germany	18.1
Germany	10.4	Denmark	9.4
Norway	8.7	Norway	8.1
United Kingdom	7.4	United Kingdom	6.9
Denmark	6.9	Netherlands	6.8
EU25	58.4	EU25	71.3

Balance of payments, reserves and aid, $bn

Visible exports fob	134.9	Overall balance	0.2
Visible imports fob	-115.2	Change in reserves	0.1
Trade balance	19.7	Level of reserves	
Invisibles inflows	78.2	end Dec.	24.9
Invisibles outflows	-69.6	No. months of import cover	1.6
Net transfers	-4.6	Official gold holdings, m oz	5.4
Current account balance	23.6	Aid given	3.36
– as % of GDP	6.7	– as % of GDP	0.94
Capital balance	-21.9		

Health and education

Health spending, % of GDP	9.1	Education spending, % of GDP	7.5
Doctors per 1,000 pop.	3.3	Enrolment, %: primary	109
Hospital beds per 1,000 pop.	3.6	secondary	103
Improved-water source access,		tertiary	66
% of pop.	100		

Society

No. of households	4.2m	Colour TVs per 100 households	97.0
Av. no. per household	2.1	Telephone lines per 100 pop.	58.2
Marriages per 1,000 pop.	4.6	Mobile telephone subscribers	
Divorces per 1,000 pop.	2.2	per 100 pop.	100.5
Cost of living, Dec. 2006		Computers per 100 pop.	76.1
New York = 100	104	Internet hosts per 1,000 pop.	357.8

SWITZERLAND

Area	41,293 sq km	Capital	Berne
Arable as % of total land	10	Currency	Swiss franc (SFr)

People

Population	7.3m	Life expectancy: men		79.0 yrs
Pop. per sq km	176.8	women		84.2 yrs
Av. ann. growth		Adult literacy		...
in pop. 2005–10	0.38%	Fertility rate (per woman)		1.4
Pop. under 15	16.7%	Urban population		75.2%
Pop. over 60	21.1%			per 1,000 pop.
No. of men per 100 women	95	Crude birth rate		9.2
Human Development Index	94.7	Crude death rate		8.1

The economy

GDP	SFr457bn	GDP per head	$50,280
GDP	$367bn	GDP per head in purchasing	
Av. ann. growth in real		power parity (USA=100)	85.1
GDP 1995–2005	1.5%	Economic freedom index	79.1

Origins of GDP[a]		Components of GDP	
	% of total		% of total
Agriculture	1.0	Private consumption	60.3
Industry, of which:	26.3	Public consumption	11.4
manufacturing	...	Investment	21.4
Services	72.7	Exports	47.9
		Imports	-41.1

Structure of employment

	% of total		% of labour force
Agriculture	4	Unemployed 2004	4.3
Industry	23	Av. ann. rate 1995–2004	3.4
Services	73		

Energy

	m TOE		
Total output	11.8	Net energy imports as %	
Total consumption	27.1	of energy use	56
Consumption per head,			
kg oil equivalent	3,672		

Inflation and finance

		av. ann. increase 2000–05	
Consumer price			
inflation 2006	1.0%	Narrow money (M1)	8.3%
Av. ann. inflation 2001–06	0.8%	Broad money	5.5%
Money market rate, 2006	1.94%	Household saving rate, 2006	7.8%

Exchange rates

	end 2006		December 2006
SFr per $	1.22	Effective rates	2000 = 100
SFr per SDR	1.84	– nominal	106.5
SFr per €	1.61	– real	116.9

Trade

Principal exports	$bn	Principal imports	$bn
Chemicals	44.1	Chemicals	26.3
Machinery	28.1	Machinery	23.8
Watches & jewellery	9.9	Motor vehicles	10.8
Metals & metal manufactures	9.4	Textiles	9.9
Precision instruments	9.2	Precision instruments	8.8
Total incl. others	**126.1**	Total incl. others	**119.8**

Main export destinations	% of total	Main origins of imports	% of total
Germany	20.0	Germany	33.3
United States	10.7	Italy	11.2
France	8.5	France	9.4
Italy	8.1	Netherlands	5.2
United Kingdom	5.1	Austria	4.6
Spain	4.3	United States	4.6
EU25	62.1	EU25	82.8

Balance of payments, reserves and aid, $bn

Visible exports fob	151.3	Overall balance	-17.7
Visible imports fob	-145.4	Change in reserves	-17.0
Trade balance	5.9	Level of reserves	
Invisibles inflows	153.8	end Dec.	57.6
Invisibles outflows	-89.7	No. months of import cover	2.9
Net transfers	-9.0	Official gold holdings, m oz	41.5
Current account balance	61.0	Aid given	1.77
– as % of GDP	16.7	– as % of GDP	0.44
Capital balance	-92.7		

Health and education

Health spending, % of GDP	11.5	Education spending, % of GDP	6.1
Doctors per 1,000 pop.	3.6	Enrolment, %: primary	108
Hospital beds per 1,000 pop.	5.7	secondary	93
Improved-water source access,		tertiary	40
% of pop.	100		

Society

No. of households	3.3m	Colour TVs per 100 households	96.8
Av. no. per household	2.2	Telephone lines per 100 pop.	69.0
Marriages per 1,000 pop.	5.3	Mobile telephone subscribers	
Divorces per 1,000 pop.	2.5	per 100 pop.	91.6
Cost of living, Dec. 2006		Computers per 100 pop.	86.2
New York = 100	112	Internet hosts per 1,000 pop.	352.2

a Latest available.

TAIWAN

Area	36,179 sq km	Capital	Taipei
Arable as % of total land	25	Currency	Taiwan dollar (T$)

People

Population	22.9m	Life expectancy:[a] men		74.7 yrs
Pop. per sq km	633.0		women	80.3 yrs
Av. ann. growth		Adult literacy		96.1%
in pop. 2005–10	0.60%	Fertility rate (per woman)		1.6
Pop. under 15	21.0%	Urban population		...
Pop. over 60	12.1%			*per 1,000 pop.*
No. of men per 100 women	104	Crude birth rate		13.0
Human Development Index	...	Crude death rate[a]		6.5

The economy

GDP	T$11,132bn	GDP per head	$15,110
GDP	$346bn	GDP per head in purchasing	
Av. ann. growth in real		power parity (USA=100)	70.0
GDP 1995–2005	4.5%	Economic freedom index	71.1

Origins of GDP		**Components of GDP**	
	% of total		*% of total*
Agriculture	1.7	Private consumption	62.1
Industry	25.0	Public consumption	13.4
Services	73.3	Investment	20.5
		Exports	65.9
		Imports	-61.7

Structure of employment

	% of total		*% of labour force*
Agriculture	8	Unemployed 2004	4.4
Industry	36	Av. ann. rate 1995–2004	3.3
Services	56		

Energy

	m TOE		
Total output	...	Net energy imports as %	
Total consumption	...	of energy use	...
Consumption per head,			
kg oil equivalent	...		

Inflation and finance

Consumer price		*av. ann. increase 2000–05*	
inflation 2006	0.6%	Narrow money (M1)	9.4%
Av. ann. inflation 2001–06	0.8%	Broad money	5.3%
Money market rate, 2006	1.75%		

Exchange rates

	end 2006		*December 2006*
T$ per $	32.59	Effective rates	*2000 = 100*
T$ per SDR	48.89	– nominal	...
T$ per €	43.03	– real	...

Trade

Principal exports		Principal imports	
	$bn fob		*$bn cif*
Machinery & electrical equipment	90.7	Machinery & electrical equipment	68.1
Base metals & manufactures	20.3	Minerals	29.9
Plastics and rubber products	14.6	Chemicals	19.5
Textiles & clothing	11.8	Metals	18.7
Vehicles, aircraft & ships	7.2	Precision instruments, clocks & watches	11.3
Total incl. others	**197.8**	Total incl. others	**182.6**

Main export destinations		Main origins of imports	
	% of total		*% of total*
China	21.6	Japan	25.3
Hong Kong	16.2	United States	11.6
United States	15.1	China	11.0
Japan	7.6	South Korea	7.3

Balance of payments, reserves and debt, $bn

Visible exports fob	198.5	Change in reserves	10.8
Visible imports fob	-180.6	Level of reserves	
Trade balance	17.9	end Dec.	253.3
Invisibles inflows	43.3	No. months of import cover	13.7
Invisibles outflows	-40.8	Official gold holdings, m oz	0.0
Net transfers	-4.3	Foreign debt	90.8
Current account balance	16.1	– as % of GDP	26
– as % of GDP	4.7	– as % of total exports	38
Capital balance	1.6	Debt service ratio	3
Overall balance	20.1		

Health and education

Health spending, % of GDP	...	Education spending, % of GDP	...
Doctors per 1,000 pop.	...	Enrolment, %: primary	...
Hospital beds per 1,000 pop.	...	secondary	...
Improved-water source access, % of pop.	...	tertiary	...

Society

No. of households	7.2m	Colour TVs per 100 households	99.3
Av. no. per household	3.2	Telephone lines per 100 pop.	59.8
Marriages per 1,000 pop.	7.5	Mobile telephone subscribers	
Divorces per 1,000 pop.	3.1	per 100 pop.	97.4
Cost of living, Dec. 2006		Computers per 100 pop.	57.5
New York = 100	85	Internet hosts per 1,000 pop.	193.0

a 2002 estimate.

THAILAND

Area	513,115 sq km	Capital	Bangkok
Arable as % of total land	28	Currency	Baht (Bt)

People

Population	64.2m	Life expectancy: men		66.5 yrs
Pop. per sq km	125.1		women	75.0 yrs
Av. ann. growth		Adult literacy		92.6%
in pop. 2005–10	0.66%	Fertility rate (per woman)		1.9
Pop. under 15	21.7%	Urban population		32.3%
Pop. over 60	11.3%			per 1,000 pop.
No. of men per 100 women	95	Crude birth rate		14.6
Human Development Index	78.4	Crude death rate		8.5

The economy

GDP	Bt7,104bn	GDP per head	$2,750
GDP	$177bn	GDP per head in purchasing	
Av. ann. growth in real		power parity (USA=100)	20.7
GDP 1995–2005	2.7%	Economic freedom index	65.6

Origins of GDP		**Components of GDP**	
	% of total		% of total
Agriculture	10.2	Private consumption	57.1
Industry, of which:	44.1	Public consumption	11.9
manufacturing	34.8	Investment	29.0
Services	45.7	Exports	73.8
		Imports	-75.1

Structure of employment

	% of total		% of labour force
Agriculture	43	Unemployed 2004	1.5
Industry	20	Av. ann. rate 1995–2004	1.9
Services	37		

Energy

	m TOE		
Total output	50.1	Net energy imports as %	
Total consumption	97.1	of energy use	48
Consumption per head,			
kg oil equivalent	1,524		

Inflation and finance

Consumer price		av. ann. increase 2000–05	
inflation 2006	4.6%	Narrow money (M1)	11.7%
Av. ann. inflation 2001–06	2.8%	Broad money	6.3%
Money market rate, 2006	4.64%		

Exchange rates

	end 2006		December 2006
Bt per $	36.05	Effective rates	2000 = 100
Bt per SDR	54.23	– nominal	...
Bt per €	47.59	– real	...

Trade

Principal exports		Principal imports	
	$bn fob		*$bn cif*
Machinery & mech. appliances	16.2	Raw materials & intermediates	49.4
Electrical appliances	8.9	Capital goods	32.0
Integrated circuits & parts	5.5	Petroleum & products	20.8
Textiles	5.5	Consumer goods	8.4
Total incl. others	**110.2**	Total incl. others	**118.2**

Main export destinations		Main origins of imports	
	% of total		*% of total*
United States	15.3	Japan	22.0
Japan	13.7	China	9.4
China	8.3	United States	7.3
Singapore	6.8	Malaysia	6.9
Hong Kong	5.6	United Arab Emirates	4.8

Balance of payments, reserves and debt, $bn

Visible exports fob	109.2	Change in reserves	2.2
Visible imports fob	-106.0	Level of reserves	
Trade balance	3.2	end Dec.	52.1
Invisibles inflows	24.0	No. months of import cover	4.5
Invisibles outflows	-33.9	Official gold holdings, m oz	2.7
Net transfers	3.0	Foreign debt	52.3
Current account balance	-3.7	– as % of GDP	32
– as % of GDP	-2.1	– as % of total exports	44
Capital balance	8.4	Debt service ratio	15
Overall balance	5.4		

Health and education

Health spending, % of GDP	3.5	Education spending, % of GDP	4.2
Doctors per 1,000 pop.	0.4	Enrolment, %: primary	94
Hospital beds per 1,000 pop.	2.2	secondary	73
Improved-water source access,		tertiary	32
% of pop.	99		

Society

No. of households	17.2m	Colour TVs per 100 households	84.9
Av. no. per household	3.6	Telephone lines per 100 pop.	11.0
Marriages per 1,000 pop.	4.6	Mobile telephone subscribers	
Divorces per 1,000 pop.	1.1	per 100 pop.	43.0
Cost of living, Dec. 2006		Computers per 100 pop.	5.8
New York = 100	69	Internet hosts per 1,000 pop.	14.6

TURKEY

Area	779,452 sq km	Capital	Ankara
Arable as % of total land	31	Currency	Turkish Lira (YTL)

People

Population	73.2m	Life expectancy: men	69.4 yrs
Pop. per sq km	93.9	women	74.3 yrs
Av. ann. growth		Adult literacy	87.4%
in pop. 2005–10	1.26%	Fertility rate (per woman)	2.1
Pop. under 15	28.3%	Urban population	67.3%
Pop. over 60	8.2%		per 1,000 pop.
No. of men per 100 women	101	Crude birth rate	18.4
Human Development Index	75.7	Crude death rate	5.9

The economy

GDP	YTL487bn	GDP per head	$4,950
GDP	$363bn	GDP per head in purchasing	
Av. ann. growth in real		power parity (USA=100)	20.1
GDP 1995–2005	4.1%	Economic freedom index	59.3

Origins of GDP		**Components of GDP**	
	% of total		% of total
Agriculture	10.3	Private consumption	68.3
Industry, of which:	29.8	Public consumption	13.2
manufacturing	...	Investment	19.8
Services	59.9	Exports	27.8
		Imports	-34.4

Structure of employment

	% of total		% of labour force
Agriculture	30	Unemployed 2005	10.3
Industry	25	Av. ann. rate 1995–2005	8.3
Services	45		

Energy

	m TOE		
Total output	24.1	Net energy imports as %	
Total consumption	81.9	of energy use	71
Consumption per head,			
kg oil equivalent	1,151		

Inflation and finance

Consumer price		av. ann. increase 2000–05	
inflation 2006	9.6%	Narrow money (M1)	41.7%
Av. ann. inflation 2001–06	17.8%	Broad money	33.0%
Money market rate, 2006	15.59%		

Exchange rates

	end 2006		December 2006
YTL per $	1.41	Effective rates	2000 = 100
YTL per SDR	2.12	– nominal	...
YTL per €	1.86	– real	...

Trade

Principal exports		Principal imports	
	$bn fob		*$bn cif*
Textiles	18.7	Chemicals & products	17.4
Motor vehicles & parts	10.2	Crude oil & natural gas	14.4
Metals	6.9	Metals	13.6
Machinery & equipment	4.9	Motor vehicles & parts	12.3
Total incl. others	**71.9**	Total incl. others	**99.0**

Main export destinations		Main origins of imports	
	% of total		*% of total*
Germany	12.9	Germany	11.7
United Kingdom	8.1	Russia	11.0
Italy	7.7	Italy	6.5
United States	6.7	China	5.9
France	5.2	France	5.0
EU25	52.3	EU25	42.2

Balance of payments, reserves and debt, $bn

Visible exports fob	76.9	Change in reserves	15.2
Visible imports fob	-109.9	Level of reserves	
Trade balance	-32.9	end Dec.	52.5
Invisibles inflows	29.5	No. months of import cover	4.8
Invisibles outflows	-21.2	Official gold holdings, m oz	3.7
Net transfers	1.5	Foreign debt	171.1
Current account balance	-23.2	– as % of GDP	59
– as % of GDP	-6.4	– as % of total exports	195
Capital balance	44.1	Debt service ratio	39
Overall balance	23.2		

Health and education

Health spending, % of GDP	7.7	Education spending, % of GDP	4.0
Doctors per 1,000 pop.	1.4	Enrolment, %: primary	101
Hospital beds per 1,000 pop.	2.6	secondary	79
Improved-water source access,		tertiary	15
% of pop.	96		

Society

No. of households	15.4m	Colour TVs per 100 households	68.2
Av. no. per household	4.7	Telephone lines per 100 pop.	25.9
Marriages per 1,000 pop.	6.5	Mobile telephone subscribers	
Divorces per 1,000 pop.	0.7	per 100 pop.	59.6
Cost of living, Dec. 2006		Computers per 100 pop.	5.1
New York = 100	85	Internet hosts per 1,000 pop.	21.6

UKRAINE

Area	603,700 sq km	Capital	Kiev
Arable as % of total land	56	Currency	Hryvnya (UAH)

People

Population	46.5m	Life expectancy: men	62.1 yrs
Pop. per sq km	77.0	women	73.8 yrs
Av. ann. growth		Adult literacy	99.4%
in pop. 2005–10	-0.76%	Fertility rate (per woman)	1.2
Pop. under 15	14.7%	Urban population	67.8%
Pop. over 60	20.6%		per 1,000 pop.
No. of men per 100 women	86	Crude birth rate	9.2
Human Development Index	77.4	Crude death rate	16.4

The economy

GDP	UAH425bn	GDP per head	$1,780
GDP	$82.9bn	GDP per head in purchasing	
Av. ann. growth in real		power parity (USA=100)	16.3
GDP 1995–2005	2.7%	Economic freedom index	53.3

Origins of GDP		Components of GDP	
	% of total		% of total
Agriculture	12.1	Private consumption	61
Industry	36.5	Public consumption	19
Services	51.4	Investment	19
		Exports	54
		Imports	-53

Structure of employment

	% of total		% of labour force
Agriculture	19	Unemployed 2004	8.6
Industry	24	Av. ann. rate 1995–2004	9.6
Services	57		

Energy

	m TOE		
Total output	76.3	Net energy imports as %	
Total consumption	140.3	of energy use	46
Consumption per head,			
kg oil equivalent	2,958		

Inflation and finance

			av. ann. increase 2000–05
Consumer price			
inflation 2006	9.0%	Narrow money (M1)	36.5%
Av. ann. inflation 2001–06	7.4%	Broad money	43.6%
Money market rate, 2006	3.58%		

Exchange rates

	end 2006		December 2006
			2000 = 100
UAH per $	5.05	Effective rates	
UAH per SDR	7.60	– nominal	95.90
UAH per €	6.67	– real	112.40

Trade

Principal exports	
	$bn fob
Metals	14.0
Machinery & equipment	4.7
Fuels & mineral products	4.4
Food & agricultural produce	4.3
Chemicals	3.0
Total incl. others	**34.2**

Principal imports	
	$bn cif
Fuels, mineral products	11.3
Machinery & equipment	10.1
Chemicals	3.1
Food & agricultural produce	2.7
Metals	2.5
Total incl. others	**36.1**

Main export destinations	
	% of total
Russia	21.9
Turkey	5.9
Italy	5.5
Germany	3.8

Main origins of imports	
	% of total
Russia	35.5
Germany	9.4
Poland	7.4
Turkmenistan	5.0

Balance of payments, reserves and debt, $bn

Visible exports fob	35.0	Change in reserves	9.9
Visible imports fob	-36.2	Level of reserves	
Trade balance	-1.1	end Dec.	19.4
Invisibles inflows	10.1	No. months of import cover	5.1
Invisibles outflows	-9.3	Official gold holdings, m oz	0.5
Net transfers	2.8	Foreign debt	33.3
Current account balance	2.5	– as % of GDP	53
– as % of GDP	3.1	– as % of total exports	89
Capital balance	8.0	Debt service ratio	13
Overall balance	10.7		

Health and education

Health spending, % of GDP	6.5	Education spending, % of GDP	6.4
Doctors per 1,000 pop.	3.0	Enrolment, %: primary	81
Hospital beds per 1,000 pop.	8.7	secondary	93
Improved-water source access,		tertiary	43
% of pop.	96		

Society

No. of households	19.8m	Colour TVs per 100 households	79.8
Av. no. per household	2.4	Telephone lines per 100 pop.	25.8
Marriages per 1,000 pop.	5.9	Mobile telephone subscribers	
Divorces per 1,000 pop.	3.7	per 100 pop.	37.0
Cost of living, Dec. 2006		Computers per 100 pop.	3.9
New York = 100	72	Internet hosts per 1,000 pop.	5.9

UNITED ARAB EMIRATES

Area	83,600 sq km	Capital	Abu Dhabi
Arable as % of total land	1	Currency	Dirham (AED)

People

Population	4.5m	Life expectancy: men	77.2 yrs
Pop. per sq km	53.8	women	81.5 yrs
Av. ann. growth		Adult literacy	...
in pop. 2005–10	2.85%	Fertility rate (per woman)	2.3
Pop. under 15	19.8%	Urban population	76.7%
Pop. over 60	1.8%		per 1,000 pop.
No. of men per 100 women	210	Crude birth rate	16.2
Human Development Index	83.9	Crude death rate	1.4

The economy

GDP	AED476bn	GDP per head	$28,820
GDP	$130bn	GDP per head in purchasing	
Av. ann. growth in real		power parity (USA=100)	60.9
GDP 1995–2005	6.4%	Economic freedom index	60.4

Origins of GDP		Components of GDP	
	% of total		% of total
Agriculture	2.9	Private consumption	44.1
Industry, of which:	50.6	Public consumption	11.1
manufacturing	13.4	Investment	21.3
Services	46.5	Exports	89.3
		Imports	-66.0

Structure of employment

	% of total		% of labour force
Agriculture	...	Unemployed 2001	2.3
Industry	...	Av. ann. rate 1995–2001	2.1
Services	...		

Energy

			m TOE
Total output	164.0	Net energy imports as %	
Total consumption	43.8	of energy use	-274
Consumption per head,			
kg oil equivalent	10,142		

Inflation and finance

			av. ann. increase 2000–05
Consumer price			
inflation 2005	7.8%	Narrow money (M1)	25.1%
Av. ann. inflation 2001–05	4.7%	Broad money	20.6%

Exchange rates

	end 2006		December 2006
AED per $	3.67	Effective rates	2000 = 100
AED per SDR	5.51	– nominal	88.5
AED per €	4.85	– real	...

Trade

Principal exports

	$bn fob
Crude oil	43.5
Re-exports	38.0
Total incl. others	**115.4**

Principal imports[a]

	$bn cif
Machinery & electrical equip.	12.4
Precious stones & metals	10.4
Transport equipment	6.4
Total incl. others	**61.6**

Main export destinations

	% of total
Japan	25.6
South Korea	9.3
Thailand	5.8
India	5.1

Main origins of imports

	% of total
China	9.9
United Kingdom	9.7
United States	9.6
India	8.9

Balance of payments, reserves and debt, $bn

Visible exports fob	115.4	Change in reserves	2.5
Visible imports fob	-71.1	Level of reserves	
Trade balance	44.3	end Dec.	21.0
Invisibles, net	-13.2	No. months of import cover	2.6
Net transfers	-5.9	Official gold holdings, m oz	0.0
Current account balance	27.2	Foreign debt	36.7
– as % of GDP	26.1	– as % of GDP	28
Capital balance	-26.9	– as % of total exports	26
Overall balance	2.6	Debt service ratio	2

Health and education

Health spending, % of GDP	2.9	Education spending, % of GDP	1.3
Doctors per 1,000 pop.	2.0	Enrolment, %: primary	94
Hospital beds per 1,000 pop.	2.2	secondary	66
Improved-water source access,		tertiary	12
% of pop.	100		

Society

No. of households	0.7m	Colour TVs per 100 households	97.3
Av. no. per household	6.5	Telephone lines per 100 pop.	27.5
Marriages per 1,000 pop.	3.1	Mobile telephone subscribers	
Divorces per 1,000 pop.	0.9	per 100 pop.	100.9
Cost of living, Dec. 2006		Computers per 100 pop.	19.8
New York = 100	70	Internet hosts per 1,000 pop.	74.6

UNITED KINGDOM

Area	242,534 sq km	Capital	London
Arable as % of total land	24	Currency	Pound (£)

People

Population	59.7m	Life expectancy: men	77.2 yrs
Pop. per sq km	246.1	women	81.6 yrs
Av. ann. growth		Adult literacy	...
in pop. 2005–10	0.42%	Fertility rate (per woman)	1.8
Pop. under 15	18.0%	Urban population	89.7%
Pop. over 60	21.2%		per 1,000 pop.
No. of men per 100 women	96	Crude birth rate	12.0
Human Development Index	94.0	Crude death rate	9.9

The economy

GDP	£1,209bn	GDP per head	$36,830
GDP	$2,199bn	GDP per head in purchasing	
Av. ann. growth in real		power parity (USA=100)	79.3
GDP 1995–2005	2.7%	Economic freedom index	81.6

Origins of GDP		**Components of GDP**	
	% of total		% of total
Agriculture	1.0	Private consumption	65.3
Industry, of which:	23.6	Public consumption	21.8
manufacturing	14.1	Investment	16.6
Services	75.4	Exports	26.1
		Imports	-30.0

Structure of employment

	% of total		% of labour force
Agriculture	1	Unemployed 2004	4.6
Industry	22	Av. ann. rate 1995–2004	6.1
Services	77		

Energy

	m TOE		
Total output	225.2	Net energy imports as %	
Total consumption	233.7	of energy use	4
Consumption per head,			
kg oil equivalent	3,906		

Inflation and finance

Consumer price		av. ann. increase 2000–05	
inflation 2006	2.3%	Narrow money (M0)	6.4%
Av. ann. inflation 2001–06	1.7%	Broad money (M4)	9.4%
Money market rate, 2006	4.77%	Household saving rate, 2006	5.3%

Exchange rates

	end 2006		December 2006
£ per $	0.51	Effective rates	2000 = 100
£ per SDR	0.77	– nominal	100.4
£ per €	0.67	– real	102.5

Trade

Principal exports

	$bn fob
Finished manufactured products	206.0
Semi-manufactured products	108.5
Fuels	39.4
Food, drink & tobacco	19.4
Basic materials	7.3
Total incl. others	**371.4**

Principal imports

	$bn fob
Finished manufactured products	285.4
Semi-manufactured products	113.6
Food, drink & tobacco	44.4
Fuels	42.9
Basic materials	12.3
Total incl. others	**483.0**

Main export destinations

	% of total
United States	14.6
Germany	10.9
France	9.4
Ireland	7.8
Netherlands	6.0
EU25	56.8

Main origins of imports

	% of total
Germany	13.8
France	7.9
United States	7.9
Netherlands	7.3
Belgium-Luxembourg	5.4
EU25	55.8

Balance of payments, reserves and aid, $bn

Visible exports fob	384.3	Overall balance	1.7
Visible imports fob	-509.4	Change in reserves	-6.1
Trade balance	-125.1	Level of reserves	
Invisibles inflows	547.6	end Dec.	43.6
Invisibles outflows	-453.8	No. months of import cover	0.5
Net transfers	-22.1	Official gold holdings, m oz	10.0
Current account balance	-53.4	Aid given	10.77
– as % of GDP	-2.4	– as % of GDP	0.47
Capital balance	60.9		

Health and education

Health spending, % of GDP	8.1	Education spending, % of GDP	5.5
Doctors per 1,000 pop.	2.3	Enrolment, %: primary	99
Hospital beds per 1,000 pop.	4.2	secondary	105
Improved-water source access,		tertiary	58
% of pop.	100		

Society

No. of households	26.1m	Colour TVs per 100 households	98.3
Av. no. per household	2.3	Telephone lines per 100 pop.	53.3
Marriages per 1,000 pop.	5.2	Mobile telephone subscribers	
Divorces per 1,000 pop.	2.9	per 100 pop.	109.8
Cost of living, Dec. 2006		Computers per 100 pop.	60.0
New York = 100	125	Internet hosts per 1,000 pop.	111.4

UNITED STATES

Area	9,372,610 sq km	Capital	Washington DC
Arable as % of total land	19	Currency	US dollar ($)

People

Population	298.2m	Life expectancy: men		75.6 yrs
Pop. per sq km	31.8	women		80.8 yrs
Av. ann. growth		Adult literacy		...
in pop. 2005–10	0.97%	Fertility rate (per woman)		2.0
Pop. under 15	20.8%	Urban population		80.8%
Pop. over 60	16.6%			per 1,000 pop.
No. of men per 100 women	97	Crude birth rate		14.0
Human Development Index	94.8	Crude death rate		8.2

The economy

GDP	$12,417bn	GDP per head	$41,640
Av. ann. growth in real		GDP per head in purchasing	
GDP 1995–2005	3.4%	power parity (USA=100)	100
		Economic freedom index	82.0

Origins of GDP		**Components of GDP**	
	% of total		% of total
Agriculture	1.0	Private consumption	70.2
Industry, of which:	18.5	Public consumption	19.1
manufacturing	12.0	Non-government investment	16.6
Services[a]	80.5	Exports	10.5
		Imports	-16.2

Structure of employment

	% of total		% of labour force
Agriculture	2	Unemployed 2004	5.5
Industry	21	Av. ann. rate 1995–2004	5.1
Services	77		

Energy

	m TOE		
Total output	1,641.0	Net energy imports as %	
Total consumption	2,325.9	of energy use	29
Consumption per head,			
kg oil equivalent	7,921		

Inflation and finance

Consumer price		av. ann. increase 2000–05	
inflation 2006	3.2%	Narrow money	2.1%
Av. ann. inflation 2001–06	2.6%	Broad money	5.7%
Treasury bill rate, 2006	4.72%	Household saving rate, 2006	-0.2%

Exchange rates

	end 2006		December 2006
$ per SDR	1.50	Effective rates	2000 = 100
$ per €	1.32	– nominal	80.2
		– real	83.0

Trade

Principal exports		Principal imports	
	$bn fob		*$bn fob*
Capital goods, excl. vehicles	361.8	Industrial supplies	520.7
Industrial supplies	231.8	Consumer goods, excl. vehicles	407.0
Consumer goods, excl. vehicles	115.5	Capital goods, excl. vehicles	379.5
Vehicles & products	97.8	Vehicles & products	240.0
Food & beverages	58.9	Food & beverages	68.1
Total incl. others	**907**	**Total incl. others**	**1,732**

Main export destinations		Main origins of imports	
	% of total		*% of total*
Canada	23.7	Canada	17.2
Mexico	13.5	China	14.5
Japan	6.2	Mexico	10.2
China	4.7	Japan	8.2
United Kingdom	4.3	Germany	5.1
EU25	20.9	EU25	18.4

Balance of payments, reserves and aid, $bn

Visible exports fob	898.5	Overall balance	-14.1
Visible imports fob	-1,677.4	Change in reserves	-2.2
Trade balance	-778.9	Level of reserves	
Invisibles inflows	851.4	end Dec.	188.3
Invisibles outflows	-777.9	No. months of import cover	0.9
Net transfers	-86.0	Official gold holdings, m oz	261.6
Current account balance	-791.5	Aid given	27.62
– as % of GDP	-6.4	– as % of GDP	0.22
Capital balance	767.0		

Health and education

Health spending, % of GDP	15.4	Education spending, % of GDP	5.9
Doctors per 1,000 pop.	2.6	Enrolment, %: primary	100
Hospital beds per 1,000 pop.	3.3	secondary	95
Improved-water source access,		tertiary	72
% of pop.	100		

Society

No. of households	112.7m	Colour TVs per 100 households	99.7
Av. no. per household	2.7	Telephone lines per 100 pop.	58.8
Marriages per 1,000 pop.	8.0	Mobile telephone subscribers	
Divorces per 1,000 pop.	3.7	per 100 pop.	71.4
Cost of living, Dec. 2006		Computers per 100 pop.	76.2
New York = 100	100	Internet hosts per 1,000 pop.[b]	822.7

a   Including utilities.
b   Includes all hosts ending ".com", ".net" and ".org" which exaggerates the numbers.

VENEZUELA

Area	912,050 sq km	Capital	Caracas
Arable as % of total land	3	Currency	Bolivar (Bs)

People

Population	26.7m	Life expectancy:	men	70.9 yrs
Pop. per sq km	29.3		women	76.8 yrs
Av. ann. growth		Adult literacy		93.0%
in pop. 2005–10	1.67%	Fertility rate (per woman)		2.6
Pop. under 15	31.3%	Urban population		93.4%
Pop. over 60	7.5%			per 1,000 pop.
No. of men per 100 women	101	Crude birth rate		21.4
Human Development Index	78.4	Crude death rate		5.1

The economy

GDP	Bs293trn	GDP per head	$5,250
GDP	$140bn	GDP per head in purchasing	
Av. ann. growth in real		power parity (USA=100)	15.8
GDP 1995–2005	1.5%	Economic freedom index	47.7

Origins of GDP		**Components of GDP**	
	% of total		% of total
Agriculture	4.0	Private consumption	47.3
Industry, of which:	40.9	Public consumption	11.3
manufacturing	16.2	Investment	21.7
Services	55.1	Exports	41.0
		Imports	-21.3

Structure of employment

	% of total		% of labour force
Agriculture	11	Unemployed 2003	16.8
Industry	20	Av. ann. rate 1995–2003	13.2
Services	69		

Energy

	m TOE		
Total output	196.1	Net energy imports as %	
Total consumption	56.2	of energy use	-248
Consumption per head,			
kg oil equivalent	2,148		

Inflation and finance

		av. ann. increase 2000–05	
Consumer price			
inflation 2006	13.6%	Narrow money	39.8%
Av. ann. inflation 2001–06	20.8%	Broad money	36.6%
Money market rate, 2006	5.26%		

Exchange rates

	end 2006		December 2006
Bs per $	2,147	Effective rates	2000 = 100
Bs per SDR	3,230	– nominal	30.2
Bs per €	2,834	– real	77.6

Trade

Principal exports		Principal imports	
	$bn fob		*$bn fob*
Oil	49.2	Machinery	3.9
Iron & steel	2.3	Vehicles	3.3
Aluminium	1.1	Electrical equipment	2.9
Total incl. others	**55.5**	Total incl. others	**21.8**

Main export destinations		Main origins of imports	
	% of total		*% of total*
United States	57.8	United States	28.9
Netherlands Antilles	4.6	Colombia	8.4
Canada	2.9	Brazil	6.0
Dominican Rep	2.8	China	3.8

Balance of payments, reserves and debt, $bn

Visible exports fob	55.5	Change in reserves	6.4
Visible imports fob	-23.7	Level of reserves	
Trade balance	31.8	end Dec.	29.8
Invisibles inflows	5.5	No. months of import cover	10.1
Invisibles outflows	-11.7	Official gold holdings, m oz	11.5
Net transfers	-0.1	Foreign debt	44.2
Current account balance	25.5	– as % of GDP	48
– as % of GDP	18.4	– as % of total exports	118
Capital balance	-16.9	Debt service ratio	9
Overall balance	5.4		

Health and education

Health spending, % of GDP	4.7	Education spending, % of GDP	...
Doctors per 1,000 pop.	1.9	Enrolment, %: primary	102
Hospital beds per 1,000 pop.	0.9	secondary	72
Improved-water source access,		tertiary	29
% of pop.	83		

Society

No. of households	5.8m	Colour TVs per 100 households	96.3
Av. no. per household	4.6	Telephone lines per 100 pop.	13.5
Marriages per 1,000 pop.	2.8	Mobile telephone subscribers	
Divorces per 1,000 pop.	0.9	per 100 pop.	46.7
Cost of living, Dec. 2006		Computers per 100 pop.	8.2
New York = 100	57	Internet hosts per 1,000 pop.	4.6

VIETNAM

Area	331,114 sq km	Capital	Hanoi
Arable as % of total land	21	Currency	Dong (D)

People

Population	84.2m	Life expectancy: men	72.3 yrs
Pop. per sq km	254.3	women	76.2 yrs
Av. ann. growth		Adult literacy	90.3%
in pop. 2005–10	1.32%	Fertility rate (per woman)	2.1
Pop. under 15	29.6%	Urban population	26.4%
Pop. over 60	7.6%		per 1,000 pop.
No. of men per 100 women	100	Crude birth rate	18.8
Human Development Index	70.9	Crude death rate	5.1

The economy

GDP	D838trn	GDP per head	$620
GDP	$52.4bn	GDP per head in purchasing	
Av. ann. growth in real		power parity (USA=100)	7.3
GDP 1995–2005	7.2%	Economic freedom index	50.0

Origins of GDP

	% of total
Agriculture	20.9
Industry	41.0
Services	38.1

Components of GDP

	% of total
Private consumption	63.6
Public consumption	6.2
Investment	33.1
Exports	69.0
Imports	-73.3

Structure of employment

	% of total		% of labour force
Agriculture	58	Unemployed 2004	2.1
Industry	17	Av. ann. rate 2003–2004	2.2
Services	25		

Energy

	m TOE		
Total output	65.3	Net energy imports as %	
Total consumption	50.2	of energy use	-30
Consumption per head,			
kg oil equivalent	611		

Inflation and finance

Consumer price			av. ann. increase 2000–05
inflation 2005	8.3%	Narrow money (M1)	21.6
Av. ann. inflation 2001–05	5.8%	Broad money	26.9
Treasury bill rate, 2005	6.13%		

Exchange rates

	end 2006		December 2006
D per $	16,054	Effective rates	2000 = 100
D per SDR	24,152	– nominal	...
D per €	21,191	– real	...

Trade

Principal exports		Principal imports	
	$bn fob		*$bn cif*
Crude oil	7.4	Machinery & equipment	5.3
Textiles & garments	4.8	Petroleum products	5.0
Footwear	3.0	Steel	3.0
Fisheries products	2.7	Textiles	2.3
Total incl. others	**31.6**	**Total incl. others**	**36.5**

Main export destinations		Main origins of imports	
	% of total		*% of total*
United States	20.6	China	17.0
Japan	13.0	Singapore	13.4
Australia	7.9	South Korea	11.7
China	7.3	Japan	10.8
Singapore	5.2	Thailand	7.1
Germany	4.9	Malaysia	4.1
United Kingdom	3.8	Hong Kong	3.9

Balance of payments, reserves and debt, $bn

Visible exports fob	32.4	Change in reserves	2.0
Visible imports fob	-33.3	Level of reserves	
Trade balance	-0.8	end Dec.	9.2
Invisibles inflows	4.5	No. months of import cover	2.8
Invisibles outflows	-6.9	Official gold holdings, m oz	0.0
Net transfers	3.4	Foreign debt	19.3
Current account balance	0.2	– as % of GDP	38
– as % of GDP	0.4	– as % of total exports	56
Capital balance	2.9	Debt service ratio	3
Overall balance	2.1		

Health and education

Health spending, % of GDP	5.5	Education spending, % of GDP	...
Doctors per 1,000 pop.	0.5	Enrolment, %: primary	108
Hospital beds per 1,000 pop.	1.4	secondary	73
Improved-water source access,		tertiary	10
% of pop.	85		

Society

No. of households	25.2m	Colour TVs per 100 households	42.2
Av. no. per household	3.3	Telephone lines per 100 pop.	18.8
Marriages per 1,000 pop.	12.1	Mobile telephone subscribers	
Divorces per 1,000 pop.	0.5	per 100 pop.	11.4
Cost of living, Dec. 2006		Computers per 100 pop.	1.3
New York = 100	62	Internet hosts per 1,000 pop.	0.2

ZIMBABWE

Area	390,759 sq km	Capital	Harare
Arable as % of total land	8	Currency	Zimbabwe dollar (Z$)

People

Population	13.0m	Life expectancy: men	44.1 yrs
Pop. per sq km	33.2	women	42.7 yrs
Av. ann. growth		Adult literacy	...
in pop. 2005–10	0.95%	Fertility rate (per woman)	3.2
Pop. under 15	45.7%	Urban population	35.9%
Pop. over 60	5.2%		per 1,000 pop.
No. of men per 100 women	99	Crude birth rate	27.9
Human Development Index	49.1	Crude death rate	17.9

The economy

GDP	Z$75,421bn	GDP per head	$260
GDP	$3.4bn	GDP per head in purchasing	
Av. ann. growth in real		power parity (USA=100)	4.9
GDP 1995–2005	-2.6%	Economic freedom index	35.8

Origins of GDP		**Components of GDP**	
	% of total		% of total
Agriculture	18	Private consumption	70
Industry, of which:	23	Public consumption	27
manufacturing	13	Investment	14
Services	59	Exports	43
		Imports	-53

Structure of employment

	% of total		% of labour force
Agriculture	...	Unemployed 2002	8.2
Industry	...	Av. ann. rate 1997–2002	7.1
Services	...		

Energy

	m TOE		
Total output	8.6	Net energy imports as %	
Total consumption	9.3	of energy use	8
Consumption per head,			
kg oil equivalent	719		

Inflation and finance

Consumer price		av. ann. increase 2000–05	
inflation 2006	1,016.7%	Narrow money (M1)	283.4%
Av. ann. inflation 2001–06	349.8%	Broad money	274.8%
Interbank rate, 2006	203.4%		

Exchange rates

	end 2006		December 2006
Z$ per $	...	Effective rates	2000 = 100
Z$ per SDR	...	– nominal	...
Z$ per €	...	– real	...

Trade[a]

Principal exports[b]

	$m fob
Gold	366
Tobacco	227
Ferro-alloys	185
Platinum	121
Total incl. others	**1,520**

Principal imports[b]

	$m cif
Fuels	413
Chemicals	401
Machinery & transport equip.	271
Manufactured products	269
Total incl. others	**1,957**

Main export destinations

	% of total
South Africa	40.7
China	8.8
Switzerland	8.6
Japan	6.9
United Kingdom	5.9

Main origins of imports

	% of total
South Africa	43.6
China	4.4
Botswana	3.3
Zambia	2.8
Mozambique	1.9

Balance of payments[a], reserves and debt, $bn

Visible exports fob	1.6	Change in reserves[d]	0.0
Visible imports fob	-2.1	Level of reserves[d]	
Trade balance	-0.5	end Dec.	0.1
Invisibles, net	-0.4	No. months of import cover[d]	0.6
Net transfers	0.3	Official gold holdings, m oz[d]	0.1
Current account balance	-0.6	Foreign debt	4.3
– as % of GDP	-16.9	– as % of GDP	85
Capital balance[c]	-0.4	– as % of total exports	228
Overall balance[c]	-0.4	Debt service ratio	13

Health and education

Health spending, % of GDP	7.5	Education spending, % of GDP	...
Doctors per 1,000 pop.	0.2	Enrolment, %: primary	97
Hospital beds per 1,000 pop.	...	secondary	36
Improved-water source access,		tertiary	4
% of pop.	81		

Society

No. of households	3.3m	Colour TVs per 100 households	2.1
Av. no. per household	4.0	Telephone lines per 100 pop.	2.8
Marriages per 1,000 pop.	...	Mobile telephone subscribers	
Divorces per 1,000 pop.	...	per 100 pop.	5.6
Cost of living, Dec. 2006		Computers per 100 pop.	7.1
New York = 100	...	Internet hosts per 1,000 pop.	1.1

a Estimates.
b 2004
c 2001 estimates.
d 2002

EURO AREA[a]

Area	2,497,000 sq km	Capital	–
Arable as % of total land	26	Currency	Euro (€)

People

Population	310.2m	Life expectancy: men	78.1 yrs
Pop. per sq km	124.2	women	84.2 yrs
Av. ann. growth		Adult literacy	...
in pop. 2005–10	0.24%	Fertility rate (per woman)	1.5
Pop. under 15	16.0%	Urban population	78.9%
Pop. over 60	22.0%		per 1,000 pop.
No. of men per 100 women	96	Crude birth rate	9.7
Human Development Index	93.7	Crude death rate[b]	9.9

The economy

GDP	€7,974bn	GDP per head	$32,130
GDP	$9,980bn	GDP per head in purchasing	
Av. ann. growth in real		power parity (USA=100)	69.6
GDP 1995–2005	2.1%	Economic freedom index	69.3

Origins of GDP		**Components of GDP**	
	% of total		% of total
Agriculture	2	Private consumption	58
Industry, of which:	26	Public consumption	21
manufacturing	19	Investment	20
Services	72	Exports	37
		Imports	-36

Structure of employment

	% of total		% of labour force
Agriculture	4.2	Unemployed 2004	9.2
Industry	28.7	Av. ann. rate 1995–2004	9.5
Services	67.1		

Energy

	m TOE		
Total output	462.9	Net energy imports as %	
Total consumption	1,245.1	of energy use	63
Consumption per head,			
kg oil equivalent	3,990		

Inflation and finance

Consumer price		av. ann. increase 2000–05	
inflation 2006	2.2%	Narrow money (M1)	10.8%
Av. ann. inflation 2000–06	2.2%	Broad money	7.7%
Repo rate, 2006	2.87%		

Exchange rates

	end 2006		December 2006
€ per $	0.76	Effective rates	2000 = 100
€ per SDR	1.14	– nominal	121.8
		– real	121.7

Trade[b]

Principal exports

	$bn fob
Machinery & transport equip.	596
Manufactures	315
Chemicals	203
Energy and raw materials	81
Food, drink & tobacco	64
Total incl. others	**1,333**

Principal imports

	$bn cif
Machinery & transport equip.	467
Energy & raw materials	372
Manufactures	352
Chemicals	117
Food, drink & tobacco	74
Total incl. others	**1,469**

Main export destinations

	% of total
United States	23.5
Switzerland	7.7
Russia	5.3
China	4.9
Japan	4.1

Main origins of imports

	% of total
United States	13.9
China	13.4
Russia	9.1
Japan	6.2
Norway	5.7

Balance of payments, reserves and aid, $bn

Visible exports fob	1,516.2	Overall balance	-23.9
Visible imports fob	-1,448.2	Change in reserves	-4.8
Trade balance	68.0	Level of reserves	
Invisibles inflows	892.2	end Dec.	377.3
Invisibles outflows	-903.4	No. months of import cover	1.9
Net transfers	-84.9	Official gold holdings, m oz	375.9
Current account balance	-28.1	Aid given	39.5
– as % of GDP	-0.3	– as % of GDP	0.41
Capital balance	93.2		

Health and education

Health spending, % of GDP	9.6	Education spending, % of GDP	4.81
Doctors per 1,000 pop.	3.9	Enrolment, %: primary	104
Hospital beds per 1,000 pop.	6.6	secondary	106
Improved-water source access,		tertiary	54
% of pop.	...		

Society

No. of households	129.6m	Colour TVs per 100 households	97.1
Av. no. per household	2.39	Telephone lines per 100 pop.	52.6
Marriages per 1,000 pop.	4.7	Mobile telephone subscribers	
Divorces per 1,000 pop.	1.9	per 100 pop.	98.9
Cost of living, Dec. 2006		Computers per 100 pop.	45.2
New York = 100	...	Internet hosts per 1,000 pop.	198.3

a   Data refer to the 12 EU members that had adopted the euro before December 31 2006.

b   EU25 data, excluding intra-trade.

WORLD

Area	148,698,382 sq km	Capital	...
Arable as % of total land	10.7	Currency	...

People

Population	6,464.7m	Life expectancy: men	65.0 yrs
Pop. per sq km	43.8	women	69.5 yrs
Av. ann. growth		Adult literacy	82.2%
in pop. 2005–10	1.17%	Fertility rate (per woman)	2.6
Pop. under 15	28.3%	Urban population	48.7%
Pop. over 60	10.3%		per 1,000 pop.
No. of men per 100 women	102	Crude birth rate	20.3
Human Development Index	74.1	Crude death rate	8.6

The economy

GDP	$44.6trn	GDP per head	$6,910
Av. ann. growth in real		GDP per head in purchasing	
GDP 1995–2005	3.1%	power parity (USA=100)	22.7
		Economic freedom index	58.4

Origins of GDP		**Components of GDP**	
	% of total		% of total
Agriculture	4	Private consumption	61
Industry, of which:	28	Public consumption	17
manufacturing	18	Investment	22
Services	68	Exports	26
		Imports	-26

Structure of employment[a]

	% of total		% of labour force
Agriculture	4	Unemployed 2004	6.4
Industry	26	Av. ann. rate 1995–2004	6.8
Services	70		

Energy

	m TOE		
Total output	11,171.2	Net energy imports as %	
Total consumption	11,026.3	of energy use	-2
Consumption per head,			
kg oil equivalent	1,793		

Inflation and finance

Consumer price		av. ann. increase 2000–05	
inflation 2006	3.5%	Narrow money (M1)[a]	9.0%
Av. ann. inflation 2000–06	3.6%	Broad money[a]	7.5%
LIBOR $ rate, 3-month, 2006	5.19%	Household saving rate, 2006[a]	4.0%

Trade

World exports

	$bn fob		$bn fob
Manufactures	7,830	Ores & metals	310
Fuels	1,040	Agricultural raw materials	210
Food	730	Total incl. others	**10,430**

Main export destinations   **Main origins of imports**

	% of total		% of total
United States	15.6	China	9.4
Germany	7.4	Germany	9.1
China	5.7	United States	9.1
France	4.9	Japan	6.2
United Kingdom	4.7	France	4.2
Japan	4.5	United Kingdom	3.5

Balance of payments, reserves and aid, $bn

Visible exports fob	10,322	Overall balance	6
Visible imports fob	-10,279	Change in reserves	435
Trade balance	43	Level of reserves	
Invisibles inflows	4,746	end Dec.	4,694
Invisibles outflows	-4,787	No. months of import cover	4
Net transfers	-9	Official gold holdings, m oz	878.2
Current account balance	-6	Aid given[b]	108.7
– as % of GDP	-0.0	– as % of GDP[b]	0.32
Capital balance	-41		

Health and education

Health spending, % of GDP	10.1	Education spending, % of GDP	4.5
Doctors per 1,000 pop.	1.5	Enrolment, %: primary	103
Hospital beds per 1,000 pop.	...	secondary	70
Improved-water source access,		tertiary	24
% of pop.	82		

Society

No. of households	...	TVs per 100 households	...
Av. no. per household	...	Telephone lines per 100 pop.	19.4
Marriages per 1,000 pop.	...	Mobile telephone subscribers	
Divorces per 1,000 pop.	...	per 100 pop.	33.9
Cost of living, Dec. 2006		Computers per 100 pop.	12.4
New York = 100	...	Internet hosts per 1,000 pop.	66.9

a   OECD countries.
b   OECD and Middle East countries.

Glossary

Balance of payments The record of a country's transactions with the rest of the world. The **current account** of the balance of payments consists of: visible trade (goods); "invisible" trade (services and income); private transfer payments (eg, remittances from those working abroad); official transfers (eg, payments to international organisations, famine relief). Visible imports and exports are normally compiled on rather different definitions to those used in the trade statistics (shown in principal imports and exports) and therefore the statistics do not match. The **capital account** consists of long- and short-term transactions relating to a country's assets and liabilities (eg, loans and borrowings). The current account and the capital account, plus an errors and omissions item, make up the **overall balance**. In the country pages of this book this item is included in the overall balance. **Changes in reserves** include gold at market prices and are shown without the practice often followed in balance of payments presentations of reversing the sign.

Big Mac index A light-hearted way of looking at exchange rates. If the dollar price of a burger at McDonald's in any country is higher than the price in the United States, converting at market exchange rates, then that country's currency could be thought to be over-valued against the dollar and vice versa.

CFA Communauté Financière Africaine. Its members, most of the francophone African nations, share a common currency, the CFA franc, which used to be pegged to the French franc but is now pegged to the euro.

Cif/fob Measures of the value of merchandise trade. Imports include the cost of "carriage, insurance and freight" (cif) from the exporting country to the importing. The value of exports does not include these elements and is recorded "free on board" (fob). Balance of payments statistics are generally adjusted so that both exports and imports are shown fob; the cif elements are included in invisibles.

Crude birth rate The number of live births in a year per 1,000 population. The crude rate will automatically be relatively high if a large proportion of the population is of childbearing age.

Crude death rate The number of deaths in a year per 1,000 population. Also affected by the population's age structure.

Debt, foreign Financial obligations owed by a country to the rest of the world and repayable in foreign currency. **The debt service ratio** is debt service (principal repayments plus interest payments) expressed as a percentage of the country's earnings from exports of goods and services.

EU European Union. Members are: Austria, Belgium, Denmark, Finland, France, Germany, Greece, Ireland, Italy, Luxembourg, Netherlands, Portugal, Spain, Sweden and the United Kingdom and, as of May 1 2004, Cyprus, Czech Republic, Estonia, Hungary, Latvia, Lithuania, Malta, Poland, Slovakia and Slovenia and, as of January 1 2007, Bulgaria and Romania.

Effective exchange rate The nominal index measures a currency's depreciation (figures below 100) or appreciation (figures over 100) from a base date against a trade-weighted basket of the currencies of the country's main trading partners. The real effective exchange rate reflects adjustments for relative movements in prices or costs.

Euro area The 13 euro area members of the EU are Austria, Belgium, Finland, France, Germany, Greece, Ireland, Italy, Luxembourg, Netherlands, Portugal and Spain and, from January 1 2007, Slovenia. Their common currency is the euro, which came into circulation on January 1 2002.

Fertility rate The average number of children born to a woman who completes her childbearing years.

GDP Gross domestic product. The sum of all output produced by economic activity within a country. GNP (gross national product) and GNI (gross national income) include net income from abroad eg, rent, profits.

Household saving rate Household savings as % of disposable household income.

Import cover The number of months of imports covered by reserves ie, reserves ÷ $\frac{1}{12}$ annual imports (visibles and invisibles).

Inflation The annual rate at which prices are increasing. The most common measure and the one shown here is the increase in the consumer price index.

Internet hosts Websites and other computers that sit permanently on the internet.

Life expectancy The average length of time a baby born today can expect to live.

Literacy is defined by UNESCO as the ability to read and write a simple sentence, but definitions can vary from country to country.

Median age Divides the age distribution into two halves. Half of the population is above and half below the median age.

Money supply A measure of the "money" available to buy goods and services. Various definitions exist. The measures shown here are based on definitions used by the IMF and may differ from measures used nationally. Narrow money (M1) consists of cash in circulation and demand deposits (bank deposits that can be withdrawn on demand). "Quasi-money" (time, savings and foreign currency deposits) is added to this to create broad money.

OECD Organisation for Economic Co-operation and Development. The "rich countries" club was established in 1961 to promote economic growth and the expansion of world trade. It is based in Paris and now has 30 members.

Opec Organisation of Petroleum Exporting Countries. Set up in 1960 and based in Vienna, Opec is mainly concerned with oil pricing and production issues. Members are; Algeria, Indonesia, Iran, Iraq, Kuwait, Libya, Nigeria, Qatar, Saudi Arabia, United Arab Emirates and Venezuela.

PPP Purchasing power parity. PPP statistics adjust for cost of living differences by replacing normal exchange rates with rates designed to equalise the prices of a standard "basket" of goods and services. These are used to obtain PPP estimates of GDP per head. PPP estimates are shown on an index, taking the United States as 100.

Real terms Figures adjusted to exclude the effect of inflation.

Reserves The stock of gold and foreign currency held by a country to finance any calls that may be made for the settlement of foreign debt.

SDR Special drawing right. The reserve currency, introduced by the IMF in 1970, was intended to replace gold and national currencies in settling international transactions. The IMF uses SDRs for book-keeping purposes and issues them to member countries. Their value is based on a basket of the US dollar (with a weight of 44%), the euro (34%), the Japanese yen (11%) and the pound sterling (11%).

List of countries

Whenever data is available, the world rankings consider 183 countries: all those which had (in 2005) or have recently had a population of at least 1m or a GDP of at least $1bn. Here is a list of them.

	Population	GDP	GDP per head	Area	Median age
	m	$bn	$PPP	'000 sq km	years
Afghanistan	29.9	7.3	800[ab]	652	16.4
Albania	3.1	8.4	5,320	29	28.6
Algeria	32.9	102.3	7,060	2,382	24.0
Andorra	0.1	2.8[a]	38,800[a]	0.4	40.0
Angola	15.9	32.8	2,330	1,247	16.6
Argentina	38.7	183.2	14,280	2,767	28.9
Armenia	3.0	4.9	4,950	30	31.7
Aruba	0.1	2.1[b]	21,800[ab]	0.2	35.5
Australia	20.2	732.5	31,790	7,682	36.7
Austria	8.2	306.1	33,700	84	40.1
Azerbaijan	8.4	12.6	5,020	87	27.7
Bahamas	0.3	5.9	17,020[b]	14	28.0
Bahrain	0.7	12.9	21,480	1	28.8
Bangladesh	141.8	60.0	2,050	144	22.2
Barbados	0.3	3.1	17,000[a]	0.4	35.5
Belarus	9.8	29.6	7,920	208	37.4
Belgium	10.4	370.8	32,120	31	40.3
Belize	0.3	1.1	7,110	23	20.9
Benin	8.4	4.3	1,140	113	17.7
Bermuda	0.1	4.5[ab]	69,900[ab]	1	39.0
Bhutan	2.2	0.8	1,400[ab]	47	22.3
Bolivia	9.2	9.3	2,820	1,099	20.8
Bosnia	3.9	10.0	7,630	51	37.1
Botswana	1.8	10.3	12,390	581	21.1
Brazil	186.4	796.1	8,400	8,512	26.9
Brunei	0.4	6.4	25,600[a]	6	26.2
Bulgaria	7.7	26.6	9,030	111	40.8
Burkina Faso	13.2	5.2	1,210	274	16.8
Burundi	7.5	0.8	700	28	17.0
Cambodia	14.1	6.2	2,730	181	20.1
Cameroon	16.3	16.9	2,300	475	18.7
Canada	32.3	1,113.8	33,380	9,971	38.6
Cayman Islands	0.0 d	1.9[ab]	43,800[ab]	0.3	37.0
Central African Rep	4.0	1.4	1,220	622	18.3
Chad	9.7	5.5	1,430	1,284	16.8
Channel Islands	0.1	4.2[a]	51,820[a]	0.2	40.0
Chile	16.3	115.3	12,030	757	30.6
China	1,315.8	2,234.3	6,760	9,561	32.5
Colombia	45.6	122.3	7,300	1,142	25.6
Congo-Kinshasa	4.0	7.1	710	2,345	18.8

	Population	GDP	GDP per head	Area	Median age
	m	*$bn*	*$PPP*	*'000 sq km*	*years*
Congo-Brazzaville	57.5	5.1	1,260	342	16.3
Costa Rica	4.3	20.0	10,180	51	26.1
Côte d'Ivoire	18.2	16.3	1,650	322	18.5
Croatia	4.6	38.5	13,040	57	40.6
Cuba	11.3	40.1[a]	3,500[a]	111	35.6
Cyprus	0.8	16.7	21,600[a]	9	35.3
Czech Republic	10.2	124.4	20,540	79	38.9
Denmark	5.4	258.7	33,970	43	39.5
Dominican Republic	8.9	29.5	8,220	48	23.9
Ecuador	13.2	36.5	4,340	272	24.0
Egypt	74.0	89.4	4,340	1,000	22.9
El Salvador	6.9	17.0	5,250	21	23.4
Equatorial Guinea	0.5	3.2	7,640[a]	28	18.7
Eritrea	4.4	1.0	1,110	117	18.1
Estonia	1.3	13.1	15,480	45	38.9
Ethiopia	77.4	11.2	1,050	1,134	17.5
Faroe Islands	0.0[d]	1.7[a]	31,000[ab]	1	34.0
Fiji	0.9	2.7	6,050	18	23.7
Finland	5.2	193.2	32,150	338	40.9
France	60.5	2,126.6[c]	30,390	544	38.9
French Polynesia	0.3	4.6[ab]	17,500[ab]	3	27.1
Gabon	1.4	8.1	6,950	268	21.5
Gambia, The	1.5	0.5	1,920	11	19.5
Georgia	4.5	6.4	3,370	70	35.5
Germany	82.7	2,794.9	29,460	358	42.1
Ghana	22.1	10.7	2,480	239	19.9
Greece	11.1	225.2	23,380	132	40.1
Greenland	0.1	1.7	20,000[ab]	2,176	34.0
Guadeloupe	0.4	8.7[b]	17,855	2	34.0
Guam	0.2	2.5[a]	15,000[a]	1	28.4
Guatemala	12.6	31.7	4,570	109	18.2
Guinea	9.4	3.3	2,320	246	18.1
Guinea-Bissau	1.6	0.3	830	36	16.2
Haiti	8.5	4.3	1,660	28	20.3
Honduras	7.2	8.3	3,430	112	19.4
Hong Kong	7.0	177.7	34,830	1	38.9
Hungary	10.1	109.2	17,890	93	38.7
Iceland	0.3	15.8	36,510	103	34.2
India	1,103.4	805.7	3,450	3,287	23.8
Indonesia	222.8	287.2	3,840	1,904	26.5
Iran	69.5	189.8	7,970	1,648	23.4

	Population	GDP	GDP per head	Area	Median age
	m	*$bn*	*$PPP*	*'000 sq km*	*years*
Iraq	28.8	33.6	3,400[a]	438	18.9
Ireland	4.1	201.8	38,500	70	33.4
Israel	6.7	123.4	25,860	21	28.8
Italy	58.1	1,762.5	28,530	301	42.0
Jamaica	2.7	9.6	4,290	11	24.7
Japan	128.1	4,534.0	31,270	378	42.9
Jordan	5.7	12.7	5,530	89	21.1
Kazakhstan	14.8	57.1	7,860	2,717	28.8
Kenya	34.3	18.7	1,240	583	18.1
Kuwait	2.7	80.8	26,320	18	29.2
Kyrgyzstan	5.3	2.4	1,930	199	23.9
Laos	5.9	2.9	2,040	237	19.2
Latvia	2.3	15.8	13,650	64	39.3
Lebanon	3.6	21.9	5,580	10	27.1
Lesotho	1.8	1.5	3,340	30	18.8
Liberia	3.3	0.5	1,000[a]	111	16.4
Libya	5.9	38.8	11,400[a]	1,760	24.1
Lithuania	3.4	25.6	14,490	65	37.9
Luxembourg	0.5	36.5	60,230	3	38.3
Macau	0.5	11.56[a]	24,300[a]	0.02	36.5
Macedonia	2.0	5.8	7,200	26	34.2
Madagascar	18.6	5.0	920	587	17.9
Malawi	12.9	2.1	670	118	16.4
Malaysia	25.3	130.3	10,880	333	24.7
Mali	13.5	5.3	1,030	1,240	16.0
Malta	0.4	5.6	19,190	0.3	37.6
Martinique	0.4	8.6[b]	19,830	1	36.4
Mauritania	3.1	1.9	2,230	1,031	19.6
Mauritius	1.2	6.3	12,710	2	30.5
Mexico	107.0	768.4	10,750	1,973	25.6
Moldova	4.2	2.9	2,100	34	32.5
Mongolia	2.6	1.9	2,110	1,565	24.2
Morocco	31.5	51.7	4,550	447	24.3
Mozambique	19.8	6.6	1,240	799	17.7
Myanmar	50.5	7.5	1,700[a]	677	26.8
Namibia	2.0	6.1	7,590	824	19.5
Nepal	27.1	7.4	1,550	147	20.1
Netherlands	16.3	624.2	32,680	42	39.1
Netherlands Antilles	0.2	2.8[ab]	16,000[ab]	1	36.4
New Caledonia	0.2	3.3[b]	15,000[ab]	19	28.8
New Zealand	4.0	109.3	25,000	271	35.5
Nicaragua	5.5	4.9	3,670	130	20.3

	Population	GDP	GDP per head	Area	Median age
	m	*$bn*	*$PPP*	*'000 sq km*	*years*
Niger	14.0	3.4	780	1,267	16.0
Nigeria	131.5	99.0	1,130	924	17.6
North Korea	22.5	40.0[a]	1,700[a]	121	32.1
Norway	4.6	295.5	41,420	324	38.0
Oman	2.6	30.8	15,360[b]	310	22.5
Pakistan	157.9	110.7	2,370	804	20.3
Panama	3.2	15.5	7,610	77	26.1
Papua New Guinea	5.9	5.0	2,560	463	19.5
Paraguay	6.2	7.3	4,640	407	21.7
Peru	28.0	79.4	6,040	1,285	24.3
Philippines	83.1	99.0	5,140	300	21.8
Poland	38.5	303.2	13,850	313	36.8
Portugal	10.5	183.3	20,410	89	39.1
Puerto Rico	4.0	72.4[a]	18,600[a]	9	33.8
Qatar	0.9	42.5	27,400[a]	11	31.1
Réunion	0.8	13.7[b]	16,150	3	29.7
Romania	21.7	98.6	9,060	238	36.7
Russia	143.2	763.7	10,840	17,075	37.3
Rwanda	9.0	2.2	1,210	26	17.4
Saudi Arabia	24.6	309.8	15,710	2,200	23.3
Senegal	11.7	8.2	1,790	197	18.5
Serbia	10.5	26.2	4,400[a]	102	36.6
Sierra Leone	5.5	1.2	810	72	18.5
Singapore	4.3	116.8	29,660	1	37.5
Slovakia	5.4	46.4	15,870	49	35.6
Slovenia	2.0	34.0	22,270	20	40.2
Somalia	8.2	4.8	600[a]	638	17.9
South Africa	47.4	239.5	11,110	1,226	23.9
South Korea	47.8	787.6	22,030	99	35.0
Spain	43.1	1,124.6	27,170	505	38.8
Sri Lanka	20.7	23.5	4,590	66	29.5
Sudan	36.2	27.5	2,080	2,506	19.4
Suriname	0.5	1.3	4,100[a]	164	25.4
Swaziland	1.0	2.7	4,820	17	18.9
Sweden	9.0	357.7	32,530	450	40.2
Switzerland	7.3	367.0	35,630	41	40.1
Syria	19.0	26.3	2,810	185	20.6
Taiwan	22.9	345.9	29,320	36	34.0
Tajikistan	6.5	2.3	1,360	143	19.2
Tanzania	38.3	12.1	740	945	17.5
Thailand	64.2	176.6	8,680	513	32.6

	Population	GDP	GDP per head	Area	Median age
	m	*$bn*	*$PPP*	*'000 sq km*	*years*
Togo	6.1	2.2	1,510	57	18.1
Trinidad & Tobago	1.3	14.4	14,600	5	28.6
Tunisia	10.1	28.7	8,370	164	26.7
Turkey	73.2	362.5	8,410	779	26.7
Turkmenistan	4.8	8.1	8,000[a]	488	23.3
Uganda	28.8	8.7	1,450	241	15.3
Ukraine	46.5	82.9	6,850	604	38.9
United Arab Emirates	4.5	104.2[b]	25,510	84	29.4
United Kingdom	59.7	2,198.8	33,240	243	38.9
United States	298.2	12,416.5	41,890	9,373	36.0
Uruguay	3.5	16.8	9,960	176	32.6
Uzbekistan	26.6	14.0	2,060	447	22.6
Venezuela	26.7	140.2	6,630	912	24.6
Vietnam	84.2	52.4	3,070	331	24.9
Virgin Islands (US)	0.1	1.6[ab]	14,500[ab]	0.4	35.0
West Bank and Gaza	3.7	3.5[b]	1,500[a]	6	16.9
Yemen	21.0	15.1	930	528	16.7
Zambia	11.7	7.3	1,020	753	16.9
Zimbabwe	13.0	3.4	2,040	391	19.0
Euro area (12)	310.7	9,950	27,350	2,497	40.4
World	6,465	44,650	9,480	148,698	29.2

a Estimate.
b Latest available year.
c Including French Guiana, Guadeloupe, Martinique and Réunion.
d Populations less than 50,000.

Sources

Airports Council International, *Worldwide Airport Traffic Report*

Amnesty International

BP, *Statistical Review of World Energy*

British Mountaineering Council

Business Software Alliance

CB Richard Ellis, *Global Market Rents*

Central banks

Central Intelligence Agency, *The World Factbook*

Confederation of Swedish Enterprise

Corporate Resources Group, *Quality of Living Report*

Council of Europe

The Economist
www.economist.com

Economist Intelligence Unit, *Cost of Living Survey*; *Country Forecasts*; *Country Reports*; *E-readiness rankings*; *Global Outlook – Business Environment Rankings*

ERC Statistics International, *World Cigarette Report*

Euromonitor, *International Marketing Data and Statistics*; *European Marketing Data and Statistics*

Europa Publications, *The Europa World Yearbook*

Eurostat, *Statistics in Focus*

Financial Times Business Information, *The Banker*

The Heritage Foundation, *Index of Economic Freedom*

IFPI

IMD, *World Competitiveness Yearbook*

IMF, *Direction of Trade*; *International Financial Statistics*; *World Economic Outlook*

International Cocoa Organisation, *Quarterly Bulletin of Cocoa Statistics*

International Coffee Organisation

International Cotton Advisory Committee, *Bulletin*

International Road Federation, *World Road Statistics*

International Rubber Study Group, *Rubber Statistical Bulletin*

International Grains Council, *The Grain Market Report*

International Sugar Organisation, *Statistical Bulletin*

International Tea Committee, *Annual Bulletin of Statistics*

International Telecommunication Union, *ITU Indicators*

ISTA Mielke, *Oil World*

Johnson Matthey

Mercer Human Resource Consulting

National statistics offices

Network Wizards

Nobel Foundation

OECD, *Development Assistance Committee Report*; *Environmental Data*

Space.com

Standard & Poor's *Emerging Stock Markets Factbook*

Taiwan Statistical Data Book
The Times, *Atlas of the World*
Time Inc Magazines, *Fortune International*
Transparency International

UN, *Demographic Yearbook; Global Refugee Trends; State of World Population Report; Statistical Chart on World Families; Survey on Crime Trends; Trends in Total Migrant Stock; World Contraceptive Use; World Population Prospects; World Urbanisation Prospects*
UNAIDS, *Report on the Global AIDS Epidemic*
UNCTAD, *Review of Maritime Transport; World Investment Report*
UNCTAD/WTO International Trade Centre
UN Development Programme, *Human Development Report*
UNESCO, website: unescostat. unesco.org
Unicef, *Child Poverty in Perspective*
Union Internationale des Chemins de Fer, *Statistiques Internationales des Chemins de Fer*
US Census Bureau
US Department of Agriculture
University of Michigan, Windows to the Universe website

WHO, *World Health Statistics Annual; World Report on Violence and Health*
The Woolmark Company
World Bank, *Doing Business; Global Development Finance; World Development Indicators; World Development Report*
World Bureau of Metal Statistics, *World Metal Statistics*
World Economic Forum/Harvard University, *Global Competitiveness Yearbook*
World Resources Institute, *World Resources*
World Tourist Organisation, *Yearbook of Tourism Statistics*
World Trade Organisation, *Annual Report*

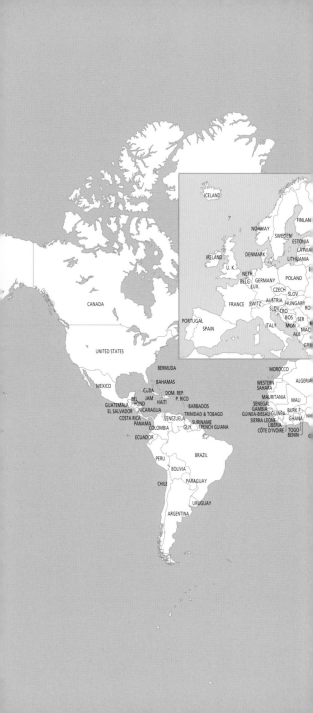